W9-BBM-708

THE BEDFORD SERIES IN HISTORY AND CULTURE

The Age of McCarthyism

A Brief History with Documents

SECOND EDITION

Ellen Schrecker

Yeshiva University

palgrave

THE AGE OF MCCARTHYISM by Ellen Schrecker

The Library of Congress has catalogued the paperback edition as follows:
200189428

PALGRAVE, 175 Fifth Avenue, New York, NY 10010

First published by PALGRAVE, 175 Fifth Avenue, New York, NY 10010. Companies and representatives throughout the world. PALGRAVE is the new global imprint of St. Martin's Press LLC Scholarly and Reference Division and Palgrave Publishers Ltd. (formerly Macmillan Ltd.).

Manufactured in the United States of America.

7 6 5 4 3 2

f e d c b a

ISBN: 0-312-29425-5

Cover photo: Joseph McCarthy, Bettmann/Corbis.

Acknowledgments

Acknowledgments and copyrights are continued at the back of the book on page 297, which constitutes an extension of the copyright page.

Foreword

The Bedford Series in History and Culture is designed so that readers can study the past as historians do.

The historian's first task is finding the evidence. Documents, letters, memoirs, interviews, pictures, movies, novels, or poems can provide facts and clues. Then the historian questions and compares the sources. There is more to do than in a courtroom, for hearsay evidence is welcome, and the historian is usually looking for answers beyond act and motive. Different views of an event may be as important as a single verdict. How a story is told may yield as much information as what it says.

Along the way the historian seeks help from other historians and perhaps from specialists in other disciplines. Finally, it is time to write, to decide on an interpretation and how to arrange the evidence for readers.

Each book in this series contains an important historical document or group of documents, each document a witness from the past and open to interpretation in different ways. The documents are combined with some element of historical narrative—an introduction or a biographical essay, for example—that provides students with an analysis of the primary source material and important background information about the world in which it was produced.

Each book in the series focuses on a specific topic within a specific historical period. Each provides a basis for lively thought and discussion about several aspects of the topic and the historian's role. Each is short enough (and inexpensive enough) to be a reasonable one-week assignment in a college course. Whether as classroom or personal reading, each book in the series provides firsthand experience of the challenge— and fun—of discovering, recreating, and interpreting the past.

Natalie Zemon Davis
Ernest R. May
Lynn Hunt
David W. Blight

Preface

The end of the cold war has not meant the end of history, as some people have predicted, but it certainly changed the writing of history—or at least of the history of the past half century. When this volume first came out, the Communist regimes in Eastern Europe and what was then the Soviet Union had only just toppled and, although historians hoped that the new governments might open their predecessors' archives, research in those sources had only just begun. Now, more than a decade into the post–cold war era, the partial opening of those archives has answered some questions and raised many more.

There is still a consensus that McCarthyism was bad, although its definition tends to vary with the political convictions of the user. It still remains easier to denounce McCarthyism than to understand it. The rampant fear of communism that unleashed a wave of political repression during the 1940s and 1950s seems almost incomprehensible in today's post–Soviet world. The most sensational events of the period—the Hollywood blacklists, the Hiss and Rosenberg cases, J. Edgar Hoover's anti-Communist obsession, the career of Senator Joseph McCarthy—have become the stuff of novels and television docudramas. But they are also an important part of our political heritage, one that requires analysis as well as retelling.

Conceived as a way to help today's students understand these ever more distant events, this volume offers an explanation of the McCarthy era together with selections from some of the documents that shaped it. Both the narrative and the readings range widely, for McCarthyism, as the term is used in this book, touched most areas of American political and cultural life. Narrower interpretations that identify what happened only with the bizarre antics of Senator McCarthy or the inquisitorial tactics of a few congressional committees do not explain why the anti-Communist furor came to dominate American political life during the early years of the cold war. But a broader investigation invites controversy. The topic remains so sensitive that reputable historians find themselves in disagreement about the nature of the Communist threat and the extent to which much of what happened was a reasonable response to that threat.

The release of previously secret Russian and American documents has corroborated many of the McCarthy-era charges of Soviet espionage. In addition to the archives of the former Soviet Union, we now have access to the so-called VENONA[1] decrypts—telegrams from the American operatives of the KGB to their superiors in Moscow that were intercepted by the U.S. intelligence community during World War II and then deciphered under the strictest secrecy during the early years of the cold war. Although this information shows that American Communists spied for the Soviet Union, it does not radically alter our interpretation of McCarthyism. These new documents, some of which are included in this edition, deal mainly with the espionage that took place during the Second World War when the United States and the Soviet Union were allies. Yet, most of what occurred during the McCarthy period had little to do with protecting America from Soviet spies. Surely, that could have been done without killing Julius and Ethel Rosenberg or firing more than ten thousand people who posed no conceivable threat to U.S. national security.

Because so many of the protagonists—on all sides—tried and still try to conceal their activities, we may never know everything that happened. There is, in addition, a strong temptation to oversimplify matters, to portray the McCarthy era as a morality play, a struggle between the "good guys" and the "bad guys." It is that—in part. But it is also a much more complicated story that forces us to confront difficult questions about the role of ideology, the power of the state, and the nature of modern American society.

Accordingly, the analytic essay in the first part of this book seeks to present both the breadth and the complexity of the McCarthyist phenomenon. Because the anti-Communist crusade of the 1940s and 1950s took many forms, this essay explores how each of its constituent elements evolved and functioned. It also looks at the well-known and the lesser-known cases of the period as well as at the specific procedures developed to handle them—the blacklists, congressional investigations, and criminal prosecutions. Finally, it explores the way in which all of the separate aspects of McCarthyism interacted with and reinforced each other.

---

[1]Terms in boldface are discussed in the glossary.

In the documents contained in the second part of this book, the actors themselves speak. Here are the voices of Communists and anti-Communists, excerpts from congressional hearings, KGB reports, Federal Bureau of Investigation (FBI) files, key presidential decrees, and Supreme Court decisions. Some of these documents have never been published; others are long out of print and all but inaccessible. Collected together, they show better than anything else the multifarious nature of McCarthyism and the enormous range of its targets.

ACKNOWLEDGMENTS

I could not have put this book together by myself. Nor, without the initial suggestion of Ernest May, would I have ever done so. I am especially grateful for the assistance I received in locating and collecting documents. My main debt is to the late Debra Bernhardt and Peter Filardo of the Tamiment Institution Library and Wagner Labor Archives at New York University. Jody Armstrong and Whitney Bagnall of the Columbia Law School Library, Don Carleton of the Center for American History of the University of Texas, Ann Fagan Ginger of the Meiklejohn Civil Liberties Institute, Victor Navasky, the late Marshall Perlin, and Walter Schneir were also helpful.

The introductory essay has benefited enormously from the generous comments made by James Barrett, Barton Bernstein, Alan Brinkley, Joanne Fraser, Joshua Freeman, Joanne Kenen, Maurice Isserman, Richard Polenberg, Steven Rosswurm, Nora Sayre, and Marilyn Young. At every stage of this book's development, I received unfailing support and encouragement from the people at Bedford/St. Martin's, among them Katherine Kurzman and Emily Berleth. Above all, I must acknowledge the extraordinary contribution of my editor, Louise Townsend, whose enthusiasm and intelligence sustained me throughout two editions' worth of the sometimes painful process of collecting and pruning documents. It also helps to have a gifted historian and experienced compiler of anthologies in the family. My husband, Marvin Gettleman, in this as in all other projects, has been a loving and supportive presence. His research skills and day-to-day nurturing contributed enormously to both editions of this book.

Ellen Schrecker

Contents

PART ONE

The Age of McCarthyism

At a few minutes before noon on October 2, 1961, a forty-one-year-old former Communist named Junius Scales mounted the steps of the Foley Square courthouse in New York City to turn himself in to the federal marshal and begin serving a six-year prison term for belonging to the American Communist party. Scales's ordeal punctures many of the myths, just as it illustrates many of the main themes, of the anti-Communist furor that swept through the United States in the 1940s and 1950s. Like most of the victims of what has come to be called *McCarthyism,* Scales never had any contact with Joe McCarthy, the senator who gave the phenomenon its name. McCarthy was a gifted demagogue whose wildly irresponsible charges of communism brought him the publicity he craved. But his antics distracted the attention of contemporaries and historians and caused them to over-look the more profound and enduring aspects of the anti-Communist crusade of the 1940s and 1950s.

Although McCarthy gained notoriety at the height of that crusade, his career as a big-league anti-Communist lasted only four years, from 1950 to 1954. The drive against communism that dominated American politics during the early years of the cold war had a much longer life, beginning as early as 1946 (or even 1939) and extending into the 1960s. Junius Scales's imprisonment four years after McCarthy's death illustrates its longevity and also reveals the role that other federal agencies played. Junius Scales never appeared before a congressional

1

investigating committee like the one Joseph McCarthy chaired. His ordeal came in the courts. He was prosecuted under a 1940 statute that made it a crime to be a member of an organization that taught or advocated the violent overthrow of the U.S. government. Though Scales had never committed an unlawful act, the Supreme Court upheld his conviction and sent him to prison.

He had been a Communist. And, in the early days of the cold war, communism was seen as so uniquely threatening to America's survival that measures that might otherwise have been considered serious violations of individual rights were justified on the grounds of national security. Although revelations from Russian and American archives show that Communists spied for the Soviet Union during World War II, they also reveal that by the late 1940s the forty to fifty thousand members of the tiny and beleaguered Communist party in the United States were no serious threat to the nation's existence. Yet the actions taken to oppose the party inflicted unnecessary injury on thousands of American citizens and did considerable damage to the political fabric of the nation. The anti-Communist crusade of the early cold war constituted what may well have been the most extensive episode of political repression in American history.

Because the anti-Communist furor of the 1940s and 1950s lasted so long and took so many different forms, it defies easy analysis. It is hard even to find a name for it. The word *McCarthyism* creates problems. Identifying the anti-Communist crusade with Senator McCarthy narrows the focus and slights the more important roles played by people like FBI Director J. Edgar Hoover and President Harry Truman. Yet there is no other term that conjures up quite as specifically all the activities that took place in the name of eliminating domestic communism during that period. Moreover, when we look beyond the imprisonment of Junius Scales and the rantings of Joe McCarthy to the thousands of unpublicized firings, FBI investigations, speakers' bans, passport denials, and other sanctions against political dissenters during this period, it becomes clear that there was not one, but many, McCarthyisms. They were all linked by a common concern with domestic communism and by a desire to eliminate its alleged threat to the American way of life.

The violations of civil liberties that occurred during the McCarthy era could not have taken place without the collaboration of the nation's political and social elites, the men and women who ran the federal government and the nation's most important public and private institutions. Most were thoughtful and responsible citizens who would not knowingly have condoned or participated in political injustice. Yet they did. To understand how McCarthyism could have happened, how otherwise decent and intelligent Americans were willing to go along with what even they in retrospect realize was political repression, we must reenter their universe and see the Communist threat through their eyes.

1

The American Communist Party

It is hard to have a witch-hunt without witches. During the late 1940s and 1950s, the American Communist party provided a fertile source of targets. Most victims of McCarthyism—the men and women who lost their jobs, went to jail, or were otherwise harassed—were Communists, former Communists, or people who worked closely with Communists. There were other cases—people whose names had gotten on the wrong mailing lists or who had the wrong kinds of friends— that triggered outrage and fed the widely shared misperception that McCarthyism targeted ordinary individuals. It did not. Most of the thousands of Americans who suffered during the anti-Communist frenzy of the 1940s and 1950s were not "innocent" victims in the way that phrase was used at the time. They had been in or near the Communist party. The political repression directed against them was justified by its perpetrators under the prevailing assumption that as "Commies" they had no rights that deserved protection.

The demonizing of communism during the early cold war has made a balanced assessment of its achievements difficult. Neither devils nor saints, American Communists were people who had committed themselves to a political movement that they hoped would make a better world. As the reminiscences of the former party members in Document 1 in Part Two reveal, individuals' motives and behavior varied, both in the party and then later as they confronted McCarthyism. They were idealistic, shrewd, foolish, rigid, brave, contentious, weak— in short, human. But their response to the persecution they faced was shaped in large part by the nature of the political movement that they had joined.

Although the Communist party did not provoke the repression visited upon it, its policies and practices could be seen as providing some justification for McCarthyism. Despite the more bizarre manifestations of the anti-Communist crusade, it was on some level a rational response to what was then perceived to be a real threat to American security. The threat was grossly exaggerated, but it was not a total fantasy. It derived in large part from the way in which the American Communist party operated. The party's secrecy and lack of internal democracy, its attempt to create a broader movement, and, above all, its connection to the Soviet Union gave plausibility to the notion that Communists endangered the United States. These practices and some of the party's other flaws made it particularly vulnerable to exposure and other techniques of repression and thus created opportunities that its opponents were to exploit during the McCarthy era.

The American Communist party had its origins in the international socialist movement that grew out of the writings of Karl Marx in the late nineteenth century. United in their opposition to capitalism and their desire to help the working class achieve power, socialists disagreed about whether they would have to use violent means. After the 1917 Bolshevik Revolution in Russia seemed to vindicate the militant strategy of V. I. Lenin and his followers, left-wing socialists throughout the world organized themselves into Communist parties. Within the United States, the new party came into being in the summer of 1919. From the start it was plagued by internal dissension and external repression. By the mid-1920s, as the euphoria of the Russian Revolution faded and the official harassment of the American Communist party eased, the party abandoned its initial preoccupation with illegal revolutionary activities and turned to other projects, especially the building of labor unions. It was still riven by internal disputes, and its leaders repeatedly turned to Moscow for help in solving them. Unfortunately, the directives from the Kremlin tended to reflect the exigencies of Soviet politics rather than any informed appreciation of the needs of the American party.

Despite the disadvantages of relying on Moscow, the party clung to its Soviet franchise. At least during its early years, when American radicals still viewed Russia as a kind of promised land of socialist revolution, the party's connection to Moscow conveyed prestige. Its membership in the **Comintern,**[1] the international organ of the Russian Revolution, gave the American Communist party its identity (and some of its funding) and enabled its few thousand adherents to feel themselves part of a worldwide movement.

The militancy of individual party members was another distinguishing feature. American Communists did much more than pay dues. As good Leninists, in accordance with Lenin's theories, they were expected

---

[1]Terms in boldface are discussed in the glossary.

to make a total commitment to the party. Not all were able to do so, but many did became **"cadres,"** the term used to describe full-time political activists working either in the party itself or for one of the many organizations that made up the broader movement of which the Communist party was the nucleus. Because it could depend on this core of experienced and dedicated activists, the party had much more influence than its small size might indicate.

In the 1930s, two events—the Depression and the rise of fascism in Europe—transformed the American Communist party from a tiny, faction-ridden sect composed primarily of radical immigrants into the most important and dynamic organization on the left. Its membership spurted from about seventy-five hundred at the start of the decade to about fifty-five thousand by the close. For many Americans disillusioned by the apparent failure of capitalism, communism offered an alternative. It also seemed effective. While other political groups talked, Communists acted. In the early 1930s, they were a visible presence in the most important social movements of the day. Communists organized demonstrations of the unemployed in Chicago, protected young African Americans against lynching in Alabama, and led strikes of California farmworkers. For many idealistic and energetic young men and women who were eager to address the stark social and economic problems of the Depression era, joining the Communist party seemed to make a lot of sense.

This appeal was especially strong during the **Popular Front** period in the late 1930s, when the Soviet Union led the opposition to Hitler's expansion and ordered Communists everywhere to give up their revolutionary rhetoric and create a broad antifascist coalition. The Spanish Civil War was crucial; like the Vietnam War, it roused an entire generation. In July 1936, General Francisco Franco mounted a military coup against the legally elected Spanish Republican government. While Hitler and Italy's Benito Mussolini rushed aid to their fellow fascist Franco, the Soviet Union was the only major power to help the democratic Loyalists. Communists everywhere flocked to the cause. Within the United States the party's support for beleaguered Spain as well as its general opposition to fascism attracted members and sympathizers, especially among students, intellectuals, Jews, and others who were worried about the rise of Hitler.

By the late 1930s, a broad left-wing movement had grown up around the Communist party. Many of the members of this movement did not belong to the party. Considering themselves communists with a small, not a capital, *C,* they sympathized with the party's goals and supported its activities, but they did not want to submit to its discipline or give up as much of their free time as the party demanded. The movement to which these people belonged encompassed dozens of organizations that not only enabled the party to extend its political influence far beyond the ranks of its own members but also created an institutional basis for an entire way of life. Besides the overtly political organizations dedicated to causes ranging from the Spanish Civil War to racial equality, there were schools, theaters, choruses, literary magazines, student groups, fraternal organizations, and summer resorts. The International Workers Order (IWO), for example, was a communist-led benevolent society organized in New York City in the early 1930s to appeal to different ethnic groups by offering cultural activities and insurance benefits. It ran summer camps and sold cemetery plots. The Joint Anti-Fascist Refugee Committee, established in 1939 after Franco's final victory in the Spanish Civil War, provided assistance to the exiled remnants of the defeated Loyalist forces.

Opponents of the Communist party, then and later, tended to view these organizations, the **"front groups"** as they were called, as evidence of the party's deviousness. They claimed that the party used these groups to attract **"fellow travelers,"** whom they characterized as unsuspecting liberals and well-meaning dupes drawn into the Communist orbit without realizing that the party was using them for its own purposes. This was seldom the case; most of these people knowingly collaborated with the party, believing it to be the most effective ally they could find.

The most important organizations with which party members became involved were trade unions. Because of the favorable climate created by the New Deal's social and economic reforms and its sympathy for organized labor, the 1930s witnessed a surge in union growth. By virtue of their experience and dedication, Communists were in great demand as organizers, especially in the campaign mounted by the newly formed **Congress of Industrial Organizations (CIO)** to unionize the nation's unskilled workers. Although they were few in number, the Communists' skill and energy gained them disproportionate influence within the CIO and its new unions. By the end of World War II, probably one-fifth of the CIO's unions were within the Communist party orbit in the sense that party members or their close allies led and staffed them. Communist influence was particularly strong within maritime and transport unions; among white-collar workers; and within the automobile, electrical, radio, food-processing, fur, metal mining, and smelting industries.

What that influence amounted to is much less clear. Even during the height of the McCarthy era, the most damaging evidence for the party's clout within the labor movement seemed to be pro-Soviet editorials in the union newspapers and resolutions about foreign policy passed at annual conventions during the 1930s and 1940s. There was no evidence that Communists had obstructed their unions' core economic activities; they had, after all, gained power because they were effective organizers dedicated to the workers they represented. In reality, many of the party's top labor leaders were unionists first, Communists second. They struggled to build their unions, not the party. Indeed, they shrank from recruiting their fellow workers into the party for fear that such recruitment might interfere with their labor organizing. For the same reason, they often concealed their party membership.

This secrecy was a problem for the entire American Communist party. While the party's top leaders were publicly known, many of its rank-and-file members hid their affiliation. Even during the height of its influence in the 1930s, communism was unpopular in America. Teachers and civil servants knew they would lose their jobs if their party membership became known. People in other fields feared, like the union activists, that they might lose their influence among their colleagues and political allies. Still, many American Communists were uncomfortable with the party's secrecy. They did not like to lie about their politics, especially when their otherwise openly expressed political views and activities made it easy for other people to tell that they were in or near the party. They recognized that the party's clandestine practices aroused suspicion. This was not a problem during periods like the Second World War when the party's relations with other political groups were good. However, when the political climate changed, the Communists' lack of openness took on sinister overtones. It also provided the party's enemies with one of their main weapons: exposure.

The American Communist party's devotion to the Soviet Union was a disaster for the party as well as the source of much of the hostility it encountered. That unwavering loyalty was, more than anything else, responsible for the party's rigidity and sudden policy changes. Decent and humane as many individual Communists were, the party itself was dictatorial and undemocratic. Its leaders scrambled to keep up with every new directive from the Kremlin and refused to allow dissent among members. Worst of all, the party's devotion to Moscow led it to condone Stalin's crimes and to ignore or apologize for Stalin's exterminations of millions of peasants in the late 1920s and early 1930s, the slave labor camps, and the paranoiac orgy of purges that cost the lives of hundreds of thousands of Russian revolutionaries and others during the late 1930s and 1940s. Even when Stalin liquidated most of his former colleagues after forcing them to confess publicly to crimes they did not commit, the American Communist party did not protest. Years later, most ex-Communists realized how wrong they had been, but at the time the self-enclosed world of American communism kept them from questioning the 1936–38 Moscow show trials. "There were many like myself," a former Communist recalled, "who believed that these people must be guilty, because we couldn't conceive that Bolsheviks who had fought together against the tsars and through civil wars would turn on each other and frame each other." It was unclear how much the rank-and-file Communists knew—or wanted to know— about the Moscow purges. Many discounted the reports as capitalist propaganda. Others seem to have ignored them or rationalized them on the grounds that the party's leaders had information they did not.

The Moscow-mandated policy shifts also hurt the American party. These reversals could be quite drastic and were to cause the party enormous difficulties internally and in their relations with other political groups. The most dramatic turnabout occurred in August 1939 when, as a result of Stalin's decision to abandon his alignment with Britain and France and sign a nonaggression treaty with Germany (the Nazi-Soviet Pact), the American Communist party suddenly dropped its campaign against Hitler and began to champion American neutrality on the grounds that the Western powers were just as bad as the Nazis. When Hitler broke the treaty and invaded Russia in June 1941, the party flipped again and began to support American intervention and aid to the Allies. The United States' entry into World War II transformed Communists into superpatriots. The American Communist party's general secretary, Earl Browder, demonstrated his newfound enthusiasm for the American way by ostensibly dissolving the party and reorganizing it as the Communist Political Association, a political pressure group dedicated to democratic reforms.

The Communist reconciliation with capitalism ended abruptly. Once the war wound down and Soviet-American tensions began to build, the party reversed itself yet again. The word came indirectly from Stalin in an April 1945 article by the French Communist leader Jacques Duclos that attacked American Communists for deviating from the proper line. The American party's leaders responded to the "Duclos Letter" that summer by adopting a militant anticapitalist stance, formally reorganizing the party, and throwing Browder out.

Over the next few years, the party became increasingly hostile to the American government and increasingly self-absorbed. The material by party chairman William Z. Foster in Document 2 gives the flavor of the party's harsh line at a time when it was attacking the Truman administration's foreign policy and throwing itself into the unsuccessful presidential campaign of the Progressive party's Henry Wallace in 1948. By then, the onset of McCarthyism had begun to aggravate the party's militance and accelerate its self-destructive decline into sectarianism and isolation. The final shock came in 1956, three years after Stalin's death, when Soviet leader Nikita Khrushchev revealed Stalin's crimes and then invaded Hungary. Ravaged by years of dogmatism and repression, the American Communist party simply fell apart.

Although most party members had usually accommodated themselves to the sudden about-faces in the party line, these reversals gravely damaged the party's relations with other left-wing and liberal political groups. When Soviet and U.S. policy dovetailed, as in the late 1930s and during World War II, liberals and moderates tolerated the party and protected it from right-wing attacks. But when the Kremlin's policy shifted, as it did after the Nazi-Soviet Pact and again at the beginning of the cold war, most of the party's erstwhile allies turned against it in disgust, leaving it unprotected in the face of its enemies.

2

The Growth of the
Anti-Communist Network

The Communists never lacked for enemies. Even before the Bolshevik Revolution gave birth to the American Communist party, many of the groups and individuals who were to become its main opponents had been actively fighting other radicals. Over the course of the twentieth century, they became increasingly concerned about Communists and by the late 1940s a wide-ranging anti-Communist network was in place whose members were to take the lead in the national crusade against domestic communism. What differentiated these people from their fellow Americans was not their anticommunism, which most Americans shared, but its intensity. Zealous partisans who often made the eradication of the so-called Communist menace a full-time career, in some respects they were the mirror image of the Communists they fought. They came into their own during the McCarthy period, staffing the main organizations in the field and imposing their agenda on the rest of the nation.

The anti-Communist network was not a monolith but a coalition that gradually attracted groups and individuals. Each element in the network appealed to a different constituency and used its own tactics; the mixture of offensives became far more potent than any single campaign would have been. Yet for all its diversity, anticommunism was indisputably a movement of the political right. Although liberals and even socialists joined the network, they did not set its tone. Instead, they enlisted in an ongoing crusade whose parameters had long been established by conservatives and whose main effect was to bolster right-wing social and economic programs. Over time, even those men and women who had originally been leftists of one kind or another often ended up on the far right.

Historians have noted the roots of American anticommunism in what they refer to as the nation's countersubversive tradition: the irrational notion that outsiders (who could be political dissidents, foreigners, or members of racial and religious minorities) threatened the nation from within. Projecting their own fears and insecurities onto a demonized "Other," many Americans have found convenient scapegoats among the powerless minorities within their midst. Native Americans, African Americans, Catholics, immigrants—all, at one time or another, embodied the threat of internal subversion. By the twentieth century, the American "Other" had become politicized and increasingly identified with communism, the party's Moscow connections tapping in conveniently with the traditional fear of foreigners.

While this countersubversive tradition cannot *in itself* explain why McCarthyism came to dominate American politics during the late 1940s and the 1950s, it does help account for its emotional impact and for its characteristic paranoia. It is also possible that, at least in part, McCarthyism was the mid-twentieth-century manifestation of a continuing backlash against the modern, secular world. Accordingly, as some historians suggest, the political demonology embodied in cold war anticommunism may well reflect deep-seated anxieties about individual autonomy, gender identity, and the perceived loss of community. Such an interpretation, though still largely speculative, is compelling. Certainly, it is not hard to conceive of the existence of the countersubversive tradition as a subterranean source of popular irrationality and xenophobia that could be exploited by ambitious politicians or special-interest groups to direct hostility against the opponents of their choice.

By far the most important of these special interests were those segments of the business community who opposed organized labor. From the 1870s until the McCarthy period, these employers identified the labor movement with the Red menace of the moment—whether anarchists, socialists, Communists, or Wobblies, as members of the radical Industrial Workers of the World were called in the early twentieth century. This tactic of Red-baiting made it possible to confront unions without having to address economic issues. Business leaders and their allies in the press insisted that workers' demands were not based on legitimate grievances but were creations of outside agitators, usually foreign-born, bomb-wielding Reds. Such charges invariably surfaced during periods of labor unrest and accompanied almost every major strike wave of the late nineteenth and early twentieth centuries.

Closely allied to the industrialists in the business of cracking down on labor militants and repressing leftists were the forces of law and order—private detective companies, local and state police, and, later, federal agencies like the FBI and military intelligence. Many of these groups had been formed specifically to fight radicalism and crush labor unrest and it was not uncommon for them to be subsidized by local businesses. But they had their own interests as well. Because of the authoritarian mind-set that law enforcement work breeds among its practitioners, opposition to radicalism was widespread. Moreover, their own bureaucratic interests, including the desire to present themselves as protecting the community against the threat of internal subversion, inspired them to exaggerate the danger of radicalism.

The obsessive anticommunism of FBI Director J. Edgar Hoover may well have been typical of the beliefs of the nation's law enforcement agents. Embracing the middle-class, small-town values of family, flag, and church, Hoover felt almost personally threatened by radical ideologies and individuals. His vision of the Communist menace extended far beyond the Communist party to almost any group that challenged the established social, economic, or racial order, and he was to dedicate his entire professional career to combatting that menace. Even when ordered to curtail his political activities, Hoover evaded his superiors and continued to keep the party and other leftists under surveillance. Because of his enormous success in building up his own power and that of the FBI, Hoover was able to transmit his own heavily ideological brand of anticommunism to the rest of the country.

His first opportunity came during the Red Scare of 1919–20 when, as a young official in the Department of Justice, Hoover helped plan a massive roundup of foreign-born radicals. The Palmer Raids, as the roundup was known, were the culmination of almost a year of near-hysteria on the part of politicians, journalists, and businesspeople who claimed that the left-wing agitation and labor unrest that had followed World War I threatened to plunge the nation into the revolutionary chaos that they claimed was sweeping Europe. The traditional targets—foreigners, radicals, and striking workers—were beaten and arrested, and many of the noncitizens among them were deported.

Although the furor soon abated, the Red Scare left an important legacy. Not only did it give J. Edgar Hoover his lifelong mission, it also fostered the development of an anti-Communist community, with an institutional base in the nation's most important patriotic organizations and small business groups. Like Hoover, the true believers within such groups as the American Legion, a veterans' organization founded in 1919, and the Chamber of Commerce, a national association of local business leaders, subscribed to an anticommunism with targets encompassing far more than the Communist party. They saw little difference between "parlor pinks" and "flaming Bolsheviks" and considered nonconformity to be as dangerous as communism. They also adhered to a dualistic view of the world in which anyone who disagreed with them was an enemy. As a result, they were often more hostile to their non-Communist critics like the **American Civil Liberties Union** (ACLU) than to the Communist party itself. Keepers of the ideological flame, these professional patriots and their associates seemed marginal during periods when the nation was concerned with other issues. But when the political atmosphere changed, as it did during the late 1930s and again during the cold war, their views entered the mainstream.

The anti-Communist network that these people nourished expanded during the labor struggles of the 1930s. Conservatives within the **American Federation of Labor (AFL)** had long struggled against radicalism within the labor movement. The presence of Communists in the CIO allowed its enemies, within both the business community and the AFL, to charge that the new unions were run by Reds. Moreover, because of the Roosevelt administration's sympathy for the CIO, anti-communism became a partisan issue. The American Legionnaires, right-wing politicians, and other spokespersons for the anti-Communist network charged that Communists had infiltrated the New Deal and were using federal agencies to further Moscow's schemes.

They received support from Congress. For years the American Legion and its allies had been demanding that the nation's lawmakers investigate communism and do something to curb it. Their efforts resulted in a few hearings with no lasting impact. By the end of the 1930s, however, as conservative lawmakers in both major parties began to turn against the New Deal, the professional patriots found a receptive audience. The result was the creation in 1938 of the **House Un-American Activities Committee** (HUAC), which was to become, along with the FBI, one of the main institutional centers of McCarthyism. For the small-town politicians in the right wing of the Republican party and their conservative southern Democratic colleagues, HUAC's anti-Communist investigations offered a more effective way to fight the New Deal than opposing its economic and social reforms. The committee also appealed to those politicians who, like its first chair, the xenophobic Texas Democrat Martin Dies, subscribed to the ideology of countersubversion.

From the start, HUAC was to focus on the alleged Communist influence in the labor movement and New Deal agencies. It took testimony from ex-Communists, American Legion officials, and other representatives of the anti-Communist right, as well as from the CIO's labor opponents. It eagerly pursued evidence that Communists had infiltrated the government. Committee staff members joined local Red squads in illegal raids on local Communist party headquarters and the offices of front groups in Philadelphia, Washington, D.C., and elsewhere. These raids produced membership lists that HUAC used to embarrass the Roosevelt administration by drawing attention to the hundreds of federal employees allegedly on them.

By the late 1930s the anti-Communist coalition had expanded far beyond the traditional right. Many of its new recruits, among them conservative trade union leaders and socialists, came from groups that had themselves once been under attack. The Catholic Church was one such group. The church had long been antagonistic to "atheistic" communism; the Spanish Civil War accentuated that hostility, for the Catholic hierarchy was as fiercely committed to Franco as the Communist party was to the Loyalist regime. The Soviet takeover of the traditionally Catholic countries of Eastern Europe after World War II and the subsequent persecution of the church there intensified Catholic anticommunism, especially within the Polish-American and other Eastern European ethnic groups.

Within the United States, Catholic anti-Communists concentrated their activities on the labor movement. The American working class was largely Catholic and, to maintain the church's influence over its flock and especially over its dwindling male membership, some Catholic activists undertook to drive the Communist party out of the labor movement. In the late 1930s, a handful of enterprising priests and laypeople began to organize anti-Communist nuclei within a few left-led unions. Although ineffectual at first, these efforts were to provide the organizational structure for later, more successful campaigns to eliminate the party's influence in the labor movement.

Perhaps the most important recruits to the anti-Communist cause during this period were former fellow travelers and ex-Communists. Some had been fairly high-ranking party leaders who were expelled from the party during the sectarian warfare of the 1920s and early 1930s. Others abandoned communism for their own ideological or personal reasons. They quickly became important members of the anti-Communist coalition, for, unlike the Legionnaires, antilabor businessmen, and right-wing politicians, they actually knew something about the party, their alleged expertise gaining greater respectability for what had been until then a rather haphazard cause. They also embarked on the task of educating the rest of the nation about the evils of communism. In the process, they made careers for themselves as witnesses, publicists, and staff members for the various organizations that made up the anti-Communist world. By the 1940s, they had become ubiquitous figures at trials, deportation proceedings, and congressional committee hearings. Excerpts from the testimony of some of these people appear in Documents 5 and 10. It is hard to conceive of McCarthyism without the former Communists; the support they gave the rest of the network was indispensable.

The career of Benjamin Mandel was typical. A former New York City high school teacher who became a full-time party activist in the 1920s, he was forced out of the party in 1929 when Stalin removed his faction from the party's leadership. After toying with a few left-wing sects during the 1930s, Mandel found a home in Congress. First with HUAC and then as the long-term research director of the **Senate Internal Security Subcommittee (SISS)**, he was to orchestrate many of the investigations and purges of the McCarthy period. The career of J. B. Matthews, Mandel's colleague on HUAC, followed a similar trajectory. A minister who had been a leading fellow traveler during the 1930s, Matthews broke with communism and began to work for HUAC. During the 1940s and 1950s, he became the power behind the throne of the anti-Communist network, supplying the Hearst Corporation and his other corporate and political clients with names and information from his famous collection of party literature and front group letterheads and other memorabilia.

By the 1940s, the professional anti-Communists had coalesced into an informal network. They shared a worldview that they assiduously sought to disseminate through whatever means they could. As journalists, consultants, and committee staffers, they worked closely together, sharing information and helping each other find jobs and publishers. They socialized frequently, conscious that they had become, as one of them jokingly suggested, "Red-Baiters Incorporated." The interconnections within the network were striking. Some of Hoover's top aides became key officials within the American Legion. Former FBI agents worked for HUAC. Father John Cronin, the Catholic Church's leading anti-Communist, wrote an influential pamphlet for the Chamber of Commerce in 1946 and then served as the liaison between the FBI and HUAC member Richard Nixon. These professionals, because they were organized, committed, and strategically placed, were to have a disproportionate influence over the ideological and institutional development of McCarthyism. Document 3, which contains excerpts from a 1948 article by the head of the American Legion, gives a sample of the views of these people.

Chronologically, the last group to join the anti-Communist coalition was the liberals. When the signing of the Nazi-Soviet Pact in August 1939 transformed American Communists from dedicated antifascists to critics of the U.S. government, the American Communist party lost many of its political allies. Most of the non-Communists who had tolerated the party because of its dedication to the antifascist cause turned against it. No longer would these liberals and moderates serve as a buffer for the party against its traditional enemies on the right. Instead, they joined them.

Despite intense opposition from isolationists who wanted the United States to stay out of the war in Europe, the American government committed itself to the support of Great Britain. Eager to squelch criticism from both the left and the right of its increasingly interventionist foreign policy, the Roosevelt administration began to treat the Communist party as a threat to the nation's security. It imprisoned the party's leader, Earl Browder, for a passport violation and tried to deport leading foreign-born Communists. Roosevelt expanded Hoover's authority to put the party under surveillance. At the same time, Congress passed several laws clearly directed against the party. The 1939 Hatch Act barred Communists, Nazis, and other totalitarians from government employment. The 1940 Voorhis Act, which stipulated that groups with foreign affiliations register with the government, was designed to force the American Communist party to sever its ties to Moscow. The 1940 Smith Act, the first peacetime sedition act in American history, authorized the government to crack down on speech as well as action by making it illegal to "teach or advocate" the overthrow of the government or to join any organization that did.

Private organizations also turned against the party during the Nazi-Soviet Pact period. Some labor unions threw party members out of leadership positions and others passed resolutions condemning Nazism, fascism, and communism. These "Communazi" resolutions popularized the concept of totalitarianism, which treated communism and fascism as but variants of the same repressive, authoritarian creed. The purges spread to the academic community where several colleges and universities, most notably the City College of New York, dismissed Communist professors. Even the American Civil Liberties Union turned anti-Communist and expelled a leading party figure from its board of directors.

For almost two years, until Hitler's invasion of the Soviet Union in June 1941 returned the Communist party to the Allied camp, American Communists were confronted with the same kind of political repression that they were to face a decade later during the McCarthy period. Abortive though that earlier campaign was, it did display all the elements of the later anti-Communist crusade. Washington's imprimatur was crucial; not only did the federal government itself crack down on the party, but in doing so it gave the stamp of approval to the previously more marginal activities of the traditional anti-Communists. In addition, the anti-Communist campaign of the Nazi-Soviet Pact period perfected many of the techniques and developed many of the institutional structures that would become crucial during the McCarthy years.

3

Communism and National Security: The Menace Emerges

The restored tolerance for American communism that grew out of the wartime alliance with the Soviet Union did not long survive the victory over Hitler in the spring of 1945. Although there was an ostensible revival of the Popular Front collaboration between Communists and liberals during the war, it was a temporary and essentially superficial phenomenon. The party's patriotism did little to overcome the hostility of its traditional enemies or make it any more popular with the general public. Once World War II ended and the cold war began, the American Communist party again came under attack.

This time, however, because of the struggle against the Soviet Union, anticommunism moved to the ideological center of American politics. The cold war transformed domestic communism from a matter of political opinion to one of national security. As U.S. hostility toward the Soviet Union intensified, members of the Communist party came increasingly to be viewed as potential enemy agents. Because that perception was to provide the justification for so much that happened during the McCarthy period, it is important to examine its development in some detail.

The cold war began even before the fighting stopped. At the **Yalta Conference** in February 1945, Roosevelt had tried to negotiate an amicable postwar settlement with Stalin, but after Roosevelt's death in April, American policymakers became concerned about the Soviet Union's obvious attempt to dominate the areas of Eastern Europe that its army controlled. As crisis followed crisis over the next few years, the world hovered on the verge of war. Each emergency heightened the tension. First came disagreements over the composition of the Polish government in 1945, then Soviet pressure on Turkey and Iran in 1946, the Greek Civil War in 1947, the Communist coup in Czechoslovakia and blockade of Berlin in 1948, the Communist takeover in China and the Soviet detonation of an atomic bomb in 1949, and, finally, the outbreak of the Korean War in 1950. At first Truman and his advisers vacillated between hoping to conciliate the Soviets and trying to strong-arm them, but by the beginning of 1946 most of the nation's policymakers had come to see the Soviet Union as a hostile power committed to a program of worldwide expansion that only the United States was strong enough to resist. This may not have been the case. Although there is no question about the horrendous repression Stalin imposed on his own people, his foreign policy may well have been motivated by a desire for security rather than conquest. American policymakers never tried to find out, assuming on the basis of the Nazi experience that totalitarian states by definition threatened the stability of the international system.

Similar assumptions pervaded the growing consensus about the dangers of American communism. Part myth and part reality, the notion that domestic Communists threatened national security was based on a primarily ideological conception of the nature of the Communist movement. The sense of urgency that surrounded the issue of communism came from the U.S. government's attempt to mobilize public opinion for the cold war. But the content, the way in which the Communist threat was defined, owed much to formulations that the anti-Communist network had pushed for years. Document 4, J. Edgar Hoover's 1947 testimony before the House Un-American Activities Committee, is an example of this type of thinking, of the vision of communism that came to shape most people's perceptions of the Red menace. It conformed to the similarly demonized view of the Soviet Union held by the Truman administration and its supporters. Although distorted in many ways, the perception of an internal Communist threat had just enough plausibility to be convincing—especially to the vast majority of Americans who had no direct contact with the party or its members. Above all, it legitimated the McCarthy era repression by dehumanizing American Communists and transforming them into ideological outlaws who deserved whatever they got.

Communist party members were believed to be part of a secret conspiracy, fanatics who would automatically do whatever Stalin told them to do. Though a wildly exaggerated caricature, the image did have some basis in reality. After all, the American Communist party was a highly disciplined organization that did have a connection to the Soviet Union. As the Russian and American documents reveal, some of the leaders of the American Communist Party did help the Soviet secret police, known as the KGB, recruit espionage agents from within the party's ranks. Whether or not they actually got orders from Moscow, those leaders also tried to ensure that the party's policies would be in accord with those of the Kremlin at least on major issues, making it possible to view the congruence between the party's line and the Soviet Union's positions as evidence of dictation.

The notion that individual American Communists were under Moscow's control had less basis in reality. True, some party members did display a Stalinist rigidity, following every zig and zag of the party line with unquestioning devotion. Many Communists did behave in what could be seen as a conspiratorial fashion, especially when they tried to conceal their political affiliation. Nonetheless, most party members were neither so rigid nor so secretive. They did not see themselves as soldiers in Stalin's army but as American radicals committed to a program of social and political change that would eventually produce what they hoped would be a better society. Even at its peak, the Communist party had a high turnover rate; and, by the early 1950s, most of the people who had once been in the party had quit, proving that they were hardly the ideological zombies they were commonly portrayed as. Nonetheless, the assumption that all Communists followed the party line all the time was to structure and justify the political repression of the McCarthy period.

Just as there was a kernel of plausibility in the demonized image of the American Communist, so too was it conceivable that individual Communists, acting as subversives, spies, and saboteurs, could threaten American security. Protecting the nation from these dangers was to become the primary justification for much of what happened during the McCarthy period. The dangers were enormously exaggerated, but they were not wholly fictitious.

Ironically, even though the party's leaders were to go to jail in the 1950s because they had supposedly advocated the violent overthrow of the American government, no one in any position of responsibility seriously worried that the party would mount a successful revolution. A far more tangible danger was the possibility that individual Communists in sensitive positions could subtly influence the nation's foreign policy or undermine its ability to defend itself. There was no evidence that this had happened. But conspiracy theories blossomed, circulated primarily by Republican politicians and their allies who wanted to discredit the Democratic party and the New Deal. Most of these theories involved charges that Communists had infiltrated the State Department, where they induced Roosevelt to give Poland to Stalin at the Yalta Conference in 1945 and then betrayed China to the Communists. Although these allegations had no basis in reality, there were enough tidbits of circumstantial evidence for people like Joe McCarthy to build their careers (and ruin those of others) by creating apparently convincing scenarios—as we see in the excerpts from the McCarthy speech in Document 16.

Communist spies were a genuine threat, however. Although never powerful enough to influence government policy, individual Communists had been involved in espionage. The notorious spy cases of the early cold war bolstered the contention that, as J. Edgar Hoover maintained, "every American Communist was, and is, potentially an espionage agent of the Soviet Union." While the FBI director was characteristically exaggerating, documents released from Russian and American archives after the cold war ended reveal that as many as two to three hundred men and women in or near the Communist party did transmit information to Moscow, including enough material about the atomic bomb to speed up the Soviet Union's acquisition of a nuclear weapon by a year or two. Most of this espionage took place during World War II when the Soviet Union and the United States were on the same side. And most of it ended abruptly in the fall of 1945 when the defections of a Soviet code clerk in Ottawa and an American courier in New York forced the KGB to break off all contact with its agents in the United States. Once the cold war began, the demonization of American communism and the federal government's purge of its left-wing employees made it impossible for the Soviet Union to recruit any more spies from the party's declining ranks.

Although the threat of espionage gained national attention, sabotage was the prime concern of policymakers. They feared that Communist-led unions might go on strike or otherwise impede the operations of the nation's vital defense industries. Here, too, the fear was wildly exaggerated. But there were just enough elements of reality to make it plausible. Although a party-dominated union like the Fur and Leather Workers posed little threat to national security, the United Electrical, Radio, and Machine Workers of America (UE) and the various maritime unions were more strategically positioned. During the Nazi-Soviet Pact period, Communist labor leaders had been involved in several highly publicized strikes in the nation's defense industries. Part of a nationwide organizing drive mounted by unions of all political persuasions, the work stoppages were triggered by economic grievances, not a desire to impede the nation's war effort. Nonetheless, because Communists had been active, these strikes were cited during the early years of the cold war as evidence that the party had tried to sabotage American rearmament. The possibility of similar job actions in the event of a conflict with the Soviet Union could easily justify cracking down on the left-led unions.

4

The State Steps In:
Setting the Anti-Communist Agenda

What transformed the Communist threat into a national obsession was not its plausibility, but the involvement of the federal government. After all, Communist parties were far more powerful in European countries, which never experienced a similar outburst of accusation and repression. McCarthyism was not a private venture. Ardent anti-Communists were found throughout American society, but the nation as a whole would not have made eliminating Communist influence such a high priority had Washington not led the way.

An important element of the power of the modern state is its ability to set the political agenda and to define the crucial issues of the moment, through its actions as well as its words. During the early years of the cold war, the actions of the federal government helped to forge and legitimize the anti-Communist consensus that enabled most Americans to condone or participate in the serious violations of civil liberties that characterized the McCarthy era. The media was the government's partner, largely because it amplified messages that came from Washington. After all, much of the news that went on the radio or onto the front pages simply reported the government's doings. Presidential orders, congressional hearings, and criminal prosecutions all told stories that, at least during the early cold war, helped construct the ideological scaffolding for McCarthyism. When in the late 1940s, for example, the Immigration and Naturalization Service (INS) began to round up foreign-born Communists and labor leaders for deportation and then detain them without bail, it was sending a very strong signal about the alien nature of communism and its dangers.

The government did not speak with a single voice. It was an amalgam of separate and often competing institutions, bureaucracies, and political parties. During the late 1940s and 1950s, almost every agency became involved in the anti-Communist crusade. From the

25

State Department and Congress to the Post Office and the Supreme Court, federal bureaucrats, politicians, and judges struggled with the issues of domestic communism as they debated and implemented policies to deal with it. On occasion, those policies came into conflict; yet—and this is crucial—they were always invested with the power of the state. Not only did this make it possible, for example, for HUAC to send recalcitrant witnesses to prison for contempt of Congress, but it also gave a legitimacy and resonance to even the wildest pronouncements of its members that the statements of private citizens did not possess.

Although the phenomenon got its name from a member of the Senate, it was the executive branch of the government that wielded the most influence over the development of McCarthyism. It stimulated concern about national security and established the main mechanisms through which the anti-Communist campaign was to operate. Much of this was the by-product of the administration's drive to enlist popular support for the cold war and obtain bipartisan backing for its foreign policy. The American people had just emerged from over a decade and a half of depression and war and the Truman administration worried that they might not be willing to sustain the effort that was deemed necessary to contain Soviet expansion.

In particular, Truman and his aides feared that the economy-minded Republican Congress that had been elected in 1946 might not allocate enough money for the struggle. As a result, the administration oversold the Soviet threat. On March 12, 1947, the president went before a special session of Congress and, using the opportunity provided by a request for aid to Greece and Turkey, formulated the **Truman Doctrine,** an unlimited commitment by the United States "to support free peoples who are resisting attempted subjugation by armed minorities or by outside pressures." A year later, Truman and his advisers were to take advantage of another crisis, the Communist takeover in Czechoslovakia, to obtain passage of the **Marshall Plan,** their program for the economic rehabilitation of Western Europe.

Ironically, although the administration won bipartisan congressional support for its foreign policy, the atmosphere of crisis that it created backfired against it. This was especially the case after Truman's surprise victory in the 1948 election revealed the unpopularity of the Republican party's traditional economic programs. Because it endorsed the administration's anti-Communist stance abroad, the Republican party sought to recoup its fortunes and embarrass the White House by focusing on communism at home. For the next four years, the Republican charge that the Democrats were "soft" on communism dominated American politics. Truman, of course, was no such thing, but to a certain extent his administration had contributed to its own difficulties by its overemphasis on the Communist threat.

The executive branch did more than provide the psychic setting for McCarthyism. The specific steps it took to combat the alleged threat of internal communism were to intensify the national preoccupation with the issue. These actions—most important were the inauguration of an anti-Communist loyalty-security program for government employees in March 1947 and the initiation of criminal prosecutions against individual Communists—not only provided specific models for the rest of the nation but also enabled the government to disseminate its version of the Communist threat. With the FBI at the heart of the federal government's internal security apparatus, the anti-Communist agenda that emerged from Washington was to be powerfully influenced by the ideologically conservative conception of anticommunism so central to the bureau's mission and so cogently expressed in Hoover's 1947 statement to HUAC, excerpted in Document 4.

Perhaps no single weapon in the federal arsenal was as powerful in the government's construction of the anti-Communist consensus as the criminal justice system. By putting Communists on trial, the Truman administration shaped the American public's view of domestic communism. It transformed party members from political dissidents into criminals—with all the implications that such associations inspired in a nation of law-abiding citizens.

As an educational venture, the criminalization of communism was a great success. The major trials of the period got enormous publicity and gave credibility to the notion that Communists threatened the nation's security. Prosecuting accused espionage agents like Alger Hiss and the Rosenbergs reinforced the image of Communists as Russian spies. Putting Communist labor leaders on trial allowed the government to raise the issue of industrial sabotage. And initiating deportation proceedings against foreign-born Communists emphasized the alien nature of the party and its ties to the Soviet Union. In the most important of the anti-Communist cases, the Smith Act trial of the top leaders of the American Communist party in 1949, the government brought all these themes together to bolster its contention that the party was an illegal conspiracy under Soviet control (see Document 10).

The government rarely lost a case at the trial stage. Treating Communists as criminals made them seem dangerous; and that perception increased the willingness of judges and juries to convict them. Communist defendants were arrested, handcuffed, fingerprinted, and often brought to their trials under guard if they were being held in jail for contempt or deportation. Moreover, because of the political nature of these trials, much of the evidence that the government produced had no relation to the case at hand but was designed to reinforce the negative image of the defendants and bolster the prosecutors' insistence on the significance of actions that might, in another context, have been considered harmless.

However, using the criminal justice system to reinforce the government's contention that communism was outside the law had its drawbacks. There were few laws under which the offenders could be tried, because being a Communist was not a crime and the statute of limitations precluded most espionage prosecutions. As a result, the charges that the cold war defendants faced—usually perjury or contempt—often bore little relation to the presumed offense for which they were on trial. In addition, it was hard to obtain the evidence necessary for a conviction. The KGB messages revealing Soviet espionage that had been intercepted by the American intelligence community during World War II and then deciphered under the so-called VENONA project in the late 1940s and 1950s were too secret to be used in court. Moreover, FBI surveillance techniques did not always fall within the law, and the bureau was reluctant to reveal the identities of its informants. Confessions, the mainstay of ordinary criminal proceedings, were hard to come by in political cases. Accordingly, prosecutors relied on the testimony of professional ex-Communists and undercover agents. Many of these people lied. Over the years, the unreliability of the government's witnesses was to invalidate many convictions, as appellate judges increasingly began to raise questions about the veracity of the professional informers.

Within the government these problems were to generate some friction as J. Edgar Hoover and his agents were often more eager to prosecute than their ostensible superiors in the Justice Department. This controversy reflected the FBI chief's growing dissatisfaction with what he believed was the Truman administration's lax attitude toward internal security. Hoover was careful to conceal his antagonism, but because of the FBI's central role in devising and implementing the federal government's internal security policies, his estrangement from the administration was to have enormous consequences.

It is hard to overestimate the importance of J. Edgar Hoover and the FBI in creating and disseminating the anti-Communist consensus.

Because of the bureau's strategic position within the government, it took control of the administration's anti-Communist effort and managed to infuse its own right-wing concerns into what otherwise might have been a rather narrow program of internal security.

The FBI came to dominate policymaking in the field of internal security for several reasons. To begin with, this was the FBI's traditional area of specialization. Hoover was a brilliant bureaucratic politician who had spent a lifetime amassing power. He had been particularly assiduous in building up his agency's image as a highly professional and impartial outfit and had actually convinced most liberals that the bureau guarded people's rights. He was to be equally energetic in publicizing the dangers of the Communist party. In 1946, motivated by his own obsession with the Red menace as well as the need to find a major postwar mission for the FBI, Hoover ordered the bureau to mount an intensive public relations campaign to alert the American people to the internal threat of communism—and to the FBI's indispensability in combatting it. By the time the rest of the Truman administration felt compelled to act against the Communist threat, Hoover had made the bureau indispensable. Moreover, having the FBI, with its vaunted reputation for expertise, handle internal security offered the hard-pressed White House a convenient way to deflect its critics' charge that it was "coddling" Communists.

By turning the official campaign against communism over to J. Edgar Hoover and his agents, the administration was giving a blank check to an organization whose conception of the Communist danger was that of the far right wing of the anti-Communist network. The bureau subscribed to and pushed the oversimplified notion that all American Communists were Soviet puppets. It also tended to assume that there was little difference between party members, fellow travelers, and left-wing liberals. The FBI tended to lump together as Communists all the people who associated with the party and its many causes and to treat them all as if they endangered American security. Document 4, Hoover's influential 1947 testimony before HUAC, shows how broadly his agency viewed the threat of communism. Bureau files reveal an underlying assumption that dissent equaled disloyalty; FBI agents apparently viewed anyone who participated in left-wing political activities as an object of suspicion and hostility.

Nor was the bureau scrupulous about protecting the rights of people under investigation. Its main priority was to protect its informants, insisting that preserving confidentiality was essential to national security. In fact, much of the bureau's passion for secrecy came from its desire to conceal its own lawbreaking. For years, Hoover had been defying his superiors in the Justice Department and had secretly put people under surveillance without authorization from above. His agents also resorted to illegal wiretaps and break-ins and leaked material from the FBI's allegedly confidential files to sympathetic journalists and politicians. Beginning in 1956, when the Supreme Court started to make anti-Communist prosecutions more difficult, the bureau embarked on COINTELPRO, a secret program of political sabotage, unauthorized surveillance, and disinformation designed to cripple the Communist party and, later, other radical groups as well.

But the FBI's illegal activities and ideological proclivities were not widely known until the 1970s. Hoover and his aides successfully concealed their dirty tricks and right-wing agenda for years even as they were proclaiming their professionalism and political neutrality. President Truman was one of the few people in power at the time to question the bureau's activities; as one of his aides noted, he wanted "to hold [the] F.B.I. down, afraid," that it would turn into a "Gestapo." But his apprehension, while sincere, did not outweigh the risk to his administration of the brutal bureaucratic struggle that reining in the FBI would have entailed. In a battle between Truman and Hoover, there is no evidence that the president would have won. The bureau had enormous popular and congressional support; and the administration, under growing Republican pressure to prove that it could handle communism, would not have taken action that might have exposed it to further attack.

Because the administration had itself subscribed to and popularized the notion that Communists threatened national security, it was in a bind. Its own activities legitimized those of its right-wing opponents. It could not deny the issue's importance without puncturing its own anti-Communist credentials. But it could not concur with the conservative view that the New Deal had been honeycombed with Communists. It took a while for this dilemma to manifest itself and, as the conflict between the Truman administration and its Republican opponents escalated in the late 1940s, the anti-Communist crusade did too. For all their differences, both sides believed that communism threatened the nation. By fighting about how to handle that threat, they merely emphasized its importance and helped disseminate anticommunism throughout society.

5

Communists in Government
and the Big Spy Cases

The most politically damaging issue confronting the Truman administration was the allegation that it was harboring Communists. This
charge was used by the Republican party to orchestrate its attacks on
the Democrats as well as to bolster the careers of individual politicians
like Richard Nixon and Joseph McCarthy. Although allegations that
Communists had infiltrated the New Deal had circulated for years, the
heightened concern about national security engendered by the cold
war made the Communists-in-government issue impossible for Washington to ignore.

There were (or there had been, during the New Deal) Communists
and people close to the Communist party in government jobs. Never
open about their party ties, these people had to hide their political
affiliations once the 1939 Hatch Act barred Communists from working
for the government. They could be fired if it became known they
belonged to the party. Many of them were on a list of more than
eleven hundred government employees that the FBI investigated in
1941 at the instigation of the **Dies Committee** (as HUAC was called
before it became a standing House committee). But the Roosevelt
administration, which did not view communism as a serious problem,
did not carry out a wholesale purge. The situation changed quickly
once World War II ended, when it became clear that the official tolerance for American communism was over. Within the next few years,
most of the suspected Communists were either fired or eased out of
their jobs if they had not already resigned. The danger had passed just
as the controversy heated up.

The Communists-in-government issue took off in the late 1940s
after several big cases seemed to show that subversives had penetrated the Roosevelt administration. The first case arose early in 1945
when an official of the **Office of Strategic Services (OSS),** the World

War II precursor of the Central Intelligence Agency (CIA), noticed that an article in *Amerasia,* a small magazine dealing with East Asian affairs, seemed to be based on one of his agency's secret reports. When the OSS investigators surreptitiously entered the *Amerasia* offices, they found hundreds of classified documents, though nothing that actually endangered the nation's security. The FBI took over the investigation; illegal searches and wiretaps turned up a handful of conspirators, including, among others, the magazine's publisher, Philip Jaffe, a close friend of Communist party leader Earl Browder, and John Stewart Service, a State Department official who claimed that he had given materials to *Amerasia* in accordance with the department's policy of maintaining good relations with the press. After delaying for several months, the Justice Department arrested six people in June.

The case never went to trial. The government's evidence was too weak for it to obtain indictments against Service and two other defendants. It decided not to prosecute the other three when one of them found out that the FBI had illegally entered his apartment. Rather than risk further disclosure of the bureau's embarrassing activities, the Justice Department dropped the case. Hoover was upset about the decision but could not reverse it. The case, however, did not disappear. It was to be disinterred repeatedly over the next few years by Truman's opponents, who felt that the failure to prosecute the *Amerasia* defendants indicated the administration's laxness about internal security. Moreover, because some of the principals were in or near the Communist party and all of them were concerned with East Asia, the case would figure prominently in McCarthy-era charges that the State Department had "lost" China.

The *Amerasia* defendants had stolen documents to publish them; there was no indication that they had handed them to the Soviets. This was not the case with the first major espionage revelation of the postwar period. Although that case occurred in Canada, it seemed to American observers to prove that Communists, whatever their nationality, were Soviet agents. The case began when a minor official named Igor Gouzenko defected from the Soviet mission in September 1945. To protect himself against reprisals, Gouzenko took with him a sheaf of coded documents that purported to give evidence of a spy ring composed mainly of party members operating within Canadian scientific and government circles. According to FBI reports, Gouzenko also claimed that there was similar espionage in the United States, including some at high levels within the State Department, but he did not produce any evidence.

The disposition of the case remains puzzling. Beyond informing the British and American governments about Gouzenko's charges, the Canadians did not make them public or (perhaps because they did not want to roil their already shaky relations with the Soviet Union) act on them until the following spring when someone in Washington leaked the story to a columnist. At that point the Canadian government set up a special investigating commission and initiated a series of prosecutions.

Despite some unanswered questions about the handling of the investigation, the combination of Gouzenko's testimony and documents and the confessions of some of the protagonists proves that some Canadian Communists and sympathizers had indeed spied for the Soviet Union during World War II. Gouzenko's revelations also bolstered the long-standing assumption of the FBI and others that American party members were also spies. The bureau's suspicions seemed to be confirmed two months after Gouzenko's defection when a distraught thirty-seven-year-old Vassar graduate named Elizabeth Bentley walked into the FBI's New York City office and began to pour out an elaborate story about her life as a courier for a Soviet spy ring in Washington, D.C.

Dubbed the "Red Spy Queen" by the media, Bentley was to become one of the McCarthy era's ex-Communist stars. She claimed she had been recruited as a Russian agent by her former lover and business associate, a party official who ran a travel agency that dealt with the Soviets. In her initial debriefing by the FBI, Bentley identified more than eighty people, including dozens of federal employees, who, she said, had been giving information to the Russians. Her most important operatives belonged to a ring headed by a Treasury Department official named Nathan Gregory Silvermaster. Within a week the FBI had dozens of agents on the case. It put all the main suspects under surveillance and encouraged Bentley to reactivate her contacts. Many of the people she had fingered, including Alger Hiss and Assistant Secretary of the Treasury Harry Dexter White, were not unknown to the FBI. They were left-wing New Dealers whose names had been on the Dies Committee list or who had been investigated for other reasons. It was clear that most of them, if not party members, had at least circulated within the world of the Popular Front during the 1930s and early 1940s. It was also clear that they knew each other both socially and professionally.

The bureau found no direct evidence of espionage, however. We now know, based on information obtained from the archives of the former Soviet Union and the VENONA documents, that most of the people

Bentley identified had, in fact, been giving information to the KGB during the Second World War. That information, which included everything from troop movements to postwar economic plans, comprised thousands of pages of documents from a wide variety of federal agencies. It is unclear, however, what the men and women who supplied it thought they were doing because few of them—then or later—ever talked about it and Bentley claimed she had tried to keep them from knowing where their information was going. In any event, her defection put an abrupt end to their unauthorized activities, as the KGB immediately broke off contact with all the people with whom she had worked. As a result, because the FBI could not catch them in the act and VENONA had yet to be deciphered, there was no way to verify Bentley's charges.

Without any corroborating evidence, it would be hard to obtain an espionage conviction. At first the bureau tried to keep the suspects on the job and under surveillance. But once it became clear that Bentley's efforts to resuscitate the Silvermaster ring had not succeeded, the bureau realized that a prosecution would fail. The Justice Department was more optimistic; it overrode Hoover's objections and early in 1947 took the case to a grand jury. For more than a year, federal attorneys grilled the alleged conspirators, all of whom either denied Bentley's charges or took the Fifth Amendment. Without any confessions or proof of espionage, the government could not obtain an indictment and there were no other statutory grounds on which the suspects could be charged.

Because it was not possible to throw the culprits in jail, Hoover was eager to have them fired. Beginning in November 1945, he regularly bombarded top officials in the Truman administration with summaries of the case. Although most of the people Bentley fingered were ultimately forced out of their jobs, it took a while. Under civil service regulations then in place, employees had the right to request a formal hearing on charges before being dismissed. Because the bureau was unwilling to open its files for such a proceeding or help officials in other agencies investigate on their own, the cases often hung in limbo. In the 1950s, Hoover and his allies in the Republican party were to claim that the Truman administration's foot-dragging in dismissing these people was an indication that it was "soft" on communism.

Enter HUAC. The House Un-American Activities Committee had, after all, been interested in the Communists-in-government issue since Martin Dies had attacked the New Deal before World War II. For Hoover and the rest of the anti-Communist network, a congressional hearing had all the publicity value of a trial without the constraints of a legal proceeding. It would alert the rest of the nation to the danger of Communist infiltration and might even goad the Truman administration into action. Revelations that emerged during a committee hearing bore an official stamp, something that could not be gained by leaking information to selected journalists, the FBI's other method of dissemination. A congressional investigation also offered the prospect of an eventual criminal prosecution for perjury or contempt of Congress. Thus, by the summer of 1948, when it became clear that Elizabeth Bentley's tale would not lead to indictments, Congress took charge of the case.

With the presidential election a few months away, the Republicans who controlled Capitol Hill were glad to air Bentley's charges. The first set of hearings was held by Michigan Senator Homer Ferguson's Government Appropriations Subcommittee in July 1948. A few days later, Bentley repeated her story to HUAC. Most of the people she named appeared as well and either denied the allegations or took the Fifth Amendment. To bolster Bentley's charges, HUAC then called up a *Time* magazine editor and former Communist named Whittaker Chambers.

As brilliant as he was unbalanced, Chambers had been an editor of several party publications in the late 1920s and 1930s until dropping out to become a self-described Soviet agent. Repelled by Stalin's terror, he abandoned his undercover activities in the late 1930s and spent the next ten years trying to warn the government about the underground Communist unit he had organized in Washington. Because Chambers had apparently been working with the Soviet military intelligence agency, the GRU, and not the KGB, there is no direct corroboration of his charges against Alger Hiss. The GRU's files are closed and, although one of the VENONA decrypts (reprinted in Document 5) and a few other KGB records do refer to Hiss, the Soviet archives have yet to produce the kinds of smoking guns that exist for the other big espionage cases. Still, the circumstantial evidence is strong, especially since the VENONA documents and Russian archives mention so many of the other people that Chambers had named.

Considering the eventual importance of the Hiss case in establishing the credibility of the charges that Communist spies had infiltrated the New Deal, it is surprising to discover the almost random way in which it developed. HUAC was probably just as interested in the former Assistant Secretary of the Treasury, Harry Dexter White, who had also been named by both Bentley and Chambers. White was the highest-ranking official to have been implicated as a Communist agent and it is possible that he would have become as notorious as Alger Hiss had he not died of a heart attack a few days after he appeared before the committee to deny the charges against him. Like White, Hiss was already out of the government by the time HUAC subpoenaed him. He had served in several New Deal agencies during the 1930s before he joined the State Department. An able administrator, Hiss participated in the Yalta Conference and then helped organize the United Nations in the spring of 1945. But the FBI's attempts to alert Hiss's superiors to the charges against him blighted his diplomatic career; and, in 1947, he left the government to head the Carnegie Endowment for International Peace.

Hiss did more than just deny Chambers's charges; he sued Chambers for slander. As his congressional testimony in Document 5 indicates, he admitted that he may have once known Chambers under another name, but he continued to maintain that he had never been in the Communist party. As the litigation proceeded, Chambers escalated his allegations. Initially he had merely charged Hiss with having been a secret Communist during the 1930s, but on November 17, 1948, he produced four penciled memoranda in Hiss's handwriting and sixty-five typewritten documents dated from January to April 1938 that he claimed Hiss had given him for transmission to the Soviets. Here, at last, was the physical evidence for espionage that the FBI had been seeking for so long. Experts identified some of the documents as having been typed on the same machine that Hiss and his wife had used in the 1930s. Because the statute of limitations for espionage had run out, Hiss was indicted for perjury. His first trial ended in a hung jury. The guilty verdict his second trial produced on January 21, 1950, seemed to prove that Communist agents had infiltrated the U.S. government and spied for the Soviet Union.

Hiss's conviction also legitimized HUAC by showing how useful a congressional investigation could be in exposing Communist subversion. Congressional Republicans had a big stake in the case, for Truman and his aides tried to downplay the disclosures as a "red herring" designed to divert attention from the feeble legislative record of the Republican-controlled 80th Congress. As the case unraveled, the committee, the FBI, and Chambers worked together with the rest of the anti-Communist network to find witnesses, develop leads, and keep the pressure on the administration. HUAC's most competent and energetic member, first-term California Representative Richard M. Nixon, took a central role in pressing the attack. Father John Cronin had been secretly leaking information from the FBI to Nixon. Nixon, who had developed an intense personal dislike for Hiss, used the bureau's material to stage a dramatic series of seemingly impromptu confrontations between the urbane Harvard Law School graduate Hiss and the disheveled, histrionic Chambers.

Although the Justice Department had copies of Chambers's incriminating documents, it did not seem eager to prosecute Hiss. Nixon also feared that the newly elected Democratic Congress might abolish HUAC. To forestall that eventuality and push the government to indict Hiss, Nixon ordered Chambers to give the rest of his documents to the committee. In a highly theatrical gesture, Chambers led two HUAC staff members to his Maryland farm on December 2, 1948, where he pulled several rolls of film out of a hollowed-out pumpkin. The "Pumpkin Papers," as these documents were called, actually contained little material that implicated Hiss, but the publicity surrounding their release forced the Justice Department to indict Hiss and saved the committee.

The continuing controversy over the Hiss case indicates its importance. Most historians now think that Chambers, despite some inconsistencies in his testimony, was essentially right. Hiss, however, maintained his innocence until the day he died and some people, including his son who has written a memoir about his father, still believe him. But the significance of the case goes far beyond the veracity of its two protagonists. Because it produced a guilty verdict (for perjury, it must be noted, not espionage), it gave credibility to the issue of Communists-in-government and made it possible for Hoover, HUAC, and the other conservatives in the anti-Communist network to force the Truman administration onto the defensive. In addition, because Hiss's credentials as a card-carrying New Dealer seemed to reveal how easily Reds could penetrate the liberal establishment, his conviction made all liberals vulnerable as well.

6

Atomic Espionage

On September 23, 1949, President Truman tersely announced that the Soviet Union had detonated an atomic device the previous month. That revelation, coming only a few months after the Communist party, under Mao Tse-tung, had taken power in China, unleashed a torrent of anxiety and finger-pointing as both policymakers and private citizens struggled to come to terms with these staggering blows to America's self-confidence and preeminence in the world. Truman and his advisers responded by stepping up the militarization of American foreign policy and authorizing the immediate development of the hydrogen bomb. Others — Republican politicians, FBI officials, and ordinary people as well — sought explanations in scenarios of Communist subversion and espionage.

They were right, at least in part. Although the Soviet Union would have become a nuclear power without outside help, espionage speeded up the process. Since 1941, Soviet agents had been eavesdropping on the **Manhattan Project,** the secret World War II crash program to build the atomic bomb. Because of that espionage, Soviet scientists were able to develop a nuclear weapon a year or two before they otherwise would have. Moscow got this information from several sources, not all of them yet known. The two physicists who delivered the most valuable materials, Klaus Fuchs and Theodore Hall, did so, as Document 6 reveals, for ideological reasons. They were Communists who believed that the world would be a better place if the Soviet Union did not have to face an American atomic monopoly after the war. Another nuclear informant was David Greenglass, a young Army machinist assigned to the weapons laboratory at Los Alamos, New Mexico. Although Greenglass's information was of little value compared to that of Fuchs and Hall, his involvement with the bomb project was to cost his sister and brother-in-law, Ethel and Julius Rosenberg, their lives.

The German-born Fuchs was the most important spy. A Communist student who fled to England after the Nazi takeover, he contacted Soviet intelligence soon after becoming involved with the early British work on the bomb. Transferred to Los Alamos as part of the British scientific delegation, he continued to feed information to the KGB. His American courier was Harry Gold, a Philadelphia chemist, who met with Fuchs several times during World War II in New York, Massachusetts, and Santa Fe. The two men would rendezvous on street corners and in movie theaters where Fuchs would turn over pages of scientific materials and try to answer the questions that Gold was relaying from his KGB superiors. Fuchs maintained a sporadic connection with Soviet intelligence after his return to England as the chief theoretical physicist on the British nuclear project. His last contact took place in April 1949. By then he was already under suspicion and by the end of the year, after intensive questioning by British intelligence agents, he was ready to confess. He received a quick trial and a fifteen-year prison term. On his release, he moved back to East Germany.

VENONA had uncovered Fuchs. It had taken several years of painstaking cryptoanalysis during the late 1940s before the American code-breakers deciphered enough of the intercepted KGB telegrams to identify him as the British spy at Los Alamos. The FBI then tracked down his courier, eventually apprehending Gold, who, like Fuchs, was willing to confess. VENONA also led to Hall, a brilliant scientific prodigy who was recruited for the bomb project while still a nineteen-year-old undergraduate at Harvard and who was also close to the Communist party. When Hall realized the implications of the work he was doing, he decided to contact the Soviet intelligence apparatus and, using several go-betweens, including his college roommate, transmitted whatever data he could from Los Alamos. When questioned by the FBI, however, neither Hall nor his couriers would talk. Because VENONA was considered too highly secret to be revealed in court, the FBI could not construct a case against the young physicist. He continued his scientific work, changing fields and eventually ending up as a respected biophysicist in Cambridge, England.

Although he had been a member of the Young Communist League, David Greenglass's involvement with atomic espionage was more fortuitous. As the VENONA decrypts in Document 6 reveal, his sister's husband Julius Rosenberg had been running a busy espionage operation composed mainly of his own left-wing engineering friends from the City College of New York. These people, who worked in a variety of defense installations and research laboratories, supplied the Soviets with technical data about the military and industrial projects on which they were employed. When his brother-in-law was serendipitously assigned to Los Alamos, Rosenberg recruited him as well, using Greenglass's wife Ruth and, on one occasion, Harry Gold as couriers. The materials that the high-school-educated technician passed on to the KGB were hardly as sophisticated as those Fuchs and Hall delivered. Still, Greenglass's activities certainly constituted espionage and they were uncovered by VENONA.

Because the Soviets had been tipped off about the VENONA project by some of their other agents, they wanted Rosenberg and Greenglass to flee the country. But they were too late. Gold's arrest and confession at the end of May 1950 led to David Greenglass; Greenglass's arrest and confession led to Julius Rosenberg. At that point the confessions stopped. Rosenberg denied everything. Because the FBI knew from VENONA that he had a lot to talk about, the authorities decided to put pressure on him by arresting his wife. Although Ethel Rosenberg, as Document 6 reveals, knew about her husband's work, she was not a spy, and, like Julius, she, too, refused to confess. The couple even denied that they were Communists. They were, they claimed, the innocent "victims of growing neo-fascism."

Until the release of the VENONA decrypts, it was possible to believe them. What kept the case alive, however, was not so much the issue of their guilt or innocence as it was the grotesquely disproportionate punishment inflicted upon them. Whatever Julius had done—and it was clear that the crude sketches his brother-in-law sent from Los Alamos did not contain the secret of the atomic bomb—neither he nor his wife deserved to die. Despite the Rosenbergs' guilt, their trial was a travesty. Because the VENONA decrypts could not be introduced in court, the only evidence against the couple was the testimony of David Greenglass who may have been willing to fabricate a story about his sister's participation to protect his wife from an indictment. The Rosenbergs insisted that they were innocent and refused to answer questions about their politics. Their attorney put up a feeble defense. Because he was afraid that it would look unpatriotic to challenge the government's assertion that the data Greenglass delivered was too vital to American security to be revealed, the Rosenbergs' attorney let the prosecution hype the case as, in J. Edgar Hoover's words, "the crime of the century." Still, given the superheated atmosphere of the period, even a more competent defense might not have prevented a guilty verdict.

The trial judge, Irving Kaufman, was illegally collaborating with the Justice Department. The death sentence that he imposed was the main fruit of that collaboration. Although the judge claimed, as Document 6 reveals, that the enormity of their crime justified their execution, he had actually imposed that sentence because J. Edgar Hoover and the prosecutors hoped it might induce Julius Rosenberg to confess. There was an open telephone line from Hoover's Washington headquarters to the death house at Sing Sing penitentiary on June 19, 1953, the evening of the couple's execution. On the list of questions that the FBI had prepared for Julius in case the imminence of the electric chair led to a change of heart was the utterly damning one: "Was your wife cognizant of your activities?"

Roughly a year after the execution, J. Robert Oppenheimer lost his security clearance. Although hardly equivalent in terms of its severity to the sentence imposed on the Rosenbergs, the refusal of the **Atomic Energy Commission (AEC)** to renew Oppenheimer's clearance was a long-awaited act of retribution on the part of the security apparatus and Oppenheimer's political enemies. Popularly reputed to be the father of the atomic bomb, Oppenheimer had directed the Manhattan Project's laboratory at Los Alamos. Security officials had been suspicious about him from the start, for the brilliant and charismatic physicist had been a prominent figure in the prewar Popular Front in Berkeley. He was not a party member, but many of the people around him were or had been, including his wife, brother, sister-in-law, former girlfriend, and some of his top students and close friends. By the time he moved to Los Alamos in 1943, he had renounced his political past. Yet he was still under suspicion by the Manhattan Project's security officers, a suspicion that intensified when he told them about having been approached on behalf of the Soviet Union early in 1943. Because he initially fabricated a story to conceal the identity of the friend who had contacted him, Oppenheimer contributed to his own later problems. During the war, however, because of his obvious indispensability to the bomb project, he did not encounter any difficulties.

Some of his students did. A group of left-wingers in or near the party, they were working for the Manhattan Project in the University of California's Radiation Laboratory at Berkeley during the war and attracted the attention of military intelligence officials and the FBI. Except for the transcript of a compromising conversation between one of these scientists and the local party leader, there was no evidence of espionage—and it may not have occurred. Not only did VENONA produce no revelations about the Berkeley lab, but the KGB replaced its San Francisco station chief in 1944 apparently because he failed to penetrate the Manhattan Project. Nonetheless, because the project's security officers assumed that Communists would automatically spy for the Soviet Union, they clung to their belief that espionage had taken place. Although they could bring no criminal charges against their suspects, they were able to have some of them removed from their posts. After the war, the FBI continued to keep tabs on these people. Then, as with the Bentley charges (see Chapter 5), HUAC took up the case. In 1948 and 1949, it called up Oppenheimer, his brother, and several other scientists. Although it claimed to be convinced that the Berkeley people "did deliver to the Soviet government every piece of scientific information they had from the Radiation Laboratory," the committee never found evidence for anything but the past party connections of some of its witnesses.

All of these stories resurfaced in 1953 when Oppenheimer's opponents within the national security establishment sought to force him out of power. They were upset about Oppenheimer's opposition to the Air Force's reliance on strategic bombing and his hesitations about the crash program to develop the hydrogen bomb. In November 1953 the former executive director of Congress's Joint Committee on Atomic Energy wrote to Hoover charging that "more probably than not J. Robert Oppenheimer is an agent of the Soviet Union." President Eisenhower then revoked Oppenheimer's security clearance pending an investigation by the AEC. During Oppenheimer's hearing before a special AEC panel in the spring of 1954, the government resuscitated all the old evidence about Oppenheimer's former left-wing ties and tried to make his clumsy efforts to conceal the identity of the man who had transmitted the Soviet request for aid appear sinister. The AEC commissioners who delivered the final verdict never questioned Oppenheimer's loyalty, but they decided that his judgment and associations—although more than a decade old—required withdrawal of his clearance. Again, as with so many of the major cases of the McCarthy period, the significance of the Oppenheimer case was largely symbolic: It showed that even someone as important as the father of the atomic bomb could not avoid punishment for having once associated with communism.

7

The Loyalty-Security Program

Given the political atmosphere of the early 1950s, it is testimony to Oppenheimer's protected status that someone with his former left-wing associations was allowed to handle atomic secrets until 1954. The federal government had long since implemented a loyalty-security program that ensured that people with such politically tainted backgrounds did not receive security clearances or remain on the official payroll. Arguably the single most important contribution the Truman administration made to the anti-Communist furor, the program screened all federal employees for evidence of Communist sympathies or affiliations. Implemented in 1947 in the hope that it would circumvent congressional action as well as keep Communists out of the government, the loyalty-security program was to legitimize the main weapon of McCarthyism: the use of political tests for employment. Moreover, by allowing the FBI to develop the criteria for those tests, the Truman administration indirectly disseminated the conservative agenda of the anti-Communist network to the rest of the nation.

By the summer of 1946, the White House was under considerable pressure to eliminate politically undesirable employees. After a brief hearing on the Communists-in-government issue in July, the House Civil Service Committee recommended that the executive branch revise its loyalty-security procedures. The Republican victory in the 1946 congressional elections and the prospect of having to face an even more unfriendly Congress goaded the administration into action. At the end of November, Truman set up a special interagency commission to handle the job. Although the FBI was not officially represented on the body, Hoover dominated its proceedings, having handpicked its chair and established its agenda. The commission worked quickly, its recommendations forming the basis of the new loyalty-security program embodied in Truman's Executive Order 9835 of March 21, 1947, the most important sections of which are in Document 7.

The program reflected the concerns and procedures of the FBI. It mandated a preliminary name check of all government employees and applicants in the files of the bureau, HUAC, and similar agencies. If any "derogatory information" turned up, the FBI would mount a full field investigation. The main innovation of Executive Order 9835 was to broaden the grounds for disqualifying government employees beyond such overtly disloyal activities as treason or espionage to membership in or "sympathetic association with" the Communist party or any one of a number of allegedly Communist, fascist, or totalitarian organizations. To help security officers administer the program, the attorney general was authorized to compile a list of the subversive groups.

If an investigation turned up enough evidence of suspicious political activities or associations to provide "reasonable grounds for belief in disloyalty," the employee would receive a written "interrogatory," a document that listed the specific charges. The employee could also request a hearing before a departmental and then a national Loyalty Review Board but could rarely find out the source of the allegations. This aspect of the program, which was to generate considerable injustice, once again reflected the preoccupations of the FBI. Protecting the bureau's informants took precedence over the civil liberties of the people under suspicion. As a result, public employees were fired on the basis of anonymous information and without being able to confront their accusers. It was, of course, possible for employees to contest the charges and retain their jobs, but the process was both humiliating and, once the government refused to provide free counsel for the suspects, expensive. As a result, roughly twelve thousand of the people involved in loyalty-security proceedings simply resigned without trying to fight for reinstatement.

The most prevalent injustices occurred as a result of the program's essentially ideological definition of what constituted an unacceptable "association." Because the executive order did not specify the exact nature of that association, the criteria were vague and came to be applied to a wide range of political beliefs and activities. Naturally, federal employees who were in or near the Communist party were especially affected. But people could lose their jobs for merely being on the "wrong" mailing lists, owning the "wrong" books, or having politically suspect relatives or friends. Because there were Communists in the leadership of the United Federal Workers (UFW), the union that represented government employees, UFW activists were particularly at risk. So, too, were people involved in fighting racial discrimination. All too often, the security officers who administered the loyalty-security program were themselves conservative and hostile to nonconformity. The case studies in Document 8 convey something of the Kafkaesque quality of the process.

Individual agencies varied in the way they administered the loyalty-security program. Oddly, the Post Office, for example, was much tougher than the State Department. In addition, as it became clear that the program had not solved Truman's Communists-in-government problem and that partisan attacks on the administration had not abated, loyalty-security officials tended to interpret the guidelines ever more stringently. People who had survived an examination in the early days of the program had their cases repeatedly exhumed. The *Amerasia* defendant John Stewart Service, who also became a symbol of the State Department's alleged "loss of China," was cleared by his superiors seven times before he was finally fired. In 1951, the criteria for dismissal changed from "reasonable grounds" for believing in someone's disloyalty to the less demanding "reasonable doubt as to loyalty." In 1953, President Eisenhower issued Executive Order 10450, which revised the program yet again to make it even easier to weed out security risks. Overall, between 1947 and 1956, approximately twenty-seven hundred federal employees were dismissed for loyalty-security reasons.

Almost from the start, the loyalty-security program came under attack, especially from liberals who deplored its reliance on "guilt by association" and its lack of procedural safeguards. Because its imposition of political tests for employment touched on important constitutional issues, the government was quickly involved in litigation. Individuals dismissed under the program sought reinstatement, and the groups on the attorney general's list contested the administration's failure to give them a hearing. During the late 1940s and early 1950s, in a pattern that was to characterize all its deliberations with regard to communism and internal security, the Supreme Court upheld the government's actions and refused to interfere with the loyalty-security program. By the mid-1950s, however, the Court under its more liberal Chief Justice Earl Warren began to question some of the more egregious dismissals of the period. In 1957 it decided to reinstate John Stewart Service. By then, however, political tests for employment had spread throughout the United States.

Executive Order 9835 was only the most well known of the federal government's cold war loyalty-security programs. These programs, all using essentially the same ideological criteria to screen people for their political views, extended far beyond the federal government.

There were, for example, security clearances required by agencies like the Department of Defense and the Atomic Energy Commission for the employees of the private companies and research laboratories that made weapons. For scientists, engineers, and the people who worked in defense plants, failure to obtain a security clearance could result in dismissal, even if their jobs did not require them to handle any sensitive materials. Left-wing unions were a particular target. In 1948 the Atomic Energy Commission refused to let the UE represent employees in its own installations or those of its contractors. When the Korean War broke out in the summer of 1950, the government expanded its political screening to the shipping industry. It gave the Coast Guard jurisdiction over a port security program that was clearly directed against the left-wing maritime unions. The State Department applied similar tests to the issuing of passports and visas; the military services, to the granting of honorable discharges.

Within a short time, state and local governments and private employers had also begun to impose political tests on their workers. Fueled largely as the Truman administration's program had been by the desire to avoid political embarrassment, school systems, social welfare agencies, movie studios, newspapers, universities—just about any institution that felt itself under pressure—adopted some kind of procedure for ensuring that no political undesirables would show up on their payrolls. The methods varied. There were loyalty oaths, background checks, and legislative investigations. Many employers simply copied the federal program and screened out people who belonged to groups on the attorney general's list.

Just as the Truman administration's loyalty-security program encouraged other employers to impose political tests on their employees, so the development of the attorney general's list was to have a similarly broad effect. Although originally designed to regularize the process of investigating federal employees, the list quickly developed a life of its own. Many of the ninety-three organizations on the original 1947 list—like the pro-Nazi German-American Bund or the North American Committee to Aid Spanish Democracy—were already defunct. Over the next few years the Justice Department continued to augment the list, until by the mid-1950s it contained nearly two hundred entries. As we can see from the version reprinted in Document 9, most of these organizations—like the International Workers Order and the Joint Anti-Fascist Refugee Committee—were the various front groups through which the party and its allies had promoted specific causes.

Nomination to the list was usually a kiss of death to an organization. For anti-Communist investigators and employers, however, the list was an enormous convenience. It was easier to identify people who had participated in the listed organizations, which operated in the open, than to find members of the secretive Communist party. Because many of these groups were run by party members, it was assumed that participating in them was the equivalent of being in the party (which was by no means always the case). In the climate of the early cold war, however, such distinctions made little difference. As the penalties for belonging to suspect organizations began to spread throughout American society, the nation of joiners began to shrink from joining anything.

8

The Assault on the Communist Party

By the late 1940s, the isolated and sectarian Communist party was about to vanish from American political life. Nonetheless, it remained a target. While partisan controversy swirled around the Communists-in-government issue and liberals criticized the loyalty-security program's lack of fairness, there was a general consensus among all political forces about the need to destroy the Communist party. Here again, federal initiatives were decisive and would be mimicked at the state and local levels as well as within the private sector. The onslaught against the party was a multipronged offensive in which almost every federal agency—from the State Department and Immigration and Naturalization Service to the Post Office and **National Labor Relations Board (NLRB)**—took part, along with a host of other private and public organizations. Well-known Communists and the organizations they worked with often found themselves fending off simultaneous attacks.

Central to the campaign were the criminal prosecutions and deportation proceedings directed against individual party leaders and key activists. The direct consequences of these proceedings—the jail sentences or deportations that were visited on these people—put them out of commission and thus deprived the party of their services. At the same time, the proceedings themselves, which invariably involved years of litigation, forced the party to devote most of its dwindling resources to its own defense. Moreover, criminalizing the Communist party as these initiatives did was a powerful way to marginalize it. The publicity that was generated reinforced the message that communism endangered the nation.

One of the federal government's main problems was that it did not want to flatly outlaw the Communist party. There was opposition to such a measure, and it was not just from leftists and civil libertarians. Not only did it seem inconsistent with American ideals and, quite possibly, with the Constitution, but it might be counterproductive as well, endowing the party with a seductive aura of martyrdom. The FBI opposed outlawing the party because an illegal, and therefore underground, organization would be much harder to keep under surveillance. Even so, Hoover was eager to find a way to make the party's activities, if not the organization itself, beyond the law. He was the most persistent advocate within the federal government of taking the party to court.

It was hard, however, to find grounds for a prosecution. After all, there was nothing intrinsically illegal about what Communists did. Nonetheless, the FBI believed that a case against the party could be made. The actual grounds for such a prosecution would be immaterial. The main function of a trial, as one of Hoover's main lieutenants explained, was educational: to show "that Communism is dangerous," that the party "advocates the overthrow of the government by force and violence," and that the "patriotism of Communists is not directed towards the United States but towards the Soviet Union." As early as 1945, the bureau had begun to recruit witnesses and collect evidence for use in a criminal proceeding. It was also pushing the Justice Department to act.

The decision to prosecute seems to have been made in a rather haphazard way, the product of bureaucratic routines rather than a high-level political decision. As pressures from Hoover, Congress, and elsewhere intensified, Attorney General Tom Clark set the apparatus in motion when he delegated several subordinates to look into the matter early in 1948. After scouring the statute books in search of an appropriate prosecution tool, the Justice Department's attorneys settled on a conspiracy charge under the 1940 Smith Act. The party was so obviously the target that the prosecutors did not decide which individuals to arraign until the very last moment. For some reason, they did not consult with their superiors when they decided in the middle of June to seek an indictment from the New York City grand jury that was hearing testimony on Elizabeth Bentley's charges. The prosecution, though a surprise to the White House, was not unwelcome to Truman and his aides; it could be used during the 1948 presidential campaign to show that the administration was tough on Communists.

On the morning of July 20, 1948, arrest warrants went out for Eugene Dennis, the party's general secretary, and eleven other National Committee members. They were charged with conspiring to "teach and advocate" the "violent overthrow" of the American government. A rather old-fashioned sedition law, the Smith Act was directed against the traditional left-wing threat of revolutionary violence. Its language, with its emphasis on the illegality of encouraging the overthrow of the government, dictated the nature of the trial. The prosecution would have to find a way to link the defendants with action that could be interpreted as advocating or teaching the violent destruction of the U.S. government.

Such an accusation was hard to prove. The Communist party's revolutionary ardor was obviously theoretical and none of the defendants had ever called for violence, let alone begun to gather guns. As the excerpts from the transcript of the trial (shown in Document 10) reveal, the prosecution relied on literary evidence—on those passages from the works of Marx, Lenin, and Stalin that advocated revolutionary violence against the bourgeois state. To link the individual defendants with the incriminating texts, the government enlisted an assortment of professional ex-Communists and FBI informants. These witnesses testified about their experiences in the party, describing the instruction they had received in the party's schools and the books they read.

The most important witness was Louis Budenz, the former managing editor of the party's newspaper, the *Daily Worker.* After his defection from the party in the fall of 1945, Budenz came under the protection of the Catholic Church, from which he received the financial and spiritual support he had once gotten from the party. Budenz was to become one of the nation's most ubiquitous witnesses, offering paid testimony on the evils of communism at most of the major cold war criminal trials, congressional hearings, and deportation proceedings. Ultimately, his willingness to embroider his testimony to suit his patrons led to such serious questions about his veracity that even the FBI, initially his most enthusiastic customer, privately admitted that "Budenz, on occasions, is inaccurate in positive statements" and stopped consulting him.

But at the first Smith Act trial, where Eugene Dennis and ten of his comrades (the party's chair, William Z. Foster, having been severed from the case because of poor health) were the defendants, Budenz's testimony was crucial. As Document 10 reveals, his main contribution was to identify the most militant passages in the literature of Marxism-Leninism and then explain how those passages—and only those passages—embodied the genuine ideology of American communism. Any less violent language was, Budenz explained, "merely window dressing asserted for protective purposes" and actually meant the opposite of what it said. In short, if Budenz was to be believed, Communists always lied except when they advocated bloodshed. Like the other prosecution witnesses, Budenz also testified to other aspects of the party's program that bolstered the government's case—the party's subservience to the Soviet Union, conspiratorial practices, and infiltration of labor unions in heavy industry.

Despite the literary nature of the government's case, the trial was a raucous affair. Both sides hoped to score political as well as legal points. Party leaders had decided to mount what they called a "labor defense" and rouse the American masses to demand an acquittal. Accordingly, party stalwarts devoted themselves to such activities as picketing the courthouse and organizing petition drives. It was a sectarian and self-defeating strategy. By scorning "bourgeois legal tricks," party leaders forfeited their best potential defense; they refused to make the civil libertarian argument that the prosecution's attack on what the defendants had read and said violated the First Amendment. Instead, they fought on the government's turf and sought to show that the party abjured force and violence.

The prosecutors also played to the public. They purposely forced several of the defendants into contempt of court by asking them questions about other people that the government's attorneys knew they would refuse to answer. The tactic gave the prosecutors a pretext for putting some of the party's leaders in jail during the trial and thus dramatizing how dangerous Communists could be. The judge, Harold Medina, was hardly impartial. He actually believed that the party leaders and their attorneys were trying to persecute *him,* and he treated them accordingly. For eleven months, in what would become the longest trial thus far in American history, attorneys, defendants, and the judge bickered, wrangled, and insulted one another. By the end of the ordeal, Medina was so furious at the party's lawyers that he cited them for contempt of court and sentenced them to jail.

Even if the trial had been more decorous and the party had mounted a more realistic defense, the outcome would still have been the same. In October 1949, when the case went to the jury, the cold war was at its zenith: The Soviet Union had just exploded its first atomic bomb and the Communists had taken over China. Within the United States, the anti-Communist furor was also at its peak. Alger Hiss's two trials were taking place in the same federal courthouse, and Judith Coplon, an employee of the Department of Justice, had just been picked up by the FBI with a sheaf of government documents in her purse that she may have been about to give to the Russian who was arrested with her. The anti-Communist furor had begun to spread beyond Washington. The guilty verdict in the *Dennis* case was no surprise, not even to the defendants.

From the start, the protagonists all knew that the case would reach the Supreme Court; and, in fact, the party's lawyers had been trying to lay the basis for an appeal throughout the trial. The issues—the constitutionality of the Smith Act and the extent to which the government could impose limits on political activity in the name of national security—could not be resolved in any other way. The Supreme Court's earlier First Amendment decisions had produced a mixed record. Most decisions had been based on the "clear and present danger" rule, which recognized that the government could limit free speech but only in the face of a serious threat. During World War II, the Court's majority did not view communism as a danger and ruled in several important deportation cases that the government had to prove that party members were actually planning to use force and violence. Yet in cases involving the wartime internment of Japanese Americans, the Court allowed massive violations of the most basic human rights in the name of national defense.

With the coming of the cold war, the Court faced the prospect of having to decide whether and to what extent it would support the government's contention that communism had become such a threat to national security that its eradication might require the abridgment of free speech. At first the justices dealt gingerly with Communist-related cases; they usually denied *certiorari,* refusing to accept jurisdiction over a case and thus letting the lower court's ruling stand. After two of the most liberal justices died unexpectedly in the summer of 1949, the Court cautiously began to accommodate itself to the changing political atmosphere. Like most Americans, the justices had come to believe that communism endangered the nation's existence and that, in the words of Justice Felix Frankfurter, it would be wrong to treat the party's advocacy of communism "as a seminar in political theory."

On June 4, 1951, the Court handed down its 6–2 decision in the *Dennis* case. In writing the majority opinion, the chief justice, a former Kentucky politician named Fred Vinson, relied heavily on the appeals court ruling that had been delivered the previous year by Learned Hand, one of the nation's most distinguished jurists. As the excerpts from the *Dennis* decision in Document 11 show, Vinson appropriated the lower court's revision of the "clear and present danger" doctrine and imposed a new test that, in Hand's words, balanced "whether the gravity of the 'evil' discounted by its improbability, justifies such invasion of free speech as is necessary to avoid the danger." The outbreak of the Korean War in June 1950 had, in both Hand's and Vinson's eyes, so increased the dangers that even though they recognized that there was no prospect of the small and unpopular Communist party overthrowing the American government, its conspiratorial nature and its ties to the Soviet Union justified its suppression. The two dissenting justices, Hugo Black and William O. Douglas, were more concerned about the damage to freedom of speech than they were about the threat posed by what Douglas labeled "the best known, the most beset, and the least thriving of any **fifth column** in history."

Besides putting the party's leaders behind bars, the decision prompted the Justice Department to initiate new Smith Act prosecutions. Within a few weeks, the rest of the party's top leadership was under indictment, as were local leaders in New York, California, Maryland, western Pennsylvania, and Hawaii. Later, cases were opened in Seattle, New Haven, St. Louis, Detroit, Philadelphia, San Juan, Cleveland, Boston, and Denver. By the time the prosecutions wound down with a final set of indictments against the Massachusetts party leaders in 1956, the government had filed Smith Act charges against nearly 150 people. Not all the defendants went to jail, however. The party's attorneys in some of these "second string" cases abandoned the unproductive courtroom tactics of the *Dennis* defendants and adopted a civil libertarian strategy. More important, the political atmosphere changed. The Court, now under Chief Justice Earl Warren, began to back away from its earlier decisions, though it did so fitfully and erratically. By that point, however, the massive legal assault on the party had done its work.

State and local officials had also gotten into the act. Ambitious politicians in Massachusetts, Pennsylvania, and elsewhere dusted off old state sedition laws and began prosecuting local party leaders and other alleged subversives. Here, however, the Supreme Court did intervene, ruling in 1956 that the federal government's predominant interest in the area of internal security overruled that of the states. But there were other laws that public officials could enforce against individual Communists. In Birmingham, Alabama, for example, the local police actually arrested someone for illegal possession of Communist literature. In venues that lacked such specific statutes, officials used ordinary criminal laws. One Ohio prosecutor, besides arresting local Communists for using false names on their drivers' licenses, actually filed a narcotics charge against a party official caught with a bottle of ulcer pills on his person. Admittedly, such types of prosecutions were extreme; but, at least during the early 1950s, individual

Communists were subject to harassment by law enforcement authorities at every level.

Contempt citations were another legal mechanism used to punish Communists and other alleged subversives. Unlike other criminal cases, contempt proceedings were not the direct result of a prosecutorial decision but the by-product of voluntary actions taken by the defendants themselves during the course of a congressional hearing, trial, or grand jury session. From the prosecution's point of view, contempt charges had considerable advantages in that there were no evidentiary problems involved in proving that a crime had been committed. The party's leaders were especially at risk during the McCarthy period. Not only were they called before dozens of tribunals, but the authorities would sometimes deliberately provoke them into contempt.

Criminal prosecutions were not the only weapons the federal government could wield against individual Communists. As early as 1946, the INS was arresting foreign-born Communists and ex-Communists for deportation. Immigration proceedings had long been a staple of federal antiradical campaigns. Sending Communists back to Moscow (or wherever they had been born) not only punished the individuals involved but reinforced the message that they belonged to an alien, un-American movement. In addition, the foreign-born had fewer constitutional rights than other Americans. A still-standing 1893 Supreme Court decision said that deportations were not criminal proceedings and thus did not have to meet the same constitutional standards of due process. In practice, this meant that the INS could round up foreign-born Communists and detain them indefinitely without bail while trying to deport them.

Deportation proceedings were similar to the other anti-Communist proceedings of the period in that they dealt with the same kinds of charges, evidence, and, when not relying on anonymous informers, even the same witnesses. The INS was, in fact, the main employer of many of the leading professional ex-Communists. During the late 1940s and early 1950s, the Supreme Court refused to seriously restrict the incarceration or expulsion of politically undesirable aliens; until 1956, it did not even stop the deportations of long-lapsed party members whose party association had been minimal. Ultimately it turned out to be technically impossible to expel most of these people; the Eastern European countries where they had been born refused to accept them. Thus, although the government initiated action against some fifteen thousand subversive aliens between 1946 and 1966, only about two hundred fifty were actually deported. Still, the proceedings were punitive in and of themselves, involving years of incarceration, litigation, unemployment, and restrictions on the travel and political activities of the people involved. Few of the foreign-born Communist leaders or their spouses were spared the ordeal.

Damaging as the government's prosecutions and immigration proceedings were to the Communist party, they did not prevent continuing demands for even stronger measures against the party. The result was the passage of the Internal Security Act of 1950, the so-called McCarran Act, named for Nevada's Pat McCarran, the powerful chair of the Senate Judiciary Committee. The measure, originally proposed by Richard Nixon and his HUAC colleague Karl Mundt in 1948, was designed to eliminate the Communist threat by forcing the party, its members, and its front groups to register with the government. The bill's advocates claimed that because the party was a secret conspiracy, exposure would inflict more damage than outlawing it, especially since failure to register would be a crime.

The Truman administration argued that the bill was unnecessary because the Smith Act prosecutions were effectively handling the Communist menace, but its opposition had little impact. Parliamentary ploys kept the measure bottled up in committee for a while, but in the anti-Communist furor that swept Congress after the outbreak of the Korean War in the summer of 1950, it was impossible to stop its passage. Even the Senate's liberals, who opposed the bill, felt themselves under so much pressure that they tried to stop it by offering a substitute that included provisions for rounding up and detaining alleged subversives during an emergency. Their strategy failed as the liberals' detention camp proposal was tacked on to the rest of the bill and, along with an assorted package of politically restrictive immigration measures, easily passed over Truman's veto.

As Truman's veto message, excerpted in Document 12, had predicted, it was clear that the registration provisions at the heart of the new measure would be hard to enforce. Nonetheless, the government set out to administer the law. Within a few weeks of passage of the McCarran Act, the Department of Justice prepared to submit a petition to the newly established **Subversive Activities Control Board (SACB)** to force the Communist party to register. The SACB hearings that the registration procedure required were in almost every respect identical to the Smith Act trials. The same literature, witnesses, and arguments were used. However, because the McCarran Act reflected a more contemporary view of the Communist menace than did the immigration laws or the Smith Act, the Justice Department's case tended to emphasize the party's conspiratorial nature and its sub-servience to Moscow rather than the harder-to-prove charge that the party sought to overthrow the government by force and violence.

The process of forcing the party to register took years, for the party appealed at every stage and the Supreme Court, which repeat-edly dealt with the case, upheld the McCarran Act in 1961 but reserved its final judgment on the constitutionality of the registration provisions. Ultimately it decided, as it had long been clear it would, that the act violated the Fifth Amendment's strictures against self-incrimination. But that decision did not come down until the mid-1960s.

By then, the Communist party had lost all its influence. While the party's own political mistakes and Soviet leader Nikita Khrushchev's 1956 revelations of Stalin's crimes contributed significantly to that decline, so too did the official campaign against it. The many prosecu-tions directed against the party, its constituent groups, and its leaders transformed it into a self-defense organization. Other activities simply fell by the wayside as Communist activists scrambled to raise money and drum up support for their beleaguered comrades. When the party's top leaders were not in prison, they were usually in court or preparing for one or another legal proceeding. Diverted from its other political tasks, the party, at least in its public face, had become a civil liberties group.

The Communist party's response to the attacks on it actually inten-sified its own internal problems. Ever since the party expelled its gen-eral secretary, Earl Browder, in 1945, its leaders had been divided about how to react to the deepening cold war and domestic political repression. Hard-liners stressed the imminence of World War III and the advent of fascism in America. The moderates, who did not want to be seen as soft on capitalism, acquiesced in the left's increasingly pes-simistic view of the political situation. Despite misgivings, they went along with preparations for going underground so that in the event of war and the outlawing of the party a remnant would survive to lead a resistance movement as the Communists had done in Nazi-occupied Europe during World War II.

The escalating assault on the party increased its leaders' paranoia. Caught off guard by the surfacing of FBI informers at the Smith Act trial in 1949, the party became obsessed about its own security. Allegedly unreliable members were purged. Recruiting came to a halt. The party was completely restructured to make it more difficult for informers to penetrate, and most of its open activities were abandoned. The Supreme Court's *Dennis* decision activated the plan to go underground. Instead of turning themselves in with their codefendants, four of the party's leaders fled. Junius Scales was among the hundreds of other trusted activists who also disappeared, abandoning their families, acquiring new identities, and moving to cities where they were unknown.

The decision to go underground was disastrous for the Communist party. Not only did it reinforce the party's image as a secret conspiracy and thus seem to justify the repression against it, but the furtive and lonely existence that characterized life underground demoralized everyone who took part in it. American communism never recovered. The shock of Khrushchev's 1956 revelations about Stalin's crimes drove its most independent members out of the party. Its formal existence continued, but it had become an ineffectual political sect.

9

The Destruction of the
Communist Fronts and Unions

A frail Communist party survived the government's attempts to destroy it, but the Communist movement was dead. The front groups that were so crucial to the political culture of American communism were already in decline by the time the Subversive Activities Control Board (SACB) decided to register them. They had been severely damaged by the attorney general's list, which publicly identified them as subversive and targeted their members for unemployment and other reprisals. Few dedicated souls were willing to take the risk that joining such organizations entailed. Dwindling memberships were not these groups' only problems. The Internal Revenue Service (IRS) revoked their tax exemptions and FBI informers pervaded their ranks. Their leaders, when not fighting criminal charges or deportation proceedings, were on regular call before HUAC and other investigating committees. In New York State, for example, the attorney general took away the charter of the American Committee for Protection of Foreign Born and the commissioner of insurance canceled the International Workers Order's license to sell insurance, thus destroying its function as a fraternal benefit society.

The SACB's registration orders were the last straw. Most of the beleaguered organizations simply folded. They no longer had the resources for another protracted battle. The few front groups that did survive were vindicated by the Supreme Court but not until the 1960s. By then the movement that had once sustained these organizations had long since vanished. Functioning primarily as alumni associations for the old left, they serviced the tiny remnants of their former clientele but had no real impact on American political life.

A similar fate befell the left-wing labor unions, the most important organizations within the Communist orbit. At the height of the party's influence in the late 1940s, Communists and their allies controlled about a dozen unions, including the CIO's third largest, the powerful United Electrical, Radio, and Machine Workers (UE), and had significant pockets of strength within other unions as well. Relatively few rank-and-file members of these unions belonged to the Communist party; its influence was concentrated at the top, among the union's officers and paid staff, a disproportionately large number of whom were party members or sympathizers. Beginning in the late 1930s employers and union rivals had been using charges of Communist influence to try to drive these people from power. However, because they were devoted and effective labor leaders, they usually retained the loyalty of their own members and the support of the CIO's liberal leaders. The cold war changed all that.

Because the left-wing unions actually gave the party some influence within American society, the campaign against them was particularly intense. Government, industry, and the rest of the labor movement all became involved. The unions often found themselves facing attacks from internal dissidents, rival unions, employers, and a variety of federal agencies all at the same time. Catholic anti-Communists organized rank-and-file opposition movements, while other unions, including other CIO unions, raided the left-led unions and tried to steal their members. The counterproductive policies of the Communist party in the late 1940s made it harder for the leaders of these unions to remain loyal to the party while maintaining their power and legitimacy within the labor movement.

Ironically, one of the weapons that the labor movement's anti-Communists used most effectively against the left-wing unions was the by-product of a legislative attack on all of organized labor. At the end of World War II, millions of workers had gone out on strike, antagonizing public opinion and sparking demands for curbing union power. When the Republican party took over both houses of Congress in 1947, restrictive legislation was inevitable. The Taft-Hartley Act, which Congress passed over Truman's veto in June, seriously curtailed union power. It also sought to eliminate Communists from leadership positions within the labor movement by requiring union officials to file an affidavit with the NLRB stating that they were not in the party.

At first, it was by no means obvious that the affidavits would have much of an impact. Labor leaders of all political persuasions opposed the Taft-Hartley law and hoped that Truman's electoral victory in 1948 would lead to its repeal. Although some union leaders signed the disclaimer, many did not, including many important non-Communists like CIO President Philip Murray, who opposed it on principle. The wording of the affidavit, its vagueness and its prohibition of "belief in" and "association with" communism, raised serious constitutional issues that both Communist-led and non-Communist unions petitioned the federal courts to decide.

The Taft-Hartley affidavits were too tempting a weapon for the foes of the left-led unions to ignore. Anti-Communist activists stepped up their campaigns for control of union locals or led their followers out of the union. Rival unions intensified their raids. In the pre-Taft-Hartley days the left-led unions had usually rebuffed such challenges, but now they could not fend off their union rivals because their failure to submit the non-Communist affidavits barred them from participating in NLRB representation elections. At the same time, some employers refused to bargain with the noncomplying unions and, deprived of assistance from the NLRB, the left-led unions had trouble fighting back. They had become less and less able to protect their members' economic interests. By mid-1949, it was clear that the Taft-Hartley Act would be neither repealed nor overturned by the Supreme Court. The recalcitrant unions capitulated. With their survival at stake, their officers signed the affidavits.

It was too late. They had lost the support of the rest of the labor movement and could not recoup. For years Murray had been under pressure to eliminate Communist influence from the CIO but had shrunk from taking any strong measures because he did not want to destroy the left-liberal alliance that had been so important to the labor movement during the Popular Front period before and during World War II. However, as the cold war intensified and the party's opposition to it seemed increasingly anti-American, the political rift between the mainstream liberalism of the CIO's leadership and the pro-Communist stance of its left-wing unions deepened. Some of the most important Communist labor leaders resolved the antagonism between their dual loyalties to the party and to the CIO by breaking with the party. Others remained loyal only to find themselves and their unions increasingly under attack from their former partners in the CIO.

The 1948 election forced the issue. The CIO had become increasingly dependent on the Truman administration, and Murray viewed the left-led unions' support for the third-party campaign of Henry Wallace and their opposition to the Marshall Plan and the rest of Truman's foreign policy as insubordination. The denouement came at the CIO's annual convention in the fall of 1949, when the delegates voted to expel the UE and another left-wing union and to authorize an official investigation into the Communist affiliations of ten others. As the resolution expelling UE in Document 13 reveals, the CIO did not criticize the unions' activities as labor organizations but rather cited convention resolutions, newspaper editorials, and contributions to groups on the attorney general's list as evidence that the left-led unions had followed the party line. The outcome of the investigations was never in doubt. With the exception of one union that ousted its politically tainted leaders, all the others were expelled from the CIO in the spring of 1950. The expulsions weakened the left-wing unions even further, enabling secessionists and raiders to intensify their attacks.

The government also stepped up its offensive. Congressional hearings, contempt citations, Smith Act prosecutions, deportations, SACB proceedings, security clearance denials, income tax audits—the assault was massive and often forced these unions and their top leaders to face several different attacks at one time. They also had to confront the various proceedings that developed out of their decision to comply with the Taft-Hartley law. After all, many of the left-wing labor officials who had signed the non-Communist affidavits had been Communists; and the NLRB refused to believe that they had all left the party. The board not only tried to decertify the unions involved but also got the Justice Department to indict some of the signers for perjury. Meanwhile, Congress, which had become equally frustrated with what it considered the ineffectiveness of the Taft-Hartley affidavits, passed the Communist Control Act of 1954 whose provisions authorized the SACB to register the left-led unions as "Communist infiltrated organizations" and thus make them ineligible for the services of the NLRB.

Legally, most of these measures failed. Only a handful of left-wing labor leaders went to jail or were deported, the SACB never registered any unions, and the NLRB did not decertify them. The federal judiciary, in the field of labor as elsewhere, was to nullify most of the official anti-Communist campaign, but it made little difference. By the time the Supreme Court issued its definitive rulings in the mid-1960s, the cumulative weight of all the private and public attacks on the left-led unions overwhelmed them. Only the West Coast longshoremen's union remained intact. The UE, which had once had close to half a million members, was down to about ninety thousand. Smaller unions simply disappeared or merged with their more successful rivals. The left-led unions were the strongest institutions within the Communist movement, and their demise was doubly disastrous. Not only did it deprive Communists and their allies of their traditional entree into the American working class, but it also deprived the rest of the movement of the concrete support and contact with reality that those unions had provided. The elimination of the party's position within the labor movement, combined with the destruction of the front groups and the marginalization of the party, meant that the anti-Communist crusade had succeeded. It had eradicated the influence of American communism.

10

Congressional Committees and Unfriendly Witnesses

The institutions that most typified the McCarthy era were congressional investigating committees. They were also the most important vehicle for extending the anti-Communist crusade throughout the rest of society. Their activities and the publicity they generated transformed what had initially been a devastating but nonetheless narrowly focused attack on a small political party and its adherents into a wide-ranging campaign that touched almost every aspect of American life.

In many respects, the operations of these committees paralleled those of the executive branch. They publicized the dangers of the Communist threat, their hearings often producing the same scenarios as trials, with many of the same charges, witnesses, and defendants. But because congressional hearings were immune from the due process requirements that accompanied criminal prosecutions, the committees had more leeway to denounce and accuse. They came to specialize in punishing individuals by exposing their alleged Communist connections and costing them their jobs. So effective had the committees become that by the height of the McCarthy era, in the mid-1950s, people were often fired simply for receiving a subpoena from HUAC or one of the other committees.

Investigating committees served more partisan functions as well. Conservatives in and outside of the Republican party used them to attack the liberalism of the New Deal and the Truman administration. On the local level, the committees often functioned as hired guns for their allies within the anti-Communist network. Conveniently timed hearings, with their highly publicized and damaging charges of Communist affiliation, could target specific groups and individuals at crucial moments, such as during strikes, union elections, or sessions of state legislatures. The committees also collected information and did research for the rest of the anti-Communist network. Their published reports and hearings were reference tools for the professional anti-Communists. HUAC was one of the network's main repositories, and, unlike the FBI, it shared its files openly with members of Congress and their constituents.

HUAC was the trailblazer, the oldest and most influential of the anti-Communist committees. Established in 1938 as part of the conservative backlash against Roosevelt's New Deal, it developed the nation's most successful techniques for exposing political undesirables. By the mid-1950s there were dozens of similar bodies at every level of government emulating HUAC's operations and procedures. The most important were Senator McCarthy's Permanent Investigating Subcommittee of the Government Operations Committee and Senator Pat McCarran's powerful Senate Internal Security Subcommittee (SISS), both of which conducted exactly the same kinds of investigations as HUAC. More than a dozen states and even a few cities had also established their own Un-American Activities Committees or authorized other investigators to make similar types of probes.

HUAC had not always been so influential. During the 1930s and early 1940s, the committee had a reputation for irresponsibility. Few members of Congress considered it a prestigious assignment and many of its mainly southern or rural members were ineffectual or worse. It recruited its staff from former FBI agents or professional ex-Communists whose ideological fervor or desire for publicity occasionally brought them into conflict with the more sedate mores of the congressional establishment. The committee's tendency to publicize unsubstantiated charges of Communist influence did not bolster its credibility. For all its fecklessness, however, nothing HUAC did seriously threatened its existence or interfered with the success of its mission. The publicity it attracted as well as its solid support from the American Legion and like-minded conservative groups ensured that few members of Congress would openly dare to oppose it or vote against its annual appropriations.

Even so, it was not until the late 1940s that HUAC gained respectability and consolidated its power. The shift in national priorities that accompanied the cold war brought the nation's political elites closer to HUAC's anti-Communist worldview. The committee thus became less marginal and got support from other institutions. This support— whether it took the form of the Supreme Court's failure to intervene against the committee's violations of civil liberties or the willingness of private employers to fire **unfriendly witnesses**—legitimized HUAC and increased its power. The Hiss case of 1948 was equally important (see Chapter 5). It convinced the public of the effectiveness of congressional investigations for uncovering Communist subversion and it showed Republicans and other conservatives how useful those investigations could be for harassing the Truman administration.

By the early 1950s, HUAC and the other committees had refined the business of exposing Communists into a science. The often frenzied improvisations that characterized HUAC's investigations during Nixon's attempt to fortify Chambers's charges against Hiss yielded to increasingly stylized rituals that all participants adhered to. (See Document 5.) The committees' basic objectives remained unchanged: They were looking for Communists—and they found them. The committees did not randomly select the subjects of their investigations. Their staff members made sure that most people questioned during the public hearings in the late 1940s and 1950s were or had been members of the party or within its political orbit.

It was not always easy for the committees to find suitably vulnerable witnesses. After all, most Communists hid their party ties. But the committees had many allies. The rest of the anti-Communist network assisted committee staffers in identifying appropriate witnesses. The FBI was especially helpful, routinely supplying the committees with information from its supposedly sacrosanct files. State and local police forces and their Red squads gave similar cooperation. The committees' staffers and their consultants also pulled names from the memories of informers and from the documents that they and other anti-Communist experts like J. B. Matthews had amassed. (See Chapter 2.) Of course, the committees pressed the people they had subpoenaed to cooperate and supply further leads.

Most committee hearings revolved around a symbolic ritual designed to expose someone as a member or former member of the Communist party. By the early 1950s these unmasking ceremonies had become almost routine. First, a cooperative ex-Communist or expert witness described the pattern of Communist infiltration in the area of American life the committee was supposedly exploring and listed the alleged infiltrators by name. Then the committee interrogated those people one by one, invariably asking them the crucial question "Are you now or have you ever been a member of the Communist party?" Witnesses who answered in the affirmative then had to name names. Although some witnesses produced the required names without assistance, the usual procedure was for the committee's counsel or another member of the staff to read out a list of alleged Communists and ask the witnesses to confirm whether these people had been members of the party. Because the committee already knew the names it was asking its witnesses to identify, it was clear that exposure, not information, was the goal.

Most of the time, these rituals took place in private, in a preliminary executive session. Witnesses who refused to answer the committee's questions were then called for a second hearing in public, while more cooperative witnesses or those who were politically spotless were sometimes excused from further testimony. The committees justified their practice of requiring witnesses to name names by explaining that it was the only way the witness could prove that he or she had really broken with the party. It was a crude political test—and one that caused enormous anguish for the committees' witnesses.

By the 1950s, many of the people who appeared before HUAC and the other committees had already dropped out of the Communist party and were no longer politically active. A few of them had decided to defy the committees for political reasons, because that seemed the best way to oppose what the investigators were doing. Others would have been willing to reveal their own past activities, even their past membership in the party, but they would not name names. They would not, as one witness explained, "crawl through the mud to be an informer." Naming names was an issue of personal morality. Playwright Lillian Hellman spoke for these witnesses when she told HUAC in a statement, reproduced in Document 14, that "I cannot and will not cut my conscience to fit this year's fashions." Their own scruples against informing as well as their political opposition to the investigations forced these people into a legal bind. The Supreme Court had left them no alternative but to refuse all cooperation with the committees.

When HUAC intensified its anti-Communist investigations in the early years of the cold war, it was by no means clear that it had the constitutional right to question people about their political beliefs and activities. The First Amendment's strictures against congressional interference with the right of free speech and assembly could easily be interpreted as preventing the committee from probing the politics of its witnesses. During 1946 and 1947, most of the men and women who refused to answer HUAC's questions assumed that they had First Amendment protection. They knew that they were taking risks. They could be cited, indicted, and tried for contempt of Congress and could well end up in prison if the Supreme Court did not overturn their convictions on constitutional grounds. But they and their lawyers expected that they would avoid that outcome.

The experiences of the Hollywood Ten were emblematic. Although their cases did not set legal precedents, these screenwriters and directors became the most notorious group of HUAC witnesses to rely on the First Amendment. They had all been in the party and, when subpoenaed to appear before the committee in October 1947, they took a confrontational stand. Like many of HUAC's other unfriendly witnesses of the period, they and their attorneys assumed that the Supreme Court would probably vindicate them; also, like the Smith Act defendants, they used their public hearings as a forum to expound their own political views. Excerpts from their testimony in Document 15 show how rancorous the sessions became. Witnesses and committee members yelled at each other, and several of the Ten were literally pulled away from the witness stand by federal marshals. A month later the full House of Representatives overwhelmingly voted to cite them for contempt. They were tried and convicted in the spring of 1948. Two years later, the Supreme Court's refusal to hear their case upheld the lower court decisions and confirmed their convictions. Had they known at the time of their hearings that they would actually go to prison, many of the Ten might have been more restrained—though probably no more cooperative.

In 1947, when the Ten appeared before HUAC, the Supreme Court had not yet ruled on the First Amendment rights of unfriendly witnesses and HUAC was still considered slightly disreputable. Because the justices at first refused to hear these cases, it was not clear how they would handle the substantive constitutional issues that the committee's activities presented. But as the official campaign against American communism intensified and public sympathy for the uncooperative witnesses began to erode, it became increasingly unlikely that the majority of the justices would take an unpopular position on any case that involved the politically sensitive issue of communism. Unlike in the *Dennis* case, there was no question of national security involved, so the Court based its reluctance to challenge what it perceived to be the will of the people—or at least of the Congress—on the doctrine of judicial restraint. That meant that the Court would not overrule the clearly expressed policies of other branches of government. Most of the justices disapproved of HUAC's heavy-handed tactics, but, as Justice Robert Jackson explained in 1949, they felt "it would be an unwarranted act of judicial usurpation to strip Congress of its investigatory power or to assume for the courts the function of supervising congressional committees." In short, HUAC had a free hand.

The Hollywood Ten were among the last unfriendly witnesses to invoke the First Amendment. By 1948, most of the people who wanted to avoid having to answer the committee's questions had begun to rely on the Fifth Amendment's privilege against self-incrimination. Among the first witnesses to use the Fifth in this way were the alleged members of the spy ring identified by Elizabeth Bentley. Although the privilege of not having to testify against oneself had developed in England during the seventeenth century expressly to shield dissidents and had been incorporated into the Bill of Rights along with other guarantees for criminal defendants, such as trial by jury, its use before congressional committees was relatively new and it was unclear just how much protection the Supreme Court would allow it to provide. Still, by the end of 1948, most witnesses had few alternatives. The federal courts were not upholding the First Amendment and people who denied the committee's charges, like Alger Hiss, were being indicted for perjury.

It took a few years for the Fifth Amendment cases to reach the Supreme Court. Once they did, the justices, who had refused to protect the First Amendment rights of unfriendly witnesses, were more willing to intervene in the apparently less sensitive terrain of procedure and uphold a witness's privilege against self-incrimination. Ironically, the Court's own decision upholding the constitutionality of the Smith Act in the *Dennis* case enabled it to extend the protection offered by the Fifth Amendment. Although the privilege ostensibly applied to criminal proceedings, not congressional hearings, the Court admitted that witnesses' answers to questions about their Communist ties could become "a link in the chain" of evidence that might make them liable for prosecution under the Smith Act. Over the next few years the federal judiciary continued to expand the protection granted by the Fifth Amendment so that eventually unfriendly witnesses did not even have to answer questions about where they lived or worked.

The Court would not protect people who refused to name names, however. The main problem here was the so-called waiver rule, under which witnesses who talked about themselves were assumed to have automatically waived their privilege against self-incrimination. Although the Supreme Court granted protection to witnesses under the Fifth Amendment, it did not allow witnesses who waived the Fifth to invoke it to avoid answering questions about other people. This rule, and their attorneys' understandable caution about it, forced many witnesses into a more uncooperative stance than they might have taken had their refusal to name names been accepted. As a result, it became impossible, for example, for many ex-Communists to give a public explanation of their experiences in the party and thus counter the demonized picture of the party that so pervaded the public discourse.

Though a legal godsend for uncooperative witnesses, the Fifth Amendment became a public relations disaster. The committees exploited the waiver doctrine to the hilt, knowing full well that few Americans understood its legal technicalities. Witnesses invoked the Fifth Amendment, the committees and their supporters claimed, because they were trying to hide something. Because many of the people who refused to testify were or had been in the party, the committees pushed the notion that everybody who took the Fifth was a "Fifth Amendment Communist." For Senator McCarthy, "A witness's refusal to answer whether or not he is a Communist on the ground that his answer would tend to incriminate him is the most positive proof obtainable that the witness is a Communist." Insisting that the people who took the Fifth were guilty of whatever it was they refused to talk about, the committees plied reluctant witnesses with damaging questions in the confident expectation that they could not answer them. Scientists could not deny outlandish charges that they had spied for the Soviet Union; teachers could not rebut similarly exaggerated allegations that they had brainwashed their students.

By the early 1950s, the disadvantages of using the Fifth encouraged some witnesses to seek alternatives. As Document 14 reveals, Lillian Hellman tried unsuccessfully to have HUAC allow her to talk about herself but not about others. Other witnesses searched for other ways to avoid naming names. Some took what came to be known as the "diminished Fifth" and denied present involvement with the party but invoked their privilege against self-incrimination with regard to the past. Others offered new technical reasons for their refusal to answer the committees' questions and, in a few cases, even reverted to the First Amendment in the hopes that the Supreme Court might reconsider its earlier position. It did a bit. Although the Court did not restore the protection of the First Amendment until the mid-1960s, it did whittle away at the committees' powers to compel testimony, usually on procedural grounds.

The protection the Court granted to unfriendly witnesses was only legal. It did not shield them from the notoriety that their refusal to cooperate with the committees ensured or from the extralegal sanctions that their employers applied. Nor did it protect them from all the unpleasantness that simply appearing before Congress entailed. Because the committees often had subpoenas served to people at their workplaces, some witnesses lost their jobs even before their hearings began. Committee procedures were intentionally disorienting. Witnesses rarely got more than a few days to prepare for a hearing. As

Document 20 reveals, finding an attorney was often difficult, especially for people who did not want to name names. Many witnesses usually ended up relying on the same small handful of left-wing and civil liberties lawyers whose identities alerted the investigators to the probable testimony their clients would give.

Even the **friendly witnesses** suffered. Although they were often spared the exposure of a public session if they agreed to name names, they usually testified under duress with the knowledge that to defy the committee would destroy their careers. Having left the party, they had no desire to martyr themselves for a cause they did not support. Still, many of them did not like becoming informers. It was, a Connecticut professor recalled, "a traumatic experience" that left him "ashamed and embarrassed."

For the unfriendly witnesses and their families the experience was, of course, even more unwelcome. Their lives were disrupted. They and their spouses often lost their jobs. People ostracized them, sometimes crossing the street to avoid an encounter. One college teacher recalled how his "old friends, fellow students, former colleagues, fled to the hills, in fact behaved like a bunch of frightened rabbits." The witnesses' children suffered too, losing playmates and even being tormented in school. The social isolation was particularly devastating for people who lived outside large cities like New York or San Francisco, where there were supportive left-wing communities. But even with such assistance, it took considerable courage to defy a committee.

What happened to the unfriendly witnesses had enormous implications. No aspect of the McCarthy era has received as much attention as the predicament that confronted the men and women subpoenaed by anti-Communist investigators. Yet all too often these people's experiences have been portrayed in both the media and the scholarly literature as individual conflicts, moments of intense personal struggle in which each witness wrestled with his or her own conscience. While not disparaging the agonizing moral dilemmas these people faced, we must recognize that their experiences had an equally important political dimension. The committees' investigations, while directly affecting the lives of their targets, indirectly affected the rest of the nation. The unfriendly witnesses were the most prominent dissenters in early cold war America. By punishing them, the committees seriously narrowed the range of political debate.

11

Red-Baiting and Careerism: Joseph McCarthy at Work

Most hearings had a specific agenda, whether it was to expose alleged Communist infiltration of a particular industry or call into question the activities of a front group or left-wing labor union. We have already seen how HUAC's pursuit of Alger Hiss reinforced the Republican party's campaign against the Truman administration (Chapter 5). Later investigations were to continue that line of attack as well as to promote charges of subversion in other areas of American life.

The spectacular publicity produced by a committee's hearings also bolstered the political careers of its members. HUAC had been an undesirable assignment at the time Representative Richard Nixon joined the committee in 1947. Six years later, he was vice president and 185 of the 221 Republicans in Congress were clamoring for a berth. Electoral geography often determined what a committee would investigate. Between January and election day 1952, HUAC held all of its hearings in the home states of its members, 27 percent of them in the members' own districts. The committees thrived on publicity and usually tried to investigate subjects that would guarantee headlines.

The personal ambitions of individual politicians and the political agendas of the Republican party and anti-Communist network often overlapped. The committee members got publicity and the right-wingers zapped their enemies. Investigating Hollywood, for example, not only influenced the studios to stop making films about controversial political or social issues but also weakened the Communist movement by attacking its wealthiest and most famous supporters (see Chapter 14). Similarly, HUAC's 1948 and 1949 hearings on atomic espionage indirectly supported the drive for military control of the nuclear weapons program (see Chapter 6). Investigations of Communist-led unions served comparable functions. Individual congressional representatives could usually track down a left-wing local to investigate in or near their home district. Such hearings were often held at the request of an anti-union employer or an anti-Communist faction within the local and were particularly effective when they occurred during a strike or union election campaign. These unions were already weakened by conflicts over the Taft-Hartley affidavits and the expulsion of unions from the CIO (see Chapter 9). Their leaders were particularly vulnerable to exposure as Communists and their committee appearances often enabled their long-term opponents to move against them or even oust them from office.

Nothing, however, could boost a politician's career as quickly as finding Communists in government. The trajectory of Senator Joseph McCarthy illustrates the power of the issue. Until he entered history on February 9, 1950, by announcing to the Women's Republican Club of Wheeling, West Virginia, that he held in his hand a list of Communist agents in the State Department, McCarthy had been a fairly undistinguished, if slightly disreputable, midwestern politician. There was nothing particularly original in his accusations; other Republicans had been making them for several years. (In fact, his attack on Alger Hiss at Wheeling came almost word for word from a speech Nixon had made the month before.) What gave McCarthy's recycled allegations force was their concreteness. He named names and gave numbers—although both the names and numbers were to change. The only copy of the Wheeling speech we have was entered into the *Congressional Record* eleven days later. That version, included here as Document 16, charged the State Department with harboring 57 subversives, although reporters who had heard the speech recalled the figure of 205. In Denver the next day, McCarthy mentioned 207. The lists he claimed to hold in his hand appear to have been extrapolated from 1946 and 1947 State Department reports on its internal loyalty-security investigations. McCarthy had no evidence that any of the people he referred to were Communists; and, in fact, when pressed, he tended to qualify his initial charges and fling new ones. Apparently, neither truth nor consistency mattered much to him.

McCarthy attracted attention precisely because of his outrageousness. He knew how to manipulate the press, taking advantage of its hunger for copy by releasing sensational accusations just in time for the evening deadlines. The blatant disregard for the accuracy of his charges that distinguished him from other politicians made McCarthy notorious and frightening. Liberals loathed him and many moderates found him distasteful as well. The leaders of the Republican party, however, recognized that McCarthy could be of use. His extravagant charges amplified their own allegations that the Truman administration had lost China to the Communists, and they encouraged him to press the attack. "If one case doesn't work out," Senator Robert Taft advised his colleague, "bring up another." McCarthy did just that and, because he had no reservations about whom he targeted, he even implied that General George Marshall, the highly respected secretary of defense, had been a traitor.

The White House responded to McCarthy's initial charges by encouraging a special subcommittee of the Senate Foreign Relations Committee to look into his claims. Chaired by the conservative Maryland Democrat Millard Tydings, the committee proved unable to squelch McCarthy's everchanging allegations and instead gave them greater currency. The Korean War broke out before the inquiry ended, intensifying the anti-Communist furor and strengthening McCarthy's position. Thus, by the time Tydings released his report in July 1950, his conclusion that the Wisconsin senator's charges were "a hoax and a fraud" had little impact. The subcommittee's Republican members refused to sign the document and in November Tydings lost his bid for reelection.

By then, despite the repugnance that many of his senatorial colleagues felt for McCarthy's methods, few of them wanted to tangle with him directly. Tydings's defeat made McCarthy seem too powerful. How much popular support he actually had is unclear; the perception of his invincibility sustained his influence. Observers assumed that the populist thrust of his attacks on Secretary of State Dean Acheson and the "striped pants diplomats" and "lace handkerchief crowd" in the State Department evoked broad support among masses of lower-middle-class voters resentful of the modern world and supposedly chafing under the stress of America's international responsibilities. There was, of course, no question about his popularity within the anti-Communist network or within the Irish-Catholic community, which welcomed him as a favorite son. Still, his showings in the polls fluctuated and, although he won reelection in 1952, he ran well behind all the other Republicans in his state.

When Dwight D. Eisenhower entered the White House in 1953, the Republican party naturally lost interest in looking for Communists in government. McCarthy, however, continued the campaign. With the Republicans in control of the Senate, McCarthy took over the Permanent Investigating Subcommittee of the Government Operations Committee and launched his own increasingly capricious search for Communists in high places. At first the Eisenhower administration tolerated him. The president wanted to avoid confrontation and maintain the unity of the Republican party. Thus, although Eisenhower personally despised McCarthy, he would not, he told his aides, "get into the gutter with that guy." But when McCarthy continued to look for subversives within the executive branch, and especially when he accused the Army of harboring Communists, the administration struck back.

McCarthy's career was to end, as it had begun, in a special Senate investigation. This time McCarthy himself was the target. A special subcommittee investigated charges that McCarthy had forced the Army to give preferential treatment to a member of his staff. When the investigation began in the spring of 1954, television was just coming into widespread use and the Army-McCarthy hearings became one of its first spectaculars. The venerated newscaster Edward R. Murrow had already presented a program critical of McCarthy and the televised hearings were even more unkind to the senator from Wisconsin. They emphasized his crude behavior and the arrogance of his young assistant Roy Cohn. Toward the end of the hearings, McCarthy charged that a young associate in the law firm of the Army's counsel, Joseph Welch, had belonged to the left-wing National Lawyers Guild while in law school. Welch had anticipated the smear and his plaintive rejoinder "Have you no sense of decency, Sir?" spoke to what millions of Americans must have felt. A few months later the rest of the Senate, by a 67–22 vote, censured McCarthy for his lack of respect. He continued to fling charges around, but he had lost his audience. Within three years he was dead, a victim of heavy drinking.

12

Congressional Investigations and the "Loss" of China

McCarthy's flamboyant career lasted only four years, but the charges on which he rode to power resonated within American politics for decades. There was nothing original in his accusation, presented in Document 16, that Communists had penetrated the State Department and subverted American foreign policy. He was simply echoing the conservative Republican position on the most sensitive issue of the early 1950s: the victory of Mao Tse-tung and the Communists in the Chinese civil war.

Americans had never viewed China realistically. Throughout the twentieth century they had subscribed to highly romanticized notions about the democratic nature of the Chinese government and the special friendship that was said to exist between the United States and China. American policymakers did not try to dispel those illusions and, in fact, encouraged them, at least during the Second World War. As a result, in the late 1940s the U.S. government found itself committed to aiding the Nationalist regime of Chiang Kai-shek in its battle against the Chinese Communist party. Many formerly isolationist Republicans who only grudgingly supported the Truman administration's containment policy in Europe and the Middle East were strongly interventionist in East Asia. Staunch supporters of Chiang Kai-shek, they refused to admit how much the Chinese government's own incompetence and corruption were contributing to its military setbacks, and they transformed America's China policy into a partisan issue.

The Truman administration had a more realistic assessment of China. Most of the East Asian experts within the State Department, while unsympathetic to Mao Tse-tung and the Communists, had become disillusioned by the Nationalists' ineptness and authoritarianism. They knew that, given China's size, nothing short of a massive infusion of American troops and dollars would affect the outcome of the civil war; and they doubted that either Congress or the American public would support such a commitment. Because of the political pressures, however, Truman and his advisers could not abandon Chiang Kai-shek or cut off the millions of dollars of aid they were sending him. By the summer of 1949, it was clear that the Nationalists were doomed. The State Department released a White Paper, an official government report designed to document Chiang's responsibility for his own defeat and exonerate the American government.

The tactic failed. The Nationalists had important defenders within what came to be known as the "China lobby," a group of businesspeople, politicians, and journalists who were quick to promote the idea that Communist influence within the State Department had engineered Chiang's defeat. The China lobby, the anti-Communist network, and the right wing of the Republican party overlapped considerably and they had a shared interest in promoting the "loss-of-China" scenario. For the China lobbyists, the attack on the State Department not only got Chiang Kai-shek off the hook but enabled them to impose their own view of East Asian affairs on the rest of the nation. For the professional anti-Communists, gaining attention for the allegation that Communist subversion had lost China increased their clout and the credibility of their other charges. For the Republicans, the loss of China provided new ammunition for a partisan attack on the Truman administration.

Probably no single figure embodied the interconnections behind the loss-of-China scenario as much as Alfred Kohlberg, a lace importer from New York. During World War II Kohlberg came to believe that Communists were subverting America's China policy. He located the source of the subversion in an organization called the Institute of Pacific Relations (IPR), a quasi-academic think tank that in the days before universities entered the field was an important source of information about East Asia for the nation's foreign-policy elite. Kohlberg soon expanded his campaign against the alleged Communists in the IPR into a full-fledged assault on the entire Red menace. He became one of the anti-Communist network's stalwarts, setting up and bankrolling several of its main organizations and publications. An indefatigable correspondent, he bombarded Republican politicians and his fellow anti-Communists with position papers, campaign contributions, and pleas for an investigation of the IPR.

He hit pay dirt with McCarthy. For Kohlberg, as for the leaders of the Republican party and the professional anti-Communists, McCarthy's genius for publicity proved invaluable in throwing the Truman administration off balance. Kohlberg and the rest of the anti-Communist network rushed to keep him supplied with material. There was nothing particularly new in most of McCarthy's allegations, but because of the notoriety he attracted, they could not be ignored. The Tydings committee inadvertently became the China lobby's forum.

McCarthy resurrected the *Amerasia* incident. (See Chapter 5.) In the aftermath of the alleged loss of China, he was able to insinuate that the administration's failure to pursue the prosecution of John Stewart Service and his fellow conspirators seemed ominous. He also attacked the State Department's other China experts. His main target, though, was Johns Hopkins University professor Owen Lattimore who, McCarthy announced, was "the architect of our far eastern policy." Editor of the IPR's scholarly journal during the 1930s, Lattimore had been an adviser to Chiang Kai-shek during the war. In the years after World War II, Lattimore had established himself as perhaps the nation's leading East Asian expert. As such, he called for a more liberal and democratic regime in China, but he had never been a Communist or a policymaker in the State Department. McCarthy charged him with being both and was able to produce the professional witness Louis Budenz to testify that his Communist party bosses considered Lattimore one of them.

Because of the outbreak of the Korean War and the partisan conflict over its report, the Tydings committee was unable to restore the reputation of the administration's China experts. Within a year the loss-of-China scenario would become the centerpiece for what was, next to HUAC's investigation of Alger Hiss, the most important congressional investigation of the entire early cold war, the probe of the IPR by Senator Pat McCarran's SISS. Inaugurated in the beginning of 1951, the investigation lasted over a year and involved dozens of witnesses and thousands of pages of testimony, all designed to gain acceptance for the contention that Communists had subverted American foreign policy in China—and indirectly caused the Korean War.

The scenario had just enough plausibility to be convincing. The interconnections between the Communist movement, the IPR, and the federal government did look suspicious. After all, there had been Communists in the IPR, including the man who had been one of its main officials and financial backers, Frederick Vanderbilt Field. One of the original founders of *Amerasia,* Field was already serving a prison sentence for contempt when he appeared before the SISS to take the Fifth Amendment. Other IPR-connected witnesses also invoked the Fifth, which of course identified them as Communists to the McCarthyites. The McCarran committee's friendly witnesses buttressed that identification. Budenz claimed to know of forty-three alleged Communists in the IPR. Harvey Matusow, a professional witness who was later to recant, also named names and stated that the party bookstore where he worked sold Lattimore's books. Even Whittaker Chambers reluctantly appeared. In addition, the SISS had commandeered the IPR's records and strengthened the testimony of its witnesses with documents that seemed to give the hearings greater substance.

The committee had no proof that the Communists in the IPR had influenced State Department decisions, but it did pounce on the fact that many of the State Department's leading China experts, including Alger Hiss and some of the people Elizabeth Bentley had named, had ties to the organization. (They would have been remiss if they had not been associated with the IPR because it was the most important private research group in the field.) The committee's conclusions were predictable: Communists had taken over the IPR and had convinced the State Department to abandon Chiang Kai-shek. McCarran then pressured the attorney general to indict Lattimore for perjury, which he did in December 1952. The charges were so flimsy that the case soon fell apart. The judge dismissed most of the counts against Lattimore, and the government eventually abandoned the prosecution in mid-1955. Lattimore suffered nonetheless; he kept his job but lost his reputation and eventually moved to England. More important, the IPR hearings gave the China lobby de facto control over the nation's East Asia policy and ensured that future administrations would never again allow themselves to become embroiled in another loss of China.

The IPR hearings were the last significant airing of the Communists-in-government scenario. In the fall of 1953, Eisenhower's attorney general, Herbert Brownell, resurrected the Harry Dexter White case, which had begun in 1945 when Elizabeth Bentley, the self-confessed Soviet agent, claimed that White, a former assistant secretary of the treasury, had belonged to her Washington spy ring. Although White had died of a heart attack a few days after he denied Bentley's charges before HUAC in August 1948, Brownell revived the case to show that Truman had been "soft" on communism because he had appointed White to high office even after he knew about the allegations against him. (See Chapter 5.) The SISS showcased the charges, but the administration shrank from the prospect of having HUAC issue a subpoena to ex-President Truman and the issue disappeared. By the time the Senate censured Joe McCarthy late in 1954, the heyday of congressional investigations was over. The nation's political elites had begun to distance themselves from the anti-Communist network. The investigating committees continued their work throughout the 1950s and, at least for the unfriendly witnesses involved, were as effective as ever. Nonetheless, these were largely mopping-up operations that concentrated on the exposure of obscure individuals rather than the development of major political themes. By the mid-1950s the Communist party was in a shambles and most of the anti-Communists' key targets had long since been obliterated. In addition, the committees were no longer in the mainstream; they were now back in the hands of militant conservatives and southern segregationists like Mississippi Senator James Eastland. The professional anti-Communists' hold on respectability and power was coming to an end.

13

Anticommunism at the
State and Local Levels

The influence of the anti-Communist crusade lingered longer outside of Washington, where state and local officials pursued the Communist menace with as much enthusiasm as their national counterparts had done. The crusades evolved differently in each region. Conservative southerners saw the Kremlin's hand in the growing civil rights movement; midwesterners were concerned about left-wing labor unions; Texans feared that progressive education was a Communist plot. The variegated and decentralized nature of the American polity allowed for a wide range of tactics and targets, with specific campaigns often depending on the ambitions of an individual politician or an especially vigorous American Legion post. Even something as idiosyncratic as how frequently its legislature met could determine the intensity of a state's crusade against communism. Michigan, with legislative sessions every year, generated much more anti-Communist activity than neighboring states such as Illinois and Wisconsin, whose lawmakers assembled less often.

The anticommunism that surfaced at the state and local levels often seemed more extreme, the laws and ordinances more foolish and reactionary. Most state legislatures were dominated by small-town businesspeople and attorneys who seemed especially responsive to pressures from groups such as the American Legion and the right-wing press. Also, their main area of concern was education, which was by its nature ideologically divisive. Public schools are cultural battlegrounds, and it is possible that local politicians and anti-Communist activists would have focused on them even if education had not been one of the few major civic functions still under state and local control. Colleges and universities posed a particular challenge. In the 1940s and 1950s they seemed to harbor populations with cosmopolitan lifestyles and liberal politics that apparently threatened the traditional values so many conservative state politicians claimed to cherish. Similar cultural conflicts also existed at the national level, but they were subordinated to national security concerns and thus received less attention.

In most other respects, however, state and local anticommunism mirrored that on the national level. Its practitioners plugged into the broader national anti-Communist network and availed themselves of its ideological resources and investigative personnel. State legislators, for example, worked with HUAC and the FBI and hired former government agents as investigators. The national organizations to which local activists belonged often supplied information about the Communist threat and guidance in how to combat it. Although their efforts in banning controversial speakers or eliminating subversive textbooks may have affected only individual communities or school systems, the same textbooks and the same speakers invariably came under attack in one community after another. One of the most common targets was a popular high school civics text, Frank A. Magruder's *American Government*. The book's supposedly socialistic endorsement of the progressive income tax and federal power projects drew attacks from American Legion posts, right-wing women's groups, and Chambers of Commerce from Chicago to Houston.

Local and national branches of the anti-Communist network collaborated closely. Whenever HUAC, McCarthy, or the SISS went on the road, committee staffers coordinated their activities with those of local politicians, journalists, labor leaders, businesspeople, and Legionnaires. In many instances, the committees came to town for a specific purpose such as helping a Catholic activist purge his union local or encouraging the state legislature to pass an antisubversive bill. In a more general, but no less important, way, the national campaign against communism benefitted the local efforts by legitimating their activities and providing models. There were few states or major cities that did not mount an anti-Communist investigation, implement a loyalty-security program, or adopt some kind of antisubversive ordinance.

Thirteen states had created their own HUACs or authorized officials to look for Communists. These investigators operated much as their congressional counterparts did in that they sought to punish alleged subversives by exposing them or forcing them into contempt. They had a similar impact; the unfriendly witnesses and the people publicly identified as Communists by these panels often lost their jobs. California's Un-American Activities Committee, founded in 1941, was the longest-lived and most influential of the state committees. Its investigations of Hollywood, higher education, and atomic spies paralleled the congressional ones, and its published reports listed even more alleged Communists and front groups than HUAC's. Washington State's more transient Un-American Activities Committee was equally vigorous. Under the leadership of a former deputy sheriff named Albert Canwell it pursued the remnants of the state's once influential Popular Front and radical professors at the University of Washington.

All of these investigations, in California, Washington, and elsewhere, used the resources of the anti-Communist network. Former military intelligence officers, FBI agents, and ex-Communists were ubiquitous. J. B. Matthews, Louis Budenz, and several other professional witnesses testified before Washington State's Canwell Committee. Matthews also served as counsel for Illinois's Seditious Activities Investigating Committee whose chair, Legionnaire Paul Broyles, was determined to root out both "overliberals" and party members. Ohio's Un-American Activities Commission also had a crew of professional witnesses on its staff. State investigators collaborated with each other. In 1949, the California and Washington committees jointly brought their colleagues to Los Angeles for an Interstate Legislative Conference on Un-American Activities, where one of the items on their agenda was a discussion of establishing a blacklist of disloyal college teachers.

Besides investigating Communists, state and local politicians tried to outlaw them. Most states already had antisedition legislation on the books but conservative activists and politicians wanted it updated to address the current menace. Most of the proposals appropriated federal models. They either mandated the installation of some kind of a loyalty-security program for state and local employees or created provisions for the registration of local Communists and the banning of their activities. Several states and cities simply duplicated the McCarran Act's registration requirements; Maryland's Ober Law, with its multipronged provisions for investigating and eliminating Communists, was also widely copied. Many of these measures were essentially symbolic expressions of community sentiment. They were rarely enforced, either because the resources to do so had not been appropriated or because the officials in charge decided to ignore them. Most of these measures were unconstitutional and were eventually voided by the federal judiciary, though often not until the mid-1960s.

The loyalty programs had more of an impact. They sought to eliminate allegedly subversive public employees through either oaths or investigations. The oaths usually called for a pledge of loyalty to the state and national constitutions and the disavowal of membership in any organization seeking the overthrow of the government by force and violence. Cheap and easy to administer, oaths were particularly popular, even though most of the people who refused to take them and thus lost their jobs were Quakers or other conscientious objectors rather than Communists. An attempt to impose a loyalty oath on the University of California's faculty in 1949 provoked a bitter controversy that nearly tore the school apart. Teachers at every level were the most common target of the many state and local loyalty oath programs. New York State, for example, enacted a law requiring public school administrators to apply the federal government's loyalty-security criteria to their staffs and dismiss Communists and people who belonged to groups on the attorney general's list. In New York City alone, the program cost more than three hundred teachers their jobs.

Unlike the federal government, state and local authorities tended to rely on symbolic legislation and economic sanctions rather than criminal prosecutions. A few people did go to prison for contempt when they refused to name names or otherwise comply with state investigators' demands for information. A few states tried to prosecute leading Communists under their already existing sedition laws. In Massachusetts, the attorney general indicted an MIT mathematician, a shoe manufacturer, and a housewife for conspiring to overthrow the commonwealth of Massachusetts by force and violence; but in 1956 the Supreme Court ruled that the federal government had exclusive jurisdiction in the area of internal security and threw such cases out.

The McCarthy years also spawned a plethora of local ordinances and other measures designed to eliminate the Communist menace. Typical of the roughly 150 municipalities that had enacted such regulations were New Rochelle, New York, which required any member of a "Communist organization" to register with the police, and Birmingham, Alabama, which imposed $100 fines and 180-day jail sentences on known Communists for every day they remained in town. Pharmacists in Texas, professional wrestlers in Indiana, and people who wanted to fish in the New York City reservoirs all had to take loyalty oaths. School libraries were particularly vulnerable; even the presumably cosmopolitan New York City school board banned copies of *The Nation* magazine. By the end of the 1950s, however, the furor began to wane. Most state and local politicians, like most national ones, had largely abandoned the anti-Communist campaign. The laws and loyalty oaths remained on the books, but the headlines were gone.

The South was a special case. It had fewer Communists, but its states enacted tougher laws against them and continued to do so even after the anti-Communist furor had receded elsewhere. Most of these measures, though ostensibly designed to eliminate the Red menace, were really directed against the civil rights movement. Accordingly, as the drive for racial equality began to intensify after the 1954 Supreme Court decision in *Brown v. Board of Education* outlawed segregated schools, white supremacists increasingly took up the weapons fashioned by the anti-Communist crusade.

There was a long-standing relationship between southern racism and anticommunism: race-baiting and Red-baiting were intertwined. The region's system of white supremacy bolstered its economic inequalities. The South's political and economic elites were almost as hostile to organized labor as they were to integration. Accordingly, even if the Communist party had not pushed for racial equality, its frontal attack on the social and economic status quo would still have earned it the undying enmity of most southern conservatives.

The party's presence in the South was small, but not completely negligible. There were few open Communists in the region; most of the party's members allied themselves organizationally with the network of southern liberals who since the late 1930s had been trying to bring the New Deal south. They were also involved in the labor movement. By the mid-1940s, in places like Winston-Salem, North Carolina, and Memphis, Tennessee, left-led unions and civil rights groups had formed the nucleus of a progressive interracial movement that was beginning to expand into areas like voting rights. Party members and their allies were also active in the third-party 1948 presidential campaign of Henry Wallace who confronted Jim Crow head on by refusing to speak to segregated audiences.

The rotten eggs, riots, and arrests that greeted the Wallace campaign throughout the South symbolized the obstacles facing the southern left, and the tiny number of votes Wallace received revealed its weakness. Destroying the minuscule southern wing of the Communist party as well as the broader left-liberal interracial coalition required very little pressure. The intervention of the national anti-Communist network was probably decisive. In June 1947 HUAC released a report on Communist infiltration in the Southern Conference for Human Welfare (SCHW), the region's most important left-liberal organization. A month later the committee subpoenaed the leaders of Local 22 of the Communist-led Food, Tobacco, Agricultural, and Allied Workers union, then in the middle of a strike against the R. J. Reynolds Tobacco Company in Winston-Salem. By 1950, both the SCHW and Local 22 were gone. The nationwide drive against communism combined with traditional racist appeals enabled southern conservatives to smash the interracial movement for social change that had seemed so promising only a few years before.

The destruction of the southern left did not end the anti-Communist crusade, for it offered southerners a respectable way to defend segregation. Southern conservatives had always claimed that the region's African Americans were perfectly content with their subordinate status and that demands for change were the product of "outside agitators." Linking those "agitators" with the Communist party, which had consistently pushed for racial equality, gave the segregationists new allies as well as a more modern rationale for their campaign against the civil rights movement. Mississippi Senator James Eastland who chaired the SISS after 1955 personified this. He repeatedly used his committee as a forum to present the segregationist case that integration was a Communist plot. J. Edgar Hoover, who secretly harassed Martin Luther King Jr. for years, also sought to expose the connections between the civil rights movement and the Communist party. That such connections were unimportant made little difference.

At the state level, anti-Communist investigators promoted similar charges. By the mid-1950s, almost every southern state had some kind of legislative investigating committee or had enacted some kind of anti-Communist registration statute. The committees, dedicated to the theory that the Communist party was behind the civil rights movement, called on professional witnesses to confirm their fears. In 1958, J. B. Matthews told state legislators in Arkansas, Mississippi, and Florida that he knew of no organization "that has been so heavily infiltrated as the NAACP [National Association for the Advancement of Colored People]"; other ex-Communists gave similar testimony. As the civil rights movement gained strength in the aftermath of the *Brown* decision, its opponents began to use the anti-Communist laws and committees to harass it. Especially common were attempts to force the NAACP to turn over its membership lists to state investigators. Though such harassment certainly hampered the activities of the civil rights movement in the 1950s, it was ultimately to fail. Unlike the anti-Communist activists in the early years of the cold war, the segregationists were not part of the mainstream of American politics and they confronted a strong mass movement that was able to win federal support. The segregationists did establish contact with the hard core of the anti-Communist network, the fanatics on the far right who continued the anti-Communist crusade long after the nation's mainstream politicians had abandoned it. By the mid-1960s, the two crusades had merged.

14

Blacklists and
Other Economic Sanctions

Even at the height of the McCarthyist furor in the early 1950s, the anti-Communist crusade was relatively mild. Many prosecutions faltered on appeal and only a few foreign-born radicals were actually deported. Only Julius and Ethel Rosenberg were put to death; and, of the roughly 150 people who went to prison, most were released within a year or two. Certainly compared to the horrors of Stalin's Russia, McCarthyism was not a drastic form of political repression. But it was an effective one.

The punishments were primarily economic. People lost their jobs. The official manifestations of McCarthyism—the public hearings, FBI investigations, and criminal prosecutions—would not have been as effective had they not been reinforced by the private sector. The political purges were a two-stage process that relied on the imposition of economic sanctions to bolster the political messages conveyed by public officials. The collaboration of private employers with HUAC and the rest of the anti-Communist network was necessary both to legitimate the network's activities and to punish the men and women identified as politically undesirable. Without the participation of the private sector, McCarthyism would not have affected the rank-and-file members of the Communist movement nor so effectively stifled political dissent.

It is hard to come up with accurate statistics for the number of politically motivated dismissals during the McCarthy period, for both the employers and the people they fired tried to conceal what was happening—the former to protect themselves against charges of violating civil liberties, the latter to obtain future jobs. Yale Law School professor Ralph Brown, who conducted the most systematic survey of the economic damage of the McCarthy era, estimated that roughly ten thousand people lost their jobs. Such a figure may be low, as even Brown admits, for it does not include rejected applicants, people who resigned under duress, and the men and women who were ostensibly dismissed for other reasons. Still, it does suggest the scope of the economic sanctions.

The two-stage nature of McCarthyism, in which political undesirables were first identified by one agency and then fired by another, increased its effectiveness. By diffusing the responsibility, the separation of the two operations made it easier for the people who administered the economic sanctions to rationalize what they were doing and deny that they were involved in the business of McCarthyism. This was especially the case with the essentially moderate and liberal men (few women here) who ran the nation's major corporations, newspapers, universities, and other institutions that fired people for their politics. Many of these administrators sincerely deplored McCarthy and HUAC and tried to conceal the extent to which their own activities bolstered the witch-hunt.

Most of the time the first stage of identifying the alleged Communists was handled by an official agency like an investigating committee or the FBI. In some areas, such as the entertainment industry, private entrepreneurs entered the field. The bureau and the congressional committees expected that the people they exposed would lose their jobs; and the evidence we have suggests that about 80 percent of the unfriendly witnesses did. The investigators often greased the wheels by warning their witnesses' employers or releasing lists of prospective witnesses to the local press. Sometimes recalcitrant witnesses who kept their jobs were recalled for a second hearing.

The FBI was also involved in the unemployment business. Throughout the late 1950s, agents routinely visited Junius Scales's employers to ensure that he could not keep a job. Naturally, the bureau operated with greater stealth than the committees, for it was not supposed to release material from its files to anyone outside the executive branch. But not only did the FBI leak selected tidbits to sympathetic journalists and members of Congress, it also inaugurated a systematic flow of information called the Responsibilities Program. The program began in 1951 when a group of liberal governors, who were worried that they might be vulnerable to right-wing charges of harboring Communists on their payrolls, asked the bureau to give them information about state employees. Deniability was the program's hallmark; FBI agents usually conveyed the requisite information to the governors or their representatives in oral reports or in the form of what the bureau called "blind memoranda," typed on plain unwatermarked paper that gave no evidence of its origins. During the four years of the program's existence, it transmitted 810 such reports, most of which resulted in the intended action.

The dismissals were usually in response to outside pressures. Most of the firings of the McCarthy era occurred after someone had refused to cooperate with an investigating committee or was denied a security clearance. Major corporations like General Electric and U.S. Steel announced that they would discharge any worker who took the Fifth Amendment, and other employers made it equally clear that they would do the same. (See Chapter 10.) Some of these employers may well have welcomed and even actually arranged for a HUAC hearing, especially when it enabled them to fire left-wing union leaders. Left to their own devices, however, most of the other employers would not have initiated political dismissals, although they were usually willing to acquiesce once they were apprised of the identities of their allegedly subversive employees.

Self-defense was the primary motivation. Even when not threatened with direct reprisals, the leaders of the nation's major corporations, universities, and other private institutions seem to have decided that good public relations demanded the dismissal of anyone openly identified as a Communist or even, in many cases, of any person who was merely controversial. In retrospect, it is clear that the fear of retaliation for retaining a Fifth Amendment witness or other political undesirable was probably exaggerated. Those few institutions that kept such people in their employ did not suffer in any noticeable way. Alumni did not withhold their donations; moviegoers did not desert the theaters. But perception in this case was more important than reality.

Ideology shored up the dismissals. The cautious college presidents and studio heads who fired or refused to hire political undesirables shared the anti-Communist consensus. They were patriotic citizens who, however squeamish they may have been about the methods of McCarthy and the other investigators, agreed that communism threatened the United States and that the crisis engendered by the cold war necessitated measures that might violate the rights of individuals. By invoking the icon of national security, they were able to give their otherwise embarrassing actions a patina of patriotism. Equally pervasive was the belief that Communists deserved to be fired. Because of their alleged duplicity, dogmatism, and disloyalty to their nation and employers, Communists (and the definition was to be stretched to include ex-Communists, Fifth Amendment Communists, and anybody who associated with Communists) were seen as no longer qualified for their jobs. Because these disqualifications usually appeared only after the until-then qualified individuals were identified by part of the anti-Communist network, these rationalizations obviously involved considerable deception and self-deception.

There were few legal restraints. The Supreme Court's refusal to interfere with the firings of public servants prefigured its attitude toward similar dismissals within other institutions. Again, the Court, which initially acquiesced in the firing of unfriendly witnesses and other political dissidents, began to change its position by the mid-1950s, but the reversals were never complete and they occurred after much of the damage had been done. In 1956, for example, the Court invalidated the dismissal of a Brooklyn College literature professor who had taken the Fifth Amendment, but because the justices admitted that there might be other reasons why he should be fired, he never got his job back. A few people whose careers had been destroyed by the entertainment industry's blacklist tried to sue for damages, but federal judges did not even recognize the existence of the blacklist until the mid-1960s.

No doubt because of the glamour of the entertainment industry, the anti-Communist firings and subsequent blacklisting of men and women in show business are well known. The movies had been a target of the anti-Communist network since the late 1930s. Investigating show business was a sure way to attract publicity. There were plenty of potential witnesses, for the film industry had a lively radical community with an active core of some three hundred Communists. In 1947, the Hollywood Ten hearings, excerpted in Document 15, precipitated the blacklist. At first it was not clear that employers would punish unfriendly witnesses. However, when the indictment of the Ten showed that the federal government's law enforcement machinery was backing HUAC, the situation changed. At the end of November, the heads of the major studios met at the Waldorf-Astoria Hotel in New York City and released a statement, reproduced as Document 17, announcing that they had fired the Ten and would not rehire them until they recanted and cleared themselves with the committee.

Over the next few years many of the film industry's more prominent leftists found it increasingly harder to get work. By 1951, when HUAC returned to Hollywood to resume the hearings it had begun four years before, the blacklist was in full operation. There was, of course, no official list and the studios routinely denied that blacklisting occurred. Still, writers stopped getting calls for work; actors were told they were "too good for the part."

The rise of television exacerbated the film industry's already serious financial slump and reinforced the major studios' reluctance to
offend any segment of their audience. Threats of boycotts by the
American Legion and other right-wing groups terrified the movie-
makers and their Wall Street backers. Imposing an anti-Communist
blacklist seemed an obvious way to avoid trouble at the box office for
an industry that had, after all, long been subject to considerable self-
censorship with regard to sexual as well as political issues.

The blacklist spread to the broadcast industry as well. Here, the
process became public in June 1950 with the publication of *Red Channels,* a 213-page compilation of the alleged Communist affiliations of
151 actors, writers, musicians, and other radio and television entertainers. The book, which appeared three days before the start of the
Korean War, was published by American Business Consultants, an outfit established in 1947 by a trio of former FBI agents who wanted to
make the public aware of the information about communism that the
bureau had collected. Initially funded by Alfred Kohlberg and the
Catholic Church, the group became one of the anti-Communist network's main enterprises, offering its services in exposing and eliminating Communists to corporations, foundations, and government
agencies. *Red Channels* was a special show-business supplement to the
exposés of individuals and organizations that appeared in the group's
regular newsletter, *Counterattack.*

The listings in *Red Channels,* some of which are reproduced in
Document 18, were compiled, so J. B. Matthews claimed, from his collection of front group letterheads, congressional and California Un-
American Activities Committee reports, and old *Daily Worker*s. They
were not always accurate, but they were devastating. By 1951, the television networks and their sponsors no longer hired anyone whose
name was in the book, and the prohibition soon spread to anyone who
seemed controversial. A tiny group of true believers enforced the
blacklist by deluging networks, advertising agencies, and sponsors
with letters and phone calls whenever someone they disapproved of
got hired. One of the blacklist's most ardent enforcers was Laurence
Johnson, a supermarket owner in Syracuse, New York, who threatened to place signs in his stores warning customers not to buy the
products of any company that sponsored a program featuring one of
"Stalin's little creatures." Although Johnson represented no one but
himself and his employees, some of the nation's largest corporations
capitulated to his demands.

Broadcasters scrambled to ensure that they did not hire the wrong kinds of talent and often enlisted professional anti-Communists to check the backgrounds of prospective employees. One of the authors of *Red Channels* charged five dollars a name; the ex-FBI agents of American Business Consultants provided similar services, sometimes, it was said, after threatening further exposures in *Counterattack.* CBS inaugurated a loyalty oath and, like the other networks and big advertising agencies, put full-time "security officers" on its payroll. In Hollywood the studios worked closely with the American Legion and the film industry's own anti-Communists and informers. The criteria for the blacklists varied. People who were cleared by one network or studio were banned by others. Even within a single network or agency, some shows hired performers that other shows refused to touch. The blacklisters' targets extended far beyond the Communist party and sometimes seemed to encompass almost every liberal in show business. As the testimony in Document 19 reveals, one producer found that a third of the performers he wanted to hire were turned down by his superiors—including an eight-year-old girl.

It is not clear exactly why the entertainment industry's blacklist had such a broad reach. Although most of the people affected by it had once been in or near the Communist party, the blacklist also encompassed some genuine innocents, people who had merely signed letters supporting the Hollywood Ten's petition for a Supreme Court hearing or attended Popular Front gatherings during World War II. No doubt the visibility of the industry played a role, as did the reluctance of studios and networks to become involved in anything that seemed controversial. As one industry executive explained, "We're a business that has to please the customers; that's the main thing we have to do, keep people happy, and, to do that, we have to stay out of trouble." Finally, the professional anti-Communists seem to have been more directly involved in administering the entertainment industry blacklist than they were with the sanctions in other fields and could thus impose their own more stringent ideological criteria.

It was possible to get removed from the blacklist. The clearance procedure was complicated, secretive, and for many people morally repugnant. The people who initiated the blacklists, such as the authors of *Red Channels,* charged a few hundred dollars to shepherd someone through the process. A loose network of lawyers, gossip columnists, union leaders, and organizations like the American Legion, Anti-Defamation League, and, it was rumored, the Catholic

Church provided similar services. Naming names was required, of course. Ex-Communists usually had to purge themselves with HUAC and the FBI before they could work again. The better known among them often had to publish articles in a mass-circulation magazine explaining how they had been duped by the party and describing its evils. For Humphrey Bogart, whose main offense was his public support for the Hollywood Ten, rehabilitation required an article in a fan magazine confessing, "I'm no Communist," just an "American dope." It was also helpful to take some kind of overtly anti-Communist actions such as opposing the antiblacklist factions within the talent unions or circulating petitions against the admission of Communist China to the United Nations. The film industry required more than three hundred people to clear themselves by writing letters, which then had to be approved by James O'Neil, the former American Legion national commander (and author of Document 3), and such anti-Communist professionals as J. B. Matthews and Benjamin Mandel. Clearance was not automatic. Even people who had no party ties had to write two or three drafts of their letters until they showed the appropriate degree of contrition.

The show-business people who couldn't or wouldn't clear themselves soon became unemployable and ostracized. Some left the country—if they could get passports. Others used subterfuges. Blacklisted writers worked under pseudonyms or hired fronts who were willing to pass off the blacklistees' scripts as their own. It was not a lucrative business. The aliases and fronts could not command the fees that the more established blacklisted writers had once earned. Producers knew what was going on and unscrupulous ones took advantage of it. The more principled ones began to chip away at the ban and hire some blacklisted writers. In 1956, the embarrassed silence that accompanied the failure of screenwriter "Richard Rich" (Dalton Trumbo, one of the Hollywood Ten) to claim his Academy Award began the process. By the mid-1960s, some of the blacklisted screenwriters were back in Hollywood.

Actors, of course, could not use fronts. Even the most talented of them had a tough time on the blacklist. Broadway, with its smaller clientele, did let them perform, but work in the legitimate theater was sporadic and much less remunerative than in movies or television. Ultimately, many of the blacklisted actors had to abandon their careers and take whatever jobs they could find. More than one blacklistee ended up waiting tables. The blacklist took a personal toll as well. Broken health and broken marriages, even suicides, were not unknown. When the blacklist lifted in the 1960s, its former victims were never able to fully resuscitate their careers. They had simply lost too much time.

The entertainment industry's blacklist was the most visible of the economic sanctions of the McCarthy era, but it was hardly unique. Most of the politically motivated dismissals affected Communists and ex-Communists and tended to be concentrated in industries where Communist-led unions had been active or in sectors of society that harbored the middle-class intellectuals and professionals who had gravitated to the party during the Popular Front. Steelworkers, teachers, sailors, lawyers, social workers, electricians, journalists, and assembly line workers were all subject to the same kinds of political dismissals and prolonged unemployment as show-business people — and the experience was just as devastating.

Considerable irony invests the McCarthy era dismissals within the academic community, for the nation's colleges and universities allegedly subscribed to the doctrines of academic freedom and to the notion that professors should not be punished for their political activities outside of class. But academia was not immune to McCarthyism, and by the late 1940s most of the nation's academic leaders believed that professors who were members of the Communist party had surrendered their intellectual independence and so were unqualified to teach. Significantly, no university administrators acted on these convictions unless pressured to do so by a state or congressional investigation or other outside agency. Until HUAC came to town or the FBI slid a "blind memorandum" across the college president's desk, there were no questions about the academic competence of the alleged subversives. At no point were any of them charged with recruiting their students or teaching the party line. Most of them were ex-Communists who, though hostile to the committees, were not especially active at the time.

The first important academic freedom case of the cold war arose in July 1948 at the University of Washington, where the state legislature's Un-American Activities Committee forced the issue by questioning a handful of faculty members. Six defied the committee and the administration filed charges against them. The faculty committee that dealt with the case in the fall recommended the retention of all but one, a professor who refused to answer any of its questions about his politics. The regents fired two others as well, because they had admitted to being members of the Communist party and were therefore, so the university's president explained, "incompetent, intellectually dishonest, and derelict in their duty to find and teach the truth." The rest of the academy agreed: Communists could not be college teachers. The academic community backed up its words with action or, rather, inaction; none of the dismissed professors was able to find a teaching job.

Within a few years the ban in academia extended to Fifth Amendment Communists. Concerned about the unfavorable publicity that unfriendly witnesses would draw to their institutions, the nation's academic leaders urged faculty members to cooperate with HUAC and the other committees. Because of the tradition of academic freedom, university administrators clothed their responses to McCarthyism in elaborate rationalizations about the academic profession's commitment to "complete candor and perfect integrity." The most authoritative such statement was released by the presidents of the nation's thirty-seven leading universities in the spring of 1953, just as the main congressional committees were about to investigate higher education. It stressed the professors' duty "to speak out"—that is, name names—and warned that "invocation of the Fifth Amendment places upon a professor a heavy burden of proof of his fitness to hold a teaching position and lays upon his university an obligation to reexamine his qualifications for membership in its society." The message was clear. College teachers subpoenaed by a congressional committee knew that if they took the Fifth Amendment or otherwise refused to testify they might lose their jobs.

The main academic purges occurred from 1952 to 1954 when the congressional committees had run out of more glamorous targets and turned to the nation's colleges and universities. Dismissals were not automatic; an academic hearing usually followed the congressional one. Although the faculty committees that mounted the investigations did not normally demand that their colleagues name names, they did expect them to cooperate and discuss their past political activities. People who refused, who felt that such questions were as illegitimate as HUAC's, were invariably fired, as were most of the others, especially at schools where conservative or politically insecure administrators and trustees refused to accept the favorable recommendations of faculty committees. In a few cases, if a professor had tenure, taught at a relatively less vulnerable private university, and cooperated fully with the institution's investigation, he or she could retain his or her job. But these were exceptional cases and they often masked the less publicized dismissals of junior professors, who were invariably let go when their contracts expired. By the time the McCarthyist furor subsided, close to a hundred academics had lost their jobs for refusing to cooperate with anti-Communist investigators. Several hundred more were probably eased out under the FBI's Responsibilities Program and similar measures.

Once fired, the politically tainted professors could rarely find other academic jobs. Like the Hollywood blacklistees, they were confronted with an unacknowledged but thoroughly effective embargo. Some emigrated, some switched fields, and some went to teach in small southern Negro colleges that were so desperate for qualified faculty members they asked no questions. The university blacklist began to subside by the early 1960s. Most of the banned professors returned to the academic world, but their careers had suffered in the interim.

Hundreds of elementary and high school teachers also lost their jobs, sometimes after an appearance before HUAC and sometimes as the result of a local loyalty probe. Social workers were similarly affected, especially in the welfare agencies of cities like New York and Philadelphia where they had formed unions and agitated on behalf of their clients. Again, a combination of outside investigations and loyalty programs cost these people their jobs. Journalists were another group of middle-class professionals who were fired when they defied congressional committees. There were only a handful of such people, their dismissals an embarrassment in an industry that presumably required so much freedom itself. The *New York Times* justified its firing of a copyreader in the foreign news department as a matter of national security; had he worked on the sports desk, the *Times* explained, he could have kept his job.

Industrial workers also faced dismissals and blacklists, especially if they were active in the locals of left-wing unions. Again, outside pressures precipitated the firings. Although alleged Communists were sometimes dropped outright (especially if found leafleting or circulating petitions outside plant gates), most of the time they lost their jobs as a result of a congressional investigation or the denial of a security clearance. Companies with defense contracts were under pressure to remove recalcitrant witnesses and other political undesirables from their payrolls; in several instances the government threatened to withdraw a contract if an offending worker was not fired. The most massive wave of dismissals occurred in the maritime industry, where the imposition of a port security program after the outbreak of the Korean War screened about fifteen hundred sailors and longshoremen off their jobs. Employers and federal authorities were not the only agencies to

impose sanctions within a factory. Unfriendly witnesses were sometimes subjected to "run-outs" organized by coworkers who beat them
up and physically forced them off their jobs.

Occasionally the fired workers were reinstated. Successful litigation
forced major revisions in the port security program, for example. In
other instances, if—and this was an increasingly big *if*—their unions
were willing to back up their grievances, some people got their jobs
back. In the late 1940s, arbitrators hearing these cases were sometimes willing to restore the jobs of people who clearly could not endanger the national security. After the outbreak of the Korean War,
however, neither their unions nor the arbitrators would support such
people's claims. In addition, workers who were fired for political reasons were often deprived of unemployment benefits.

Economic sanctions affected independent professionals and businesspeople in different ways. Being self-employed, they did not have
to worry about being fired, but they had to endure other injuries. In
some occupations, licensing requirements enabled the states to impose
political tests, usually by making applicants take some kind of loyalty
oath. Unfriendly witnesses could lose their licenses or, if they did
work for a state or local government, have their contracts canceled.

Lawyers were particularly affected, especially those who defended
people in anti-Communist proceedings. Whatever their own political
beliefs, such lawyers were perceived as sharing those of their clients.
Of course, some attorneys were or had been Communists. Like other
middle-class professionals, many lawyers had been attracted to the
party during the 1930s and 1940s. Many of them belonged to the cohort of talented liberal and left-wing attorneys who had staffed the
New Deal agencies or worked with the CIO. By the late 1940s most of
them had left the government and the mainstream unions and were
trying to establish themselves in private practice. The few members of
the legal profession willing to handle the cases of Communists suffered economically. Their other clients, fearful of being stigmatized by
attorneys who were publicly identified with the national enemy, went
elsewhere. The political dissidents, deportees, and left-led unions that
provided the core of their business were usually too insolvent to pay
much, if anything.

Worse than the loss of clients and income was the possibility that
defending the party might land them in jail or get them disbarred.
The lawyers who represented the *Dennis* defendants were not the only
attorneys to be charged with contempt of court as the result of their
efforts during a Communist trial. (See Chapter 8.) Nor were they the

only lawyers threatened with disbarment because of their politics. As the testimony of a Bay Area attorney in Document 20 reveals, the problems such lawyers faced made it particularly difficult for the protagonists in anti-Communist proceedings to find legal representation, especially if they did not want a known left-winger. Some of the defendants in the second round of Smith Act trials were rejected by more than two hundred attorneys.

Unlike the academic world and film industry, which were under outside pressure, the legal profession undertook to oust its tainted members on its own. The initiatives came from conservative attorneys associated with the anti-Communist network. The American Bar Association (ABA) set up a Special Committee on Communist Tactics, Strategy, and Objectives to ensure that alleged subversives did not penetrate the legal profession. The ABA also adopted resolutions against allowing Communists and, later, Fifth Amendment witnesses to practice law. These resolutions, coming as they did from the organized voice of a highly respected profession, carried considerable weight. To implement them, national and local bar associations worked closely with HUAC, the FBI, and the rest of the anti-Communist network to screen applicants and begin disbarment proceedings against the more radical members. Few succeeded.

Important members of the legal establishment (and not just the targeted attorneys) opposed these ousters. After all, lawyers did have a traditional commitment to and understanding of civil liberties, as well as a professional responsibility to represent all types of clients. By the mid-1950s some eminent lawyers were concerned about protecting the public's right to counsel and refused to countenance political disbarments. Even more important, in a few instances local bar associations and attorneys from major law firms in cities like Philadelphia, Denver, and Cleveland had begun to take on Communist cases. Such gestures, coming from leading members of the bar, contributed to the lessening of the McCarthyist furor—even if they did not necessarily win their clients' acquittal.

15

Liberals and the
Struggle against McCarthyism

The establishment attorneys who had agreed to represent some of the Smith Act defendants were careful to distance themselves from their clients. Even so, their willingness to support Communists' right to a fair trial exposed them to attack. The controversy was instructive, for their colleagues rallied behind the attorneys and ostracized their critics. But that occurred in 1956. Perhaps an earlier defense of the civil rights of Communists and other political undesirables by similar establishment figures might also have won support. We will never know. Instead of fighting McCarthyism, most members of the American elite—the business and professional leaders who wielded influence within American society—collaborated with it, if not directly by firing or blacklisting people, then indirectly by their silence.

The failure of leading liberals and the organizations associated with them to offer more than rhetorical opposition was particularly damaging. To a certain extent it was caused by a failure of nerve. The Democratic party, the traditional political home of the nation's liberals, was under heavy partisan attack by the late 1940s. Many of its leaders feared that taking a strong stand against McCarthyism might cost them their political lives. To defend themselves against charges that they were soft on Communists, they flaunted their own anticommunism. The Senate liberals' unsuccessful attempt to defeat the 1950 McCarran Act by substituting a harsher measure was emblematic. They opposed the bill yet voted for it anyhow, an action that, as one of them later confessed, "troubled me more than any vote I made during my entire period in the Senate."

There was more than cowardice behind the failure to stand up to McCarthyism. Although deploring the excesses of the anti-Communist crusade, many politicians, union leaders, and intellectuals supported its underlying goals. Known as "cold war liberals," these people were fervently committed to the struggle against communism at home and abroad. Many of them, like Minnesota Senator and future Vice President Hubert H. Humphrey, who had gained prominence after ejecting Communists from his state's Democratic party, also wanted to expand the welfare state and eliminate racial segregation. In their speeches and writings and in the pronouncements of the Americans for Democratic Action (ADA), an organization Humphrey and his allies founded in 1946 to promote their political agenda, the cold war liberals insisted that their combination of moderate social reform and muscular anti-communism was a more effective counter to the Communist threat than the unenlightened frenzy of the anti-Communist extremists. They also argued that the best way for liberals to protect the nation from the evils of right-wing McCarthyism was to carry out the anti-Communist purges themselves.

Such an enterprise was tricky, for there was considerable overlap between the causes that the Communist party supported and the domestic reforms that organizations like the ADA espoused. This programmatic affinity, many cold war liberals believed, made it imperative for them to police their own ranks to ensure that they would not be duped by the Communists. Insufficient vigilance during the 1930s, these people insisted, had allowed the party to gain entry into mainstream institutions. Such naiveté was dangerous, they claimed, not only because it helped Communists, but also because it gave the right-wingers justifiable grounds for their suspicion of liberals. Unfortunately, in their eagerness to distance themselves from anything that might be remotely connected with communism, many of the cold war liberals abandoned their original concern with social reform. By the late 1960s they had become neo-conservatives; but even before they shed their liberalism, as the excerpts from a 1950 article by Sidney Hook in Document 21 indicate, it was clear that their anticommunism had displaced most of their other political concerns.

Because of the defection of so many liberals, most of the opposition to the anti-Communist crusade was marginal and weak. Except for a handful of committed civil libertarians, the opposition's most conspicuous members were themselves victims of McCarthyism. After all, many of the men and women who defied HUAC or the SISS did so to register their opposition to the committees' activities. In many cases, they viewed their struggles to retain their jobs and overcome the blacklist as more than just their private business. Targets and challengers, they were both the strongest opponents of McCarthyism and its main casualties. Many of these people tried to coordinate their individual resistance with a broader movement. But because tangling with the anti-Communist crusade turned them into social pariahs, they could find few allies.

More important, the institutional basis for a viable opposition movement simply did not exist. If private individuals were to mount an effective campaign against the anti-Communist furor, they needed to work as part of an organization. But except for a handful of left-wing groups, which were themselves under attack, the established liberal and professional organizations that would have ordinarily defended the civil liberties of the victims of McCarthyism shrank from the task. Thus, although thousands of Americans were upset about what was going on and might even have expressed their opposition openly, the absence of effective collective outlets for that opposition seriously diminished it.

If any organization could have been expected to lead the fight against McCarthyism, it was the American Civil Liberties Union (ACLU). Yet the ACLU remained detached from the fray. It did not participate directly in the major Communist trials of the period, choosing instead to submit friend of the court briefs, supplementary arguments that supported the general principle of free speech but avoided any controversial stands. The organization did not become involved with the Rosenbergs, and its national leaders hesitated for so long over whether to support Owen Lattimore's battle against the obviously trumped-up perjury charges against him that Lattimore's attorney, future Supreme Court Justice Abe Fortas, finally told the ACLU not to bother. (See Chapter 12.)

The organization's waffling stemmed from the serious divisions within its board of directors. Many board members were typical cold war liberals, ardent anti-Communists who feared that taking a strong stand against McCarthyism might dilute the ACLU's opposition to what they felt was the greater evil of communism. One of the ACLU's main leaders, the New York attorney Morris Ernst, was an unofficial apologist for the FBI and worked secretly with Hoover to maintain the bureau's reputation among liberals. The refusal of Ernst and his allies within the ACLU to support anything that might help the party simply paralyzed the organization. Thus, for example, when the ACLU decided to study the entertainment industry's blacklist in preparation for taking legal action, a conservative on the board aborted the project. The commitment to civil liberties at the rank-and-file level was considerably stronger; the ACLU's local affiliates and members successfully opposed the board's attempt to impose an anti-Communist affidavit on the membership, but they could not force the national organization to take positive action on other issues.

The nation's main professional organizations were equally passive. As Chapter 14 explains, the ABA accommodated itself to the anti-Communist crusade. Within higher education, where the widespread dismissals of tenured professors would ordinarily have precipitated some kind of organized protest, the lethargy of the American Association of University Professors (AAUP), the main organization devoted to the defense of academic freedom, crippled collective action. The AAUP traditionally responded to violations of academic freedom by investigating them and then censuring the schools involved. Although AAUP censure was a largely symbolic action that probably would not have restored many jobs, during the height of the McCarthy period, between 1949 and 1956, the association did not even report on the political dismissals. Unlike the ACLU leadership, which was paralyzed for ideological reasons, the national leaders of the AAUP opposed McCarthyism but were at the mercy of their incompetent and ailing executive director, who did nothing to oppose the universities' acquiescence in McCarthyism. Because most of the academics who opposed the political dismissals understandably expected the AAUP to lead the fight, its failure to act made it hard to mobilize opposition to the academic firings and blacklists.

Within the entertainment world, the obstacles to a successful struggle were even greater, for a strong nucleus of anti-Communist activists had entrenched themselves within the industry. One powerful union, the Screen Actors Guild (SAG), then headed by Ronald Reagan, imposed loyalty oaths on its members and joined forces with the studios in trying to purge the film industry of Communists. "If any actor by his own actions outside of union activities has so offended American public opinion that he has made himself unsaleable at the box office," the SAG warned its members in 1951, "the Guild cannot and would not want to force any employer to hire him." The other talent unions were equally reluctant to confront the blacklist. In 1955 a group of insurgents within the broadcast industry organized a slate of candidates to challenge the pro-blacklist leadership of the American Federation of Television and Radio Artists (AFTRA). The candidates won their election only to find themselves on the blacklist. (See Document 19.)

Elsewhere the few groups that actively opposed the anti-Communist crusade quickly became its targets. One was the National Lawyers Guild (NLG), an organization established in 1936 by a coalition of left-wing and liberal attorneys expressly to combat the conservatism and anti-Semitism of the mainstream American bar. Communists were active in the NLG, but so were many of the nation's most dedicated non-Communist civil libertarians. Most of the attorneys willing to represent Communists were guild members; and the organization submitted friend of the court briefs in many key cases. Because of the NLG's long-standing criticism of the FBI, it became a major target of bureau harassment. Unable to get the NLG placed on the attorney general's list of subversive organizations, the FBI conducted a massive campaign of illegal surveillance and media disinformation designed to discredit it. In September 1950, HUAC released a report on the NLG, calling it "The Legal Bulwark of the Communist Party," just a few days before the NLG was to submit an exposé of the FBI's lawbreaking. A few years later the Eisenhower administration tried to put the NLG on the attorney general's list. Although the guild's fight against the list succeeded, the accompanying publicity along with the earlier HUAC report essentially gutted the organization. By the mid-1950s the NLG had lost more than half of its local chapters and four-fifths of its members.

What happened to the NLG happened to all the organizations that vigorously tried to oppose McCarthyism. Hounded by the FBI, HUAC, and the rest of the anti-Communist network, they encountered enormous problems simply getting their message across. The FBI's intervention often made it impossible for such groups even to obtain meeting halls or hold press conferences; HUAC routinely subpoenaed their leaders. Just as debilitating was the Red-baiting by anti-Communist liberals. As a result, organizations like the Emergency Civil Liberties Committee, established in 1951 to take on the cases that the ACLU was ducking, were put on the defensive and essentially marginalized. Even an organization like the Ford Foundation's Fund for the Republic, which sponsored research on civil liberties issues, came under congressional attack.

Litigation was by far the most successful form of opposition. The McCarthy era may well have been one of the few times when the slowness of the legal process produced a positive outcome because the delays ensured that few Communist defendants actually went to prison. Most of the protagonists in the criminal prosecutions and deportation proceedings of the time won their cases. The struggle often took years, however, and even though they prevailed, the extralegal sanctions inflicted on them as well as the expense and constant uncertainty of their cases may well have caused more suffering than six months in jail. People who tried to use the legal system to contest their dismissals and subsequent blacklisting fared less well. Suits against public employers had somewhat more success than those in the private sector. Attempts by blacklisted writers and actors to obtain monetary damages for their exclusion from the entertainment industry, for example, floundered until the mid-1960s. Significantly, juries often supported the plaintiffs' claims, only to have judges reverse them—an indication that ordinary Americans may not have backed the anti-Communist crusade as strongly as the elites did. It was not until 1962, as the excerpts from the trial testimony in Document 19 indicate, that John Henry Faulk, a Texas radio and television personality who had led the AFTRA battle, finally won his suit against his blacklisters. By then, of course, Faulk's once-promising career was over.

16

The Legacy of McCarthyism

In the late 1950s a group of graduate students at the University of Chicago wanted to have a soft drink vending machine installed outside the Physics Department for the convenience of people who worked there late at night. They started to circulate a petition to the Buildings and Grounds Department, but their colleagues refused to sign. They did not want to be associated with the allegedly radical students whose names were already on the document.

This incident—and it is not unique—exemplifies the kind of timidity that came to be seen, even at the time, as the most damaging consequence of the anti-Communist furor. Because political activities could get you in trouble, prudent folk avoided them. Instead, to the despair of intellectuals, middle-class Americans became social conformists. A silent generation of students populated the nation's campuses, while their professors shrank from teaching anything that might be construed as controversial. "The Black Silence of Fear" that Supreme Court Justice William O. Douglas deplores (in Document 22) seemingly blanketed the nation, and meaningful political dissent had all but withered away.

Was McCarthyism to blame? Obviously the congressional hearings, loyalty programs, and blacklists affected the lives of the men and women caught up in them. Beyond that, however, it is hard to tell. The statistics are imprecise. Ten thousand people may have lost their jobs. Is that few or many? It may be useful to reflect on an earlier debate among historians about the application of sanctions—in this case the apparently low number of whippings administered under slavery—to realize that it may not be necessary to whip many slaves to keep the rest of the plantation in line.

Quantification aside, it may be helpful to look at the specific sectors of American society that McCarthyism touched. Such an appraisal, tentative though it must be, may offer some insight into the extent of the damage and into the ways in which the anti-Communist crusade influenced American society, politics, and culture. McCarthyism's main impact may well have been in what did not happen rather than in what did—the social reforms that were never adopted, the diplomatic initiatives that were not pursued, the workers who were not organized into unions, the books that were not written, and the movies that were never filmed.

The most obvious casualty was the American left. The institutional toll is clear. The Communist party, already damaged by internal problems, dwindled into insignificance and all the organizations associated with it disappeared. The destruction of the front groups and the left-led unions may well have had a more deleterious impact on American politics than the decline of the party itself. With their demise, the nation lost the institutional network that had created a public space where serious alternatives to the status quo could be presented. Moreover, with the disappearance of a vigorous movement on their left, moderate reform groups were more exposed to right-wing attacks and thus rendered less effective.

In the realm of social policy, for example, McCarthyism may have aborted much-needed reforms. As the nation's politics swung to the right after World War II, the federal government abandoned the unfinished agenda of the New Deal. Measures like national health insurance, a social reform embraced by the rest of the industrialized world, simply fell by the wayside. The left-liberal political coalition that might have supported health reforms and similar projects was torn apart by the anti-Communist crusade. Moderates feared being identified with anything that seemed too radical, and people to the left of them were either unheard or under attack. McCarthyism further contributed to the attenuation of the reform impulse by helping to divert the attention of the labor movement, the strongest institution within the old New Deal coalition, from external organizing to internal politicking.

The impact of the McCarthy era was equally apparent in international affairs. Opposition to the cold war had been so thoroughly identified with communism that it was no longer possible to challenge the basic assumptions of American foreign policy without incurring suspicions of disloyalty. As a result, from the defeat of third-party presidential candidate Henry Wallace in the fall of 1948 until the early 1960s, effective public criticism of America's role in the world was essentially nonexistent. Within the government, the insecurities that McCarthyism inflicted on the State Department lingered for years, especially with regard to East Asia. Thus, for example, the campaign against the "loss" of China left such long-lasting scars that American policymakers feared to acknowledge the official existence of the People's Republic of China until Richard Nixon, who was uniquely impervious to charges of being soft on communism, did so as president in 1971. And it was in part to avoid a replay of the loss-of-China scenario that Nixon's Democratic predecessors, Kennedy and Johnson, dragged the United States so deeply into the quagmire of Vietnam.

The nation's cultural and intellectual life suffered as well. While there were other reasons that television offered a bland menu of quiz shows and westerns during the late 1950s, McCarthy-era anxieties clearly played a role. Similarly, the blacklist contributed to the reluctance of the film industry to grapple with controversial social or political issues. In the intellectual world, cold war liberals also avoided controversy. They celebrated the "end of ideology," claiming that the United States' uniquely pragmatic approach to politics made the problems that had once concerned left-wing ideologists irrelevant. Consensus historians pushed that formulation into the past and described a nation that had supposedly never experienced serious internal conflict. It took the civil rights movement and the Vietnam War to end this complacency and bring reality back.

Ironically, just as these social commentators were lauding the resilience of American democracy, the anti-Communist crusade was undermining it. The political repression of the McCarthy era fostered the growth of the national security state and facilitated its expansion into the rest of civil society. On the pretext of protecting the nation from Communist infiltration, federal agents attacked individual rights and extended state power into movie studios, universities, labor unions, and many other ostensibly independent institutions. The near universal deference to the federal government's formulation of the Communist threat abetted the process and muted opposition to what was going on.

Moreover, even after the anti-Communist furor receded, the antidemocratic practices associated with it continued. We can trace the legacy of McCarthyism in the FBI's secret COINTELPRO program of harassing political dissenters in the 1960s and 1970s, the Watergate-related felonies of the Nixon White House in the 1970s, and the Iran-Contra scandals in the 1980s. The pervasiveness of such wrongdoing reveals how seriously the nation's defenses against official illegalities had eroded in the face of claims that national security took precedence over ordinary law. McCarthyism alone did not cause these outrages; but the assault on democracy that began during the 1940s and 1950s with the collaboration of private institutions and public agencies in suppressing the alleged threat of domestic communism was an important early contribution.

PART TWO

The Documents

A Note about the Text:

Two objectives guided the selection of materials for this volume. The first was to include those documents that, like Senator McCarthy's February 1950 speech in Wheeling, West Virginia, Alger Hiss's testimony before the House Un-American Activities Committee, and the Supreme Court decision in the case of the Communist party's top leaders, shaped the events of the era. The second was to offer a representative sampling of materials that would illustrate the different forms McCarthyism took and allow its many voices to be heard. Because it was so extensive, the cold war Red Scare generated literally dozens, if not hundreds, of documents that I could have selected. I tried to choose ones that were both important and emblematic.

These materials come from a wide variety of published and unpublished sources. Some, like playwright Lillian Hellman's 1952 letter to the House Un-American Activities Committee, have been reprinted many times, while others, like the recollections of former American Communists from the transcripts of a documentary film on deposit at the Tamiment Library at New York University, have never been published. Most are official documents, generated by congressional hearings, FBI investigations, and judicial proceedings. Others are texts that, like the Hollywood producers' press release announcing the entertainment industry's blacklist or the CIO resolution expelling one of its left-wing unions, constitute an informal record of McCarthyism's spread into the private sector. I found those types of documents in many different types of publications, from newspapers and pamphlets to the official proceedings of meetings and the appendices of books. Finally, I have included excerpts from a few contemporary magazine articles that present the views of important protagonists and observers.

1

The World of American Communism: Party Members Talk about Their Experiences

People joined the American Communist party for all kinds of reasons, and their experiences once they became members were just as varied. This document contains the first-person accounts of several Communists and ex-Communists who discuss why they joined the party and what they did in it. The material comes from a set of oral history interviews conducted in the late 1970s and 1980s by filmmakers Julia Reichert and James Klein, whose documentary *Seeing Red* (1984) explores the lives of these and other Communists and ex-Communists. Similar in tone and content to the published memoirs of other party activists, these reminiscences, though not uncritical of the party, reflect the idealism of most American Communists and the energy that they poured into their political work.[1]

---

[1]The most interesting of these ex-Communist memoirs are listed in "Interpreting McCarthyism: A Bibliographic Essay," starting on page 284 in the back of the book.

Howard Johnson, David Friedman, Marge Frantz, and Rose Krysak, Oral History Transcripts, interviews by James Klein and Julia Reichert for *Seeing Red,* Oral History of the American Left, Tamiment Institute Library, Elmer Holmes Bobst Library, New York University.

HOWARD JOHNSON

A Communist in Harlem

November 16, 1979

A leader of the Young Communist League in Harlem in the 1930s, John-son remained a full-time cadre until he left the Communist party in the 1950s.

. . . When I joined, [it was] as if all of a sudden my life had been taken out of a small box and I had plugged into the entire globe internationally. Because in a very short space of time I had participated in a demonstration around Ethiopia, you know, shouting, picket signs "Get Mussolini out of Ethiopia."[2]. . .

Immediately my life took on a new dimension that reminded me of some novels I had read as a teenager, like Jack London's *Martin Eden* and his whole description of what socialism was to him. So I was, you know, getting out of the books and beginning to live a life that I had always dreamed of—being in contact with the world. So it was really a very powerful experience. Very powerful. . . .

. . . The first thing that impressed me about all the party members that I came in contact with was the range of their conversation and their interests. They seemed to be informed about everything that was going on. They could talk about music. There was a Marxist analysis of music. They could talk about art. There was a Marxist analysis of art. They could talk about the international situation. The meaning and significance of collective security. They were so well informed.

[Johnson is asked about the party's goal of overthrowing the government.]

. . . I didn't look on it that way. I saw it as an action organization. Things were happening. And the kind of things that were happening I didn't regard as subversion of the government, I regarded it as good for me and for other blacks. . . .

---

[2]In 1935 the Italian dictator Benito Mussolini invaded Ethiopia. The Western democracies, including the United States, did not take any serious action against this act of aggression. The American Communist party openly opposed the move and used demonstrations against Mussolini to rally support from the African American community.

The job struggles. The campaign against Jim Crow and baseball. Putting people who had been evicted by the City Marshall back in their buildings. Uh, the interracial activities that they developed. . . . I remember organizing youth in the Harlem Vocational School in 1940, and publicizing the fact that the black youth in the Harlem Vocational School were not really getting training for jobs. . . .

. . . By 1943 there were fourteen hundred members in the party, organized in clubs, sections, and all of them, the majority of them were activists who could be called to a demonstration [or] to a mobilization. We would picket stores that were discriminating. Oh, the most famous was the Empire Cafeteria, which didn't employ black—right in the middle of Harlem, 125th Street and Lenox Avenue. And the police tried to break up our picket lines. But we finally won and got blacks in there. Can you imagine? The police trying to prevent blacks from picketing, or blacks and whites from picketing, to get jobs for blacks in a cafeteria in Harlem. . . .

. . . Most of the black intellectuals joined the party because they were attracted to it for the same reasons that I was. It was one organization that was really doing something, that was there. That was picketing, that was demonstrating, that was getting jobs for blacks in this union and that union—especially the unions where there was left leadership, like the furriers union, the united electrical workers union, auto workers, the hotel and restaurant club employees union, Local 6. These were under Communist leadership.

[Johnson responds to a question about lifestyles in the party.]

. . . I didn't see recruiting people into the party to turn them into grim puritans. . . .

. . . You know, why join a movement that wasn't having any fun? Well I came into the party at a time that it was attempting to change that grim look, what some of us call the Communist International look. We came in after the Seventh World Congress, which put forward a broad line to make friends with everyone that was against war and fascism, even if they didn't understand the party line. And the Young Communist League did more in terms of putting that style into life than the party. So my early training in the movement was as part of the Young Communist League. . . . We put on a musical at one of the national conventions called "Socialism to Swing." And there was dancing in it, swinging, and we took a song that was popular—Ella Fitzgerald was singing it with Chick Webb's band—called "A-Tisket

A-Tasket." And we wrote antifascist words to it. "A tisket, a tasket, put Hitler in a casket. And tell that meanie, Mussolini, and his henchman, Franco."

DAVID FRIEDMAN

A New York City Schoolteacher in the Party

October 23, 1979

Friedman's experiences were typical of the many Jewish professionals who joined the Communist party in the 1930s.

. . . My father was an old time socialist. I guess when he came from Russia—many Jews did who lived in the Lower East Side—they brought with them a socialist tradition. . . . And . . . the days when I was a teenager the Socialist party was pretty active. . . . And I used to hear the speakers—some of them very well known—of the Socialist party on the street corners. . . .

. . . And Friday and Saturday nights there were always crowds looking to speakers on four corners, and always a Socialist party speaker. . . . I was only a kid, an adolescent, but I remember listening to their talk about the oppression. And I knew from my own of the struggle of people in a rich country to have to contend with actual poverty, actual deprivation. . . . And I used to listen avidly to those speakers. And my father used to read the Socialist newspaper, the *Forward*. . . .

. . . Well I began to teach in 1926, and I started as a substitute, and I was a substitute for maybe two or three months in various schools in Harlem, where I was appalled at the fact that some of the schools had as much as one-third or almost one-half substitute teachers, . . . regularly assigned substitute teachers . . . that you paid . . . a fraction of the salary that you would a regular . . . In other words, these were inexperienced teachers mostly, brand new teachers as I was, so that the Harlem schools were considered a place where you didn't worry too much about the quality of education. . . . And only the teachers union brought to my attention the extensive nature of this phenomenon there. And seeing also that the textbooks we had, some of them were thirty years old, they were falling apart.... I know there were shops that had inadequate materials, lavatories with practically no equipment, uh, old run-down buildings that still had outside toilets.... There was a group in the union that wanted to deal with these issues and bring them before the Board of Education and to mobilize parents, mobilize other trade unions to try to change these conditions... and there must have been Communists because I know some of them were militant and they talked about not just the issue of what was happening in the Harlem schools, but related it to the broader question of, you know, discrimination and prejudice against the blacks in general throughout the history of the country....

... They were stimulating, and they got me thinking.... And I got involved in the group in the trade union that was trying to oust the leadership and getting leadership that would not be so willing to cooperate with the Board of Education and was willing to raise issues such as this about the condition in the Harlem schools....

People began to reveal themselves [as Communists] when they saw that I was an active union member. The union was the base where the focus of my interest was. And I got on committees, and I got involved in activities, and I realized that the people that I later found out and subsequently or almost immediately found out were party people, certainly sympathetic to the party, were the most active and the most dedicated, the ones who would sweat it out all kinds of hours and come in on Saturdays and would work on the mimeograph machine or writing statements or trying to mobilize committees all hours of the late afternoon and into the evening. And I developed a very high respect for many of these people. And I realized that they were the kind of people that I was glad to work with.

... They would bring me the *Daily Worker,* these friends, and they would give me the *Daily Worker* and I got a subscription to the *Daily Worker* before I joined the party, and saw that they were dealing with a question that in a way would, uh, that made sense to me in terms of the fact that here was the strongest economic power—"strongest" in the world and was going through a cataclysm where millions of people were literally trying to make a living selling apples for a nickel apiece to each other. Millions of people who had never thought of themselves as incompetent or inefficient were made to feel that something was wrong with them and that they couldn't make a living and that they were jobless. And the inequity of it and the fact that the society was doing things like burning wheat and spilling milk in order to keep the price from going too low, pouring out milk, you know, on the highways and undercutting crops in order to prevent the price of products from dropping because of the situation so there would be artificial scarcity.[3] The insanity of that was brought home to me and reinforced by pamphlets . . . that I got from these party people and from the reading that I did. . . .

. . . Then the years that followed Hitler began to come on the scene, and the threat of fascism, and Mussolini had been in power for a number of years, and the Hitler phenomenon with its destruction of trade unions, its obvious threat to the welfare or even the existence of the Jews in its control in Germany. . . .

And the threat of these things as a Jew and as a worker, as a person with some social awareness to me was something that . . . wasn't of peripheral interest but something that began to absorb my attention. . . .

. . . I joined a branch in Brooklyn. And I was assigned to an area near Red Hook. . . . I would go to speak to people to try to get them interested in subscribing to the *Daily Worker* and try to get them into coming to meetings to talk about not just the economic problems but about the threat of fascism as it was being displayed in the invasion of Ethiopia. . . .

. . . I was quite active. My wife and I were quite active. We were in the first couple years in the street branch, what's called the street branch, where people from the community of all occupations—housewives and so on—were members of this same, in the same branch. And, uh, we were very much involved then in trying to help financially and in any other way we could the activities of the CIO union that were then busy trying to organize. The auto workers and the steelworkers and the other . . . and electrical workers. . . . [We] were very much caught up with the whole organization of the CIO union in financial support, in legislation—you know, in getting letters and getting resolutions from groups that we belonged to, the teachers union in my case, trying to get them involved, other union members, get their AFL unions to support the . . . if they couldn't do it directly, get them sympathetic to pressures to help the new CIO unions in their efforts. That

---

[3]During the Depression, the prices for agricultural products were so low that the farmers protested by pouring out surplus milk, and the Agriculture Department paid for and then destroyed crops and livestock to try to raise prices.

was in the middle '30s, '36, '37, '38, the sit-down strikes were going on.[4] So there was money, literature distribution at plants that people were trying to organize in Brooklyn. And, uh, many, many meetings and firming up friendships with other party people where we became very close not only in terms of our party activity. . . .

. . . Getting American foreign policy to be helpful, to not refuse to sell arms and to sell supplies to the legitimate Spanish Republican government. That took tremendous energy, tremendous activity, meetings of all kinds and petitions and trying to get people . . . fundraising for supplies for the medical needs, which was one thing that could be done without running afar with the State Department. The medical committee helped the Spanish refugees and Republicans. . . . Tried to mobilize support for aid to the whole movement for a pact between the democratic countries and the Soviet Union to stop Hitler.

So we were involved in mass meetings and literature distribution and all types of activities that had to do with trying to set up a situation where the Western democracy—then the Soviet Union—would combine to have some type of power or policy, or even an alliance, which would maybe stop the Hitler movement and the expansion of the fascist pressure in Europe and throughout the world. . . .

Well there were about four or five meetings a week, and Sunday going up into the tenement houses of the Lower East Side selling or distributing the *Daily Worker* and pamphlets, trying to get people to subscribe, trying to get people to come to meetings. And for a few years I was in the teachers' branch where we dealt mainly with the problems that had to do with the teachers' profession, with the question of low salaries—there hadn't been a teachers' wage increase in many years—and the high number of substitutes.

---

[4]During the sit-down strikes of the late 1930s, workers occupied factories, especially in the automobile industry, to force management to recognize their unions.

A Longtime Woman Activist
in the Party

August 22, 1981

Frantz, whose father, Joseph Gelders, was an important secret party member in Alabama in the 1930s, joined the party when she was in her teens; she left in the 1950s.

It took infinitely more courage to leave the party than to stay in the party. Because all the people you love and respect, or many of the people you love and respect, are still there. You're leaving behind an extremely safe, comfortable home to go out into, you know, to sort of move out to nowhere. . . .

By the '50s we weren't doing anything except barely trying to stay alive. We weren't really having any, you know, we were trying to fight against McCarthyism—fairly ineffectually. . . . We were fighting a very principled fight against McCarthyism . . . but in retrospect I don't think we did that altogether well by any means. But in any case . . . we weren't out in the world doing things in the '50s. And increasingly I began to feel less and less efficacious, I mean less and less accomplished, that I was accomplishing less and less. So that the rewards of staying in the party seemed fewer and fewer. . . . We should have been up front about our politics and then nobody would have cared, you know. They would have lost their power. Their power was a power of exposure. . . .

Well, there's nothing like being actively engaged in the life of what's happening in your time. I mean, you didn't live, it wasn't a trivial life, you know. . . . It did feel like a very useful worthwhile life. And, uh, you know, there's nothing like the comfort and security of something you really believe in. You know, there were also a lot of horrible things that happen when you believe that strongly in something, too. . . . It was narrow in a sense.

We didn't have enough reality checks. We got totally caught up in our, you know, in the elaborations of our theory. . . . And we simply, um, we were not open to fundamental challenges. We didn't listen to other people. We thought we had the truth. And the truth is not that simple. So essentially, for me, we were, you know, looking back we were just incredibly simplistic in our thinking. . . . We just, everything, people were either good guys or bad guys. There was nothing in between.

ROSE KRYSAK

A Rank-and-File Communist in the 1950s

October 31, 1979

Krysak exemplifies the dedicated rank-and-file activist who remained a loyal party member throughout the 1950s.

Well, it wasn't a happy thing, I mean it wasn't a very easy thing, but it's very funny that sometimes stress strengthens you. Now I think maybe I've said that when I first was approached by the FBI, and when people told me the FBI had visited them and told them about me, that I was a Communist or whatever, it was very disconcerting, in fact frightening. But as it kept getting repetitive and repetitive I, it got to be you got used to it and it got less and less frightening.

[Krysak is asked about her reactions to Khrushchev's revelations about Stalin.]

I personally was shocked like most people were because we just didn't believe it, and when you are suddenly confronted with something, it was almost like a betrayal of your loyalty. But that was because we didn't learn yet . . . to think for ourselves or to question certain things, and so it was very painful, but on the other hand after we adjusted to the situation and we began to think things through it had certain positive elements to it. . . .

. . . I think it is sad because [the people who left the party] took this sad incident in the history and forgot one thing, even Stalin built the revolution. And I think that played a big role. You can't throw everything, Stalin, out with the revolution and all, he did participate in building the revolution, now what happened in subsequent years where he made a very serious mistake and did harm in many ways, if you are going to use this as a basis for being in or out, then you are really losing sight of the main objective of the Communist movement. . . .

I was a very devoted member. At the beginning almost without questioning. I never questioned them because I really, I felt they had all the answers. As I grew older and things develop[ed] I learned to question a little bit, but I always felt that on any shortcomings the party had, I felt in essence they are going toward their goal [which] was a good one and I want to be part of it. So that when people are critical I say yes that's from a mistake maybe, but that's not the important, the important thing [is] what is the ultimate goal. And that's why I think I was a good Communist and *am* a good Communist. . . .

I did everything that had to be done. If they had a demonstration at the ship that we had, I forgot the name, that German ship, I'd be there and I was considered very devoted and loyal a person. And they'd ask us to come out at eleven o'clock at night at Times Square to demonstrate against fascism. We would be there, and I was part of the organizing on that level.

2

From the Communist Party's Perspective: William Z. Foster Looks at the World in 1947

William Z. Foster's rise to the leadership of the American Communist party in mid-1945 indicated that the party had changed its line. It abandoned its wartime efforts to collaborate with capitalism and became increasingly hostile to the American government. The following excerpts from Foster's 1947 book *The New Europe* give the flavor of the party's dogmatic line during the early years of the cold war.

WILLIAM Z. FOSTER

The New Europe

1947

... The masses in Europe are again striking at the root evil that is producing the ever-more disastrous series of devastating world wars, economic crises, and tyrannous governments, namely, the monopoly controlled capitalist system itself. They do not accept the stupid notion, current in some American political circles, to the effect that the capitalist system is a sort of divinely ordained institution which can do no harm, and that the war was caused merely by Hitler and a few other unscrupulous and ambitious men in the fascist countries. Instead, they are trying to abolish the real evil, the capitalist system. ...

William Z. Foster, *The New Europe* (New York: International Publishers, 1947), 14–17, 23, 96–98, 104–5.

. . . The reactionary imperialist offensive of the United States in Europe and throughout the world, is writing upon the agenda of all the new democracies several new and urgent tasks, chief among them being the need to protect themselves against the threatening economic crisis in the United States, to fight against the American-stimulated, fascist-like reaction in their countries, to defend their national independence from Wall Street imperialism, and to combat the threat of a third world war that the American atom bomb maniacs are preparing. All these pressures, from within and without, are surely pushing the peoples of Europe, in varying tempos of development, towards the eventual adoption of socialism.

There is a growing understanding among the peoples all over Europe of these elementary facts: (a) that the private profit interests of the big capitalists conflict basically with the interests of the nation; (b) that the big capitalists are the source of the major economic and political evils that modern society is a prey to—industrial stagnation, mass pauperization, political reaction, imperialism, and war; and (c) that to abolish these evils the power of the monopolist capitalists must be broken and the people take full command of society's industrial and governmental machine. The various economic and political changes now being made in European countries have the foregoing general purposes in view.

All this goes to show the hollowness of the propaganda of the big American capitalists who, through their hosts of stooges and mouthpieces in politics, the press, the radio, the pulpit, and even in the ranks of organized labor, are flamboyantly boasting of their own patriotism and insolently challenging the patriotism of the Communists. All over Europe the democratic masses of the people are awakening to the antisocial role of these very same monopolists who sold out their peoples to Hitler. . . .

One hears these days a lot of talk about the so-called iron curtain in Europe, and the import of this is that it is a device of the Russians, to hide their "political sins" from the eyes of the world. But the only "iron curtain" in reality has been created by the Anglo-American press and diplomatic circles to obscure from the peoples of the world the vitally important democratic developments now taking place in Central and Eastern Europe, not to mention those in the U.S.S.R. . . .

The propaganda of violent threats now being carried on against the U.S.S.R. by capitalist forces in the United States, curiously enough, is based on fear of that country—not fear that the Soviets will attack us, as the Soviet-baiters allege—but fear that the socialist economic system of the U.S.S.R. is fundamentally superior to the prevailing capitalist economic order in the United States. The capitalists of this country and their mouthpieces and pen pushers, for all their shrieking to the contrary, are not at all sure of the soundness of their economic system. They are observant enough to know that while the United States is openly exposed to shattering economic breakdowns, with their mass unemployment and all the rest of the human tragedies attendant upon cyclical capitalist economic crises, the U.S.S.R. is quite immune to such economic disasters. The Soviet Union, by its very nature, does not and *cannot* have cyclical economic crises and mass unemployment due to overproduction. . . .

Besides this economic fear, the big American capitalists also have a profound political fear. They view with the gravest alarm the rising democratic tide throughout Europe and the world, and they know that the U.S.S.R. is the main bulwark of this new world democracy. They correctly see in this expanding democracy a formidable threat to their perspective of imperialist expansion. In the reactionary spirit of Hitler, therefore, they have embarked upon a crusade to crush democracy and socialism and to set up reactionary political systems that will conform with their plans for establishing world domination by Wall Street.

. . . The Truman Doctrine,[1] in substance, means the throwing of the gigantic financial, industrial, and military might of the United States government behind European reactionary minorities, even to the point of promoting civil war and undermining world peace. Besides the serious dangers inherent in the arming of a fascist country like Turkey a grave menace is involved in undermining the power and prestige of the United Nations as the United States did by taking the unilateral action of giving military aid to Greece and Turkey. The success of the Truman Doctrine, in its wider implications, would imply the systematic organization of a fascist Europe. Characteristically, the Truman Doctrine has as its slogan the old reactionary watchword of Hitler and Mussolini; that is, to stop the advance of communism. The Truman Doctrine is the Wall Street counterpart of Hitler's Anti-Comintern Pact[2] and has no more chance of success.

---

[1]The Truman Doctrine was the name given to the American policy of supporting anti-Communist governments. It had been articulated by President Truman in a March 1947 speech to Congress calling for economic and military aid to Greece and Turkey.

[2]The Anti-Comintern Pact sealed the alliance among Germany, Italy, and Japan during World War II.

3

The Communist Menace:
An American Legion View

The following selection is representative of the literature produced by
professional anti-Communists in the McCarthy era. Written by the
national commander of the American Legion, James F. O'Neil, it tells
Legionnaires how to fight communism. Like J. Edgar Hoover's 1947
statement to HUAC in Document 4, it stresses the dangers posed by
liberal gullibility and the need to expose the Communists' tricks.
Throughout the 1940s and 1950s, the Legion worked closely with the
FBI and the rest of the anti-Communist network, often spearheading
local campaigns against alleged Communist influence in schools or
other institutions. O'Neil himself became an important figure in the
unofficial program set up by the professional anti-Communists to
administer the Hollywood blacklist and help its victims "rehabilitate"
themselves.

JAMES F. O'NEIL

How You Can Fight Communism
August 1948

The rape of Czechoslovakia and the president's message to Congress
on March 16th pointing out the now clear menace of world communism poses a serious question for the Legion. Are we doing all we can
at post and community level in combating and exposing Communist

James F. O'Neil, "How You Can Fight Communism," *American Legion Magazine,* Aug.
1948, 16–17, 42–44.

activities? Or are we complacently "letting George do it"? Resolutions and oratorical efforts are obviously not enough. Strong arm methods and various other attempts to prevent Communist or near-Communist meetings are both beneath Legion dignity and counter to fundamental constitutional American rights. . . .

What then can Legionnaires effectively do to combat these Fifth Columnists in our midst and yet stay strictly within the law of land and bounds of patriotic propriety? Plenty! First let us briefly analyze the problem. The nature and purposes of world communism are now generally understood by all literate, informed Americans. Communists, no matter what their pretenses, are foreign agents in any country in which they are allowed to operate. The Canadian spy trials[1] more than proved that point. But while they are plotters for revolution and ultimate seizure of power, it obviously would be foolish for them openly to advocate anything so unwanted, unpopular, and repugnant.

So the first step is to disguise, deodorize, and attractively package Moscow's revolutionary products. Next the salesmen and peddlers themselves must be skillfully disguised, deodorized, and glamorized. Hence Communists always appear before the public as "progressives." Yesterday they were "20th century Americans," last week they were "defenders of all civil liberties," tonight they may be "honest, simple trades unionists." They are "liberals" at breakfast, "defenders of world peace" in the afternoon, and "the voice of the people" in the evening. These artful dodges and ingenious dissimulations obviously make it difficult for the average trusting citizen to keep up with every new Communist swindle and con game.

Here is where the American Legion can serve exactly the same important public service that Better Business Bureaus have done in the past in warning and protecting the public against all manner of swindles and rackets. . . . It does not require four years of college to be able to spot new commie fronts and to keep abreast of the ever-changing party line. But it does require a few hours of serious study and reading each week plus consultation with recognized experts. Legionnaires cannot devote themselves to any more valuable public service. . . .

Most cities today contain a nucleus of former F.B.I. men, Army or Navy intelligence officers, former C.P. [Communist party] members who have come over to our side, and other trained or experienced

---

[1]In 1946, as a result of the revelations of a defector from the Soviet embassy in Ottawa, the Canadian government charged a dozen men and women with spying for the Soviet Union. See pages 32–33.

men, many of them Legionnaires. They should be contacted and organized into an unofficial advisory committee. Experts on communism are available; it is your job to locate them in your department and community. These experts generally all know each other and should be used to check on the credibility of doubtful and unknown "anti-Communists."

You cannot fight knowledge with ignorance. Communist propaganda is generally craftily conceived and is carried out with diabolic cunning and guile. Most Communists spend years in study and training for their subversive roles. You cannot expect to outwit and thwart them by reading a couple of pamphlets or even a book. You will simply have to know your stuff. Merely hating them is not enough. . . .

. . . When a known pro-Soviet apologist is slated to lecture in your city, to address a meeting, speak over a local station, or make any kind of public appearance, form a small delegation, assemble all your facts (having first made doubly sure that they are facts), then call upon those responsible for importing the out-of-town peddler of Soviet propaganda and in a friendly, helpful manner call their attention to the fact that they evidently have been misinformed as to the background and record of the individual in question or to the true intent and purpose of the allegedly bona fide organization.

Or if some of your local prominent people have sponsored or lent their names or contributed money to indubitable c.p. fronts, perform the same friendly advisory service. Remember that you are trying to protect a local citizen from being made the fool, so belligerence and blustering are entirely out of order. If your local organization or citizen rejects your friendly, documented advice then obviously you are dealing with a willful fool or with people who know exactly what they are doing and don't care. In other words you will have uncovered another c.p. fronter.

. . . Many newspapers and other publicity media have secret Communists on their staffs who regularly slip in a neat hypodermic needle full of Moscow virus. They simply neglect to mention that "So and So" is a well known Communist or that "Such and Such Organization" is a Communist front and a fraud. Call their attention to their "mistakes" in a friendly manner. Honest and patriotic people appreciate such friendly tips. Those who go right on making similar "mistakes" should have their employers or sponsors notified. . . .

. . . Never forget the fact that Communists operating in our midst are in effect a secret battalion of spies and saboteurs parachuted by a foreign foe inside our lines at night and operating as American citizens under a variety of disguises just as the Nazis did in Holland and Belgium. Every art of human cunning is therefore necessary on their part to protect themselves and their subversive mission from exposure.

Far from their homeland and base of supplies, they are totally dependent on us for cover, food, munitions, and transport. The front organizations continually set up by the C.P. are therefore nothing more than screening auxiliary forces which keep the secret battalion supplied, clothed, and fed. Mercilessly and tirelessly exposing and putting these fronts out of business is manifestly almost as vital as detecting and exposing actual Communists and spies. Actual *official investigation* is obviously beyond our jurisdiction and under the law it is the proper field of the F.B.I., while the *exposure* of front organizations and Communist supporters is the function of the House Un-American Activities Committee.

All departments and posts should be eternally vigilant against any attempts to sabotage or wreck the House Un-American Activities Committee, the Washington State Legislative Committee on Subversive Activities, or the Fact Finding Committee of the California Legislature, also known as the Tenney Committee. . . . The American Legion should be in the forefront in demanding that similar subversive investigating committees be set up by the state legislatures in every department where communism is a serious threat. . . .

The American Legion is composed of men who risk[ed] their lives on the field of battle for their country, in two world wars. Military wars of aggression have now been replaced by a far more insidious form of warfare—political or psychological war. Shooting wars have been turned by the Communists into "cold wars." Cold wars require even a greater degree of vigilance and militancy on our part than shooting wars. The fight against America's enemies goes on.

There is work, important work, for every loyal Legionnaire as I have outlined in this article. Everyone is now familiar with the Communists' fanaticism and their ruthless, dynamic drive for power. If 75,000 fanatical Communists can indoctrinate, control, and activate an estimated million dupes and camp followers, surely the American Legion's more than three million members can arouse, warn, and instruct the remaining 139 millions of our citizens. The task is clear, the weapons and tools are available—let's go!

4

To Quarantine Communism: J. Edgar Hoover Speaks to the American People

Because J. Edgar Hoover rarely appeared before congressional committees, his 1947 HUAC testimony was unprecedented. The FBI director's stature and alleged expertise ensured that the views he expressed in this statement received wide circulation. Politicians, journalists, academics, and opinion leaders of all political persuasions adopted his formulations and recycled them in countless speeches, position papers, judicial decisions, and magazine and newspaper articles. Hoover's testimony is also part of the FBI's campaign to criminalize the Communist party by prosecuting it under the 1940 Smith Act's provisions against teaching and advocating the overthrow of the government "by force and violence." As the excerpts in Document 10 from the transcript of the 1949 Smith Act trial of the party's top leaders reveal, many of the arguments the FBI director presented to HUAC were repeated almost word for word by the prosecutors and their witnesses two years later.

Hoover also used his HUAC appearance to call for supplementing the government's legal assault on communism with an organized campaign to weaken the party by exposing its members and its alleged machinations. His testimony about the party's infiltration of the labor movement, film industry, and federal government points to what would become the main battlegrounds of the McCarthy era, just as his final invocation of "old-fashioned Americanism" reveals the traditional mentality that undergirded so much of the anti-Communist crusade.

J. Edgar Hoover, testimony, House Committee on Un-American Activities, *Hearings on H.R. 1884 and H.R. 2122,* 80th Cong., 1st sess., 26 Mar. 1947.

J. EDGAR HOOVER

Testimony before HUAC

March 26, 1947

... The aims and responsibilities of the House Committee on Un-American Activities and the Federal Bureau of Investigation are the same—the protection of the internal security of this Nation. The methods whereby this goal may be accomplished differ, however. I have always felt that the greatest contribution this committee could make is the public disclosure of the forces that menace America—Communist and Fascist. . . . This committee renders a distinct service when it publicly reveals the diabolic machinations of sinister figures engaged in un-American activities. . . .

The Communist movement in the United States began to manifest itself in 1919. Since then it has changed its name and its party line whenever expedient and tactical. But always it comes back to fundamentals and bills itself as the party of Marxism-Leninism. As such, it stands for the destruction of our American form of government; it stands for the destruction of American democracy; it stands for the destruction of free enterprise; and it stands for the creation of a "Soviet of the United States" and ultimate world revolution.

The historic mission: The preamble of the latest constitution of the Communist Party of the United States, filled with Marxian "double talk," proclaims that the party "educates the working class, in the course of its day-to-day struggles, for its historic mission, the establishment of socialism."

The phrase "historic mission" has a sinister meaning. To the uninformed person it bespeaks tradition, but to the Communist, using his own words, it is "achieving the dictatorship of the proletariat"; "to throw off the yoke of imperialism and establish the proletarian dictatorship"; "to raise these revolutionary forces to the surface and hurl them like a devastating avalanche upon the united forces of bourgeois reaction, frenzied at the presentment of their rapidly approaching doom."

In recent years, the Communists have been very cautious about using such phrases as "force and violence"; nevertheless, it is the subject of much discussion in their schools and in party caucus where they readily admit that the only way in which they can defeat the present ruling class is by world revolution.

The Communist, once he is fully trained and indoctrinated, realizes that he can create his order in the United States only by "bloody revolution."

Their chief textbook, *The History of the Communist Party of the Soviet Union,* is used as a basis for planning their revolution. Their tactics require that to be successful they must have:

1. The will and sympathy of the people.
2. Military aid and assistance.
3. Plenty of guns and ammunition.
4. A program for extermination of the police as they are the most important enemy and are termed "trained Fascists."
5. Seizure of all communications, buses, railroads, radio stations, and other forms of communications and transportation.

They evade the question of force and violence publicly. They hold that when Marxists speak of force and violence they will not be responsible—that force and violence will be the responsibility of their enemies. They adopt the novel premise that they do not advocate force and violence publicly but that when their class resists to defend themselves then they are thus accused of using force and violence. A lot of double talk. . . .

. . . The American Communist, like the leopard, cannot change his spots.

The party line: The Communist Party line changes from day to day. The one cardinal rule that can always be applied to what the party line is or will be is found in the fundamental principle of Communist teachings that the support of Soviet Russia is the duty of Communists of all countries.

One thing is certain. The American progress which all good citizens seek, such as old-age security, houses for veterans, child assistance, and a host of others is being adopted as window dressing by the Communists to conceal their true aims and entrap gullible followers. . . .

The numerical strength of the party's enrolled membership is insignificant. But it is well known that there are many actual members who because of their position are not carried on party rolls.

. . . The *Daily Worker* boasts of 74,000 members on the rolls.

What is important is the claim of the Communists themselves that for every party member there are 10 others ready, willing, and able to do the party's work. Herein lies the greatest menace of communism. For these are the people who infiltrate and corrupt various spheres of

American life. So rather than the size of the Communist Party, the way to weigh its true importance is by testing its influence, its ability to infiltrate.

The size of the party is relatively unimportant because of the enthusiasm and iron-clad discipline under which they operate. In this connection, it might be of interest to observe that in 1917 when the Communists overthrew the Russian Government there was one Communist for every 2,277 persons in Russia. In the United States today there is one Communist for every 1,814 persons in the country.

One who accepts the aims, principles, and program of the party, who attends meetings, who reads the party press and literature, who pays dues, and who is active on behalf of the party "shall be considered a member." The open, avowed Communist who carries a card and pays dues is no different from a security standpoint than the person who does the party's work but pays no dues, carries no card, and is not on the party rolls. In fact, the latter is a greater menace because of his opportunity to work in stealth.

Identifying undercover Communists, fellow travelers, and sympathizers: The burden of proof is placed upon those who consistently follow the ever-changing, twisting party line. Fellow travelers and sympathizers can deny party membership, but they can never escape the undeniable fact that they have played into the Communist hands thus furthering the Communist cause by playing the role of innocent, gullible, or willful allies.

Propaganda activities: The Communists have developed one of the greatest propaganda machines the world has ever known. They have been able to penetrate and infiltrate many respectable and reputable public opinion mediums. . . .

The Communist propaganda technique is designed to promote emotional response with the hope that the victim will be attracted by what he is told the Communist way of life holds in store for him. The objective, of course, is to develop discontent and hasten the day when the Communists can gather sufficient support and following to overthrow the American way of life.

Communist propaganda is always slanted in the hope that the Communist may be alined [*sic*] with liberal progressive causes. The honest liberal and progressive should be alert to this, and I believe the Communists' most effective foes can be the real liberals and progressives who understand their devious machinations.

The deceptiveness of the Communist "double talk" fulfills the useful propaganda technique of confusion. In fact, Lenin referred to their peculiar brand of phraseology as "... that cursed **Assopian** [*sic*] **language** ... which ... compelled all revolutionaries to have recourse, whenever they took up their pens to write a legal work."

Lenin used it for the purpose of avoiding "censorship." Communists today use it to mislead the public.

The use of the term "democracy" by the Communists, we have learned to our sorrow, does not have the meaning to them that it does to us. To them it means communism and totalitarianism and our understanding of the term is regarded by them as imperialistic and Fascist. ...

Motion pictures: The American Communists launched a furtive attack on Hollywood in 1935 by the issuance of a directive calling for a concentration in Hollywood. The orders called for action on two fronts. (1) An effort to infiltrate the labor unions; (2) infiltrate the so-called intellectual and creative fields. ...

... The entire industry faces serious embarrassment because it could become a springboard for Communist activities. Communist activity in Hollywood is effective and is furthered by Communists and sympathizers using the prestige of prominent persons to serve, often unwittingly, the Communist cause.

The party is content and highly pleased if it is possible to have inserted in a picture a line, a scene, a sequence, conveying the Communist lesson, and more particularly, if they can keep out anti-Communist lessons.

Infiltration: The Communist tactic of infiltrating labor unions stems from the earliest teachings of Marx, which have been reiterated by party spokesmen down through the years. They resort to all means to gain their point and often succeed in penetrating and literally taking over labor unions before the rank and file of members are aware of what has occurred.

With few exceptions the following admonitions of Lenin have been followed:

> It is necessary to be able to withstand all this, to agree to any and every sacrifice, and even—if need be—to resort to all sorts of devices, maneuvers, and illegal methods, to evasion and subterfuge, in order to penetrate into the trade-unions, to remain in them, and to carry on Communist work in them at all costs. (p. 38, Left-Wing Communism, an Infantile Disorder. V. I. Lenin, 1934, International Publishers Co., Inc.)

I am convinced that the great masses of union men and women are patriotic American citizens interested chiefly in security for their families and themselves. They have no use for the American Communists but in those instances where Communists have taken control of unions, it has been because too many union men and women have been outwitted, outmaneuvered, and outwaited by Communists.

The Communists have never relied on numerical strength to dominate a labor organization. Through infiltration tactics they have in too many instances captured positions of authority. Communists have boasted that with 5 percent of the membership the Communists with their military, superior organizational ability and discipline could control the union. . . .

If more union members took a more active role and asserted themselves it would become increasingly difficult for Communists to gain control. Patriotic union members can easily spot sympathizers and party members in conventions and union meetings because invariably the latter strive to establish the party line instead of serving the best interests of the union and the country. . . .

. . . The party for the past 18 months has been giving special attention to foreign language groups. . . . The Communists now seek strength from foreign groups who may have relatives in countries which Russia seeks to influence.

Government: The recent Canadian spy trials revealed the necessity of alertness in keeping Communists and sympathizers out of Government services. . . .

Since July 1, 1941, the FBI has investigated 6,193 cases under the Hatch Act, which forbids membership upon the part of any Government employee in any organization advocating the overthrow of the government of the United States. . . .

One hundred and one Federal employees were discharged as a result of our investigation, 21 resigned during the investigation, and in 75 cases administrative action was taken by the departments. A total of 1,906 individuals are no longer employed by the Government while 122 cases are presently pending consideration in various Government agencies.

The FBI does not make recommendations; it merely reports facts, and it is up to the interested Government department to make a decision. Almost invariably, of course, subjects of investigations deny affiliation with subversive groups, often despite strong evidence to the contrary. . . .

Mass and front organizations: . . . The Communist Party in the United States immediately took up the [united front] program and a systematic plan was worked out of infiltrating existing organizations with Communists. . . .

. . . Front organizations . . . solicited and used names of prominent persons. Literally hundreds of groups and organizations have either been infiltrated or organized primarily to accomplish the purposes of promoting the interests of the Soviet Union in the United States, the promotion of Soviet war and peace aims, the exploitation of Negroes in the United States, work among foreign-language groups, and to secure a favorable viewpoint toward the Communists in domestic, political, social, and economic issues.

The first requisite for front organizations is an idealistic sounding title. Hundreds of such organizations have come into being and have gone out of existence when their true purposes have become known or exposed while others with high-sounding names are continually springing up. . . .

. . . I feel that this committee could render a great service to the Nation through its power of exposure in quickly spotlighting existing front organizations and those which will be created in the future. . . .

The Communist Party of the United States is a fifth column if there ever was one. It is far better organized than were the Nazis in occupied countries prior to their capitulation.

They are seeking to weaken America just as they did in their era of obstruction when they were alined [*sic*] with the Nazis. Their goal is the overthrow of our Government.

There is no doubt as to where a real Communist's loyalty rests. Their allegiance is to Russia, not the United States. . . .

. . . What can we do? And what should be our course of action? The best antidote to communism is vigorous, intelligent, old-fashioned Americanism with eternal vigilance. I do not favor any course of action which would give the Communists cause to portray and pity themselves as martyrs. I do favor unrelenting prosecution wherever they are found to be violating our country's laws.

As Americans, our most effective defense is a workable democracy that guarantees and preserves our cherished freedoms.

I would have no fears if more Americans possessed the zeal, the fervor, the persistence, and the industry to learn about this menace of Red fascism. I do fear for the liberal and progressive who has been hoodwinked and duped into joining hands with the Communists. I confess to a real apprehension so long as Communists are able to secure ministers of the gospel to promote their evil work and espouse a cause that is alien to the religion of Christ and Judaism. I do fear so long as school boards and parents tolerate conditions whereby Communists and fellow travelers, under the guise of academic freedom, can teach our youth a way of life that eventually will destroy the sanctity of the home, that undermine[s] faith in God, that causes them to scorn respect for constituted authority and sabotage our revered Constitution.

I do fear so long as American labor groups are infiltrated, dominated, or saturated with the virus of communism. I do fear the palliation and weasel-worded gestures against communism indulged in by some of our labor leaders who should know better but who have become pawns in the hands of sinister but astute manipulations for the Communist cause.

I fear for ignorance on the part of all our people who may take the poisonous pills of Communist propaganda. . . .

The Communists have been, still are, and always will be a menace to freedom, to democratic ideals, to the worship of God, and to America's way of life.

I feel that once public opinion is thoroughly aroused as it is today, the fight against communism is well on its way. Victory will be assured once Communists are identified and exposed, because the public will take the first step of quarantining them so they can do no harm. Communism, in reality, is not a political party. It is a way of life—an evil and malignant way of life. It reveals a condition akin to disease that spreads like an epidemic and like an epidemic a quarantine is necessary to keep it from infecting the Nation.

5

Communist Spies in the
State Department:
The Emergence of the Hiss Case

The following selections illustrate different aspects of the Alger Hiss case. Hiss had been under suspicion for several years before the accusations against him became public at a HUAC hearing in August 1948 when the confessed ex-Communist Whittaker Chambers claimed that Hiss and several other former New Deal officials had once been in the Communist party. At first Hiss denied knowing Chambers and then sued him for slander for having accused him of being a Communist. Chambers retaliated by producing copies of government documents that he claimed Hiss had given him for transmission to the Soviets. Hiss's eventual conviction for perjury in January 1950 (the statute of limitations for espionage having run out) seemed to prove that Communists were Soviet agents, thus legitimizing much of the anti-Communist furor that followed.

The first document is the text of an intercepted 1945 telegram that the head of the Soviet intelligence bureau in Washington sent to Moscow describing the operations of an American with the cover name of ALES who was spying for the GRU, or Soviet military intelligence. Intercepted during World War II, this message was deciphered by the top-secret VENONA project several years later. Because Alger Hiss's travels at that time paralleled those of the individual referred to in this document, it is likely that he was ALES. Although none of the

Washington KGB to Moscow, March 30, 1945, No. 1822, VENONA files; Alger Hiss and Whittaker Chambers, testimony, House Committee on Un-American Activities, *Hearings Regarding Communist Espionage in the United States Government,* 80th Cong., 2nd sess. (Washington, D.C., and New York City) 3, 5, 7, 16, 17 Aug. 1948; Frank G. Johnstone (Special Agent, Baltimore), Summary Report, 4 Dec. 1948, Alger Hiss FBI File, in *In Re Alger Hiss,* ed. Edith Tiger (New York: Hill and Wang, 1979), 269–72.

Soviet or American records released after the cold war contain direct evidence of Hiss's espionage activities as they do for some of the other espionage agents, the indirect evidence from this and other documents tends to support Chambers's story.

The next five documents are excerpts from the original HUAC testimony of Chambers and Hiss. These transcripts show how the case unfolded as the discrepancies between Hiss's testimony and that of Chambers emerged. Under the prodding of Richard Nixon, Chambers seemed to reveal details about Hiss's personal life that contradicted Hiss's initial denial that he knew Chambers.

The final document comes from an FBI report that contained a signed statement Chambers made the day after he turned over several rolls of film, the so-called Pumpkin Papers, to HUAC. Chambers had already produced several typewritten and handwritten documents that he claimed Hiss and other members of his espionage ring had given him for transmission to the Soviets. In this statement Chambers describes his espionage activities and the materials that he received from Hiss and others.

WASHINGTON KGB

Telegram to Moscow
March 30, 1945

VENONA

MGB[1]

From: WASHINGTON

To: MOSCOW

No. 1822

30 March 1945

Further to our telegram No. 283(a). As a result of "(D% A.'s)" (i) chat with "ALES" (ii) the following has been ascertained:

1.   ALES has been working with the NEIGHBORS (SOSEDI) (iii) continuously since 1935.

2.   For some years past he has been the leader of a small group of the NEIGHBORS' probationers (STAZhERY),[2] for the most part consisting of his relations.

3.   The group and ALES himself work on obtaining military information only. Materials on the "BANK" (iv) allegedly interest the NEIGHBORS very little and he does not produce them regularly.

4.   All the last few years ALES has been working with "POL" (v) who also meets other members of the group occasionally.

---

[1]During the course of its existence, the Soviet Union's secret police changed its name several times. MGB was the KGB's acronym during World War II.

[2]"Probationers" was the code word that the KGB used to refer to its American agents.

5.   Recently ALES and his whole group were awarded Soviet decorations.

6.   After the YaLTA conference,[3] when he had gone on to MOSCOW, a Soviet personage in a very responsible position (ALES gave to understand that it was Comrade VYShINSKIJ) allegedly got in touch with ALES and at the behest of the Military NEIGHBORS passed on to him their gratitude and so on.

No. 431   VADIM (vi)
Notes: (a) not available
Comments:
   (i)   A.: "A." seems the most likely garble here although "A." has not been confirmed elsewhere in the WASHINGTON traffic.
  (ii) ALES: Probably Alger HISS
 (iii) SOSEDI: Members of another Soviet Intelligence organization, here probably the GRU.
 (iv) BANK: The U.S. State Department.
  (v) POL': i.e. "PAUL," unidentified cover-name.
 (vi) VADIM: Anatolij Borisovich GROMOV, MGB resident in WASHINGTON

8 August 1969

---

[3]Roosevelt, Churchill, and Stalin met at the Soviet resort town of Yalta in February 1945 to discuss the final stages of the war and the future of postwar Europe.

WHITTAKER CHAMBERS

Testimony before HUAC

August 3, 1948

Chambers: I joined the Communist Party in 1924.

[HUAC counsel Robert] Stripling: How long did you remain a member of the Communist Party?

Chambers: Until 1937.

... For a number of years I had myself served in the underground, chiefly in Washington, D.C.... I knew it at its top level, a group of seven or so men, from among whom in later years certain members of Miss Bentley's[4] organization were apparently recruited. The head of the underground group at the time I knew it was Nathan Witt, an attorney for the National Labor Relations Board. Later, John Abt[5] became the leader. Lee Pressman[6] was also a member of this group, as was Alger Hiss, who, as a member of the State Department, later organized the conferences at Dumbarton Oaks, San Francisco, and the United States side of the Yalta Conference.[7]

The purpose of this group at that time was not primarily espionage. Its original purpose was the Communist infiltration of the American Government. But espionage was certainly one of its eventual objectives. Let no one be surprised at this statement. Disloyalty is a matter of principle with every member of the Communist Party. ...

Originally I came to Washington to act as a courier between New York and Washington, which in effect was between this apparatus and New York.

Stripling: You were a member of the Communist Party?

Chambers: I was.

---

[4]Elizabeth Bentley was a self-confessed Soviet agent who accused many former government employees of having spied for the Soviet Union during World War II.

[5]John Abt was a Communist attorney who often represented the party.

[6]Lee Pressman was the chief counsel of the CIO. He later admitted to HUAC that he had been in the Communist party.

[7]The Dumbarton Oaks conference in Washington, D.C., in 1944 created the United Nations, which met for the first time in May 1945 in San Francisco. At the Yalta Conference in February 1945, Joseph Stalin, Winston Churchill, and Franklin D. Roosevelt discussed postwar arrangements in Europe and East Asia.

Stripling: Were you a paid functionary of the Communist Party?

Chambers: Yes.

Stripling: Did you meet with all these men you mentioned?

Chambers: Yes.

Stripling: Where did you meet with them?

Chambers: At the home, the apartment of Henry Collins, which was at St. Matthew's Court here in Washington. . . .

Stripling: Mr. Chambers, when you would meet at the apartment of Mr. Collins and he would turn over Communist Party dues, would he turn over any other information to you, any other dues or information other than from these seven people?

Chambers: Well, the dues were not simply from the seven people, I believe. Dues were from the whole apparatus, cells which were headed by these seven people. . . .

[Representative Karl E.] Mundt: Miss Bentley testified before our committee and said that in her capacity as courier between Communist headquarters in New York and Washington, I think chronologically she followed you as courier and did that work, she mentioned that she also brought Communist literature and instructions from New York to Washington. Did you also do that?

Chambers: I did. . . .

Stripling: When you left the Communist Party in 1937 did you approach any of these seven to break with you?

Chambers: No. The only one of those people whom I approached was Alger Hiss. I went to the Hiss home one evening at what I considered considerable risk to myself and found Mrs. Hiss at home.

. . . Mrs. Hiss attempted while I was there to make a call, which I can only presume was to other Communists, but I quickly went to the telephone and she hung up, and Mr. Hiss came in shortly afterward, and we talked and I tried to break him away from the party.

As a matter of fact, he cried when we separated[,] when I left him, but he absolutely refused to break.

. . . I was very fond of Mr. Hiss.

ALGER HISS

Testimony before HUAC

August 5, 1948

Hiss: I am here at my own request to deny unqualifiedly various statements about me which were made before this committee by one Whittaker Chambers the day before yesterday. I appreciate the committee's having promptly granted my request. I welcome the opportunity to answer to the best of my ability any inquiries the members of this committee may wish to ask me.

I am not and never have been a member of the Communist Party. I do not and never have adhered to the tenets of the Communist Party. I am not and never have been a member of any Communist-front organization. I have never followed the Communist Party line, directly or indirectly. To the best of my knowledge, none of my friends is a Communist. . . .

To the best of my knowledge, I never heard of Whittaker Chambers until in 1947, when two representatives of the Federal Bureau of Investigation asked me if I knew him and various other people, some of whom I knew and some of whom I did not know. I said I did not know Chambers. So far as I know, I have never laid eyes on him, and I should like to have the opportunity to do so. . . .

Mundt: . . . I want to say for one member of the committee that it is extremely puzzling that a man who is senior editor of *Time* magazine, by the name of Whittaker Chambers, whom I had never seen until a day or two ago, and whom you say you have never seen—

Hiss: As far as I know, I have never seen him.

Mundt: Should come before this committee and discuss the Communist apparatus working in Washington, which he says is transmitting secrets to the Russian Government, and he lists a group of seven people—Nathan Witt, Lee Pressman, Victor Perlo,[8] Charles Kramer, John Abt, Harold Ware, Alger Hiss, and Donald Hiss—

Hiss: That is eight.

Mundt: There seems to be no question about the subversive connections of the six other than the Hiss brothers, and I wonder what possible motive a man who edits *Time* magazine would have for

---

[8]Perlo was a left-wing economist who worked in the U.S. government during the war. He was named by both Bentley and Chambers in HUAC testimony.

mentioning Donald Hiss and Alger Hiss in connection with those other six.

Hiss: So do I, Mr. Chairman. I have no possible understanding of what could have motivated him. There are many possible motives, I assume, but I am unable to understand it.

. . . I wish I could have seen Mr. Chambers before he testified. . . .

Stripling: You say you have never seen Mr. Chambers?

Hiss: The name means absolutely nothing to me, Mr. Stripling.

Stripling: I have here, Mr. Chairman, a picture which was made last Monday by the Associated Press. I understand from people who knew Mr. Chambers during 1934 and '35 that he is much heavier today than he was at that time, but I show you this picture, Mr. Hiss, and ask you if you have ever known an individual who resembles this picture.

Hiss: I would much rather see the individual. I have looked at all the pictures I was able to get hold of in, I think it was, yesterday's paper which had the pictures. If this is a picture of Mr. Chambers, he is not particularly unusual looking. He looks like a lot of people. I might even mistake him for the chairman of this committee. [Laughter.] . . .

Stripling: Mr. Chairman, there is very sharp contradiction here in the testimony. I certainly suggest Mr. Chambers be brought back before the committee and clear this up.

WHITTAKER CHAMBERS

Testimony before HUAC

August 7, 1948

This testimony comes from a private hearing in New York City conducted by a HUAC subcommittee under Richard M. Nixon.

Nixon: Mr. Chambers, you are aware of the fact that Mr. Alger Hiss appeared before this committee, before the Un-American Activities Committee, in public session and swore that the testimony which had been given by you under oath before this committee was false.

The committee is now interested in questioning you further concerning your alleged acquaintanceship with Mr. Alger Hiss so that we can determine what course of action should be followed in this matter in the future. . . .

At what period did you know Mr. Hiss? What time?

Chambers: I knew Mr. Hiss, roughly, between the years 1935 to 1937.

Nixon: Do you know him as Mr. Alger Hiss?

Chambers: Yes.

Nixon: Did you happen to see Mr. Hiss's pictures in the newspapers as a result of these recent hearings?

Chambers: Yes; I did.

Nixon: Was that the man you knew as Alger Hiss?

Chambers: Yes; that is the man.

Nixon: You are certain of that?

Chambers: I am completely certain.

Nixon: During the time that you knew Mr. Hiss, did he know you as Whittaker Chambers?

Chambers: No, he did not.

Nixon: By what name did he know you?

Chambers: He knew me by the party name of Carl.

Nixon: Did he ever question the fact that he did not know your last name?

Chambers: Not to me.

Nixon: Why not?

Chambers: Because in the underground Communist Party the principle of organization is that functionaries and heads of the group, in other words, shall not be known by their right names but by pseudonyms or party names. . . .

Nixon: Do you have any other evidence, any factual evidence, to bear out your claim that Mr. Hiss was a member of the Communist Party?

Chambers: Nothing beyond the fact that he submitted himself for the two or three years that I knew him as a dedicated and disciplined Communist.

Nixon: Did you obtain his party dues from him?

Chambers: Yes, I did. . . . Mr. Hiss would simply give me an envelope containing party dues. . . .

I must also interpolate there that all Communists in the group in which I originally knew him accepted him as a member of the Communist Party. . . .

Nixon: Could this have possibly been an intellectual study group?

Chambers: It was in nowise an intellectual study group. Its primary function was not that of an intellectual study group. I certainly supplied some of that intellectual study business, which was part of my function, but its primary function was to infiltrate the Government in the interest of the Communist Party.

[Nixon then asks questions designed to find out what Chambers knows about Hiss's personal life.]

Nixon: What name did Mrs. Hiss use in addressing Mr. Hiss?

Chambers: Usually "Hilly.". . .

Nixon: Not "Alger"?

Chambers: Not "Alger."

Nixon: What nickname, if any, did Mr. Hiss use in addressing his wife?

Chambers: More often "Dilly" and sometimes "Pross." Her name was Priscilla. They were commonly referred to as "Hilly" and "Dilly.". . .

Nixon: Did you ever spend any time in Hiss's home?

Chambers: Yes.

Nixon: Did you stay overnight?

Chambers: Yes; I stayed overnight for a number of days. . . . I have stayed there as long as a week. . . .

[HUAC staff member Benjamin] Mandel: Did Mr. Hiss have any hobbies?

Chambers: Yes; he did. They both had the same hobby—amateur ornithologists, bird observers. They used to get up early in the morning and go to Glen Echo, out the canal, to observe birds.

I recall once they saw, to their great excitement, a prothonotary warbler.

[Congressman John] McDowell: A very rare specimen?

Chambers: I never saw one. I am also fond of birds.

ALGER HISS

Testimony before HUAC

August 16, 1948

Hiss testified before an executive session in Washington, D.C.

Nixon: As of course, Mr. Hiss, you are aware, the committee has a very difficult problem in regard to the testimony which has been submitted to the committee by Mr. Chambers and by yourself....

We have come to the conclusion . . . that the individual who has come before the committee and has given false testimony must, if possible, answer for that testimony.

For that reason we are going this afternoon to go into a number of items which I can assure you have a direct bearing on that problem. . . .

As you have probably noted from press accounts of the hearings, Whittaker Chambers during the period that he alleges that he knew you was not known by the name of Whittaker Chambers. He has testified that he was known by the name of Carl. Do you recall having known an individual between the years 1934 and 1937 whose name was Carl?

Hiss: I do not recall anyone by the name of Carl that could remotely be connected with the kind of testimony Mr. Chambers has given. . . .

Nixon: I am now showing you two pictures of Mr. Whittaker Chambers, also known as Carl, who testified that he knew you between the years 1934–37, and that he saw you in 1939.

I ask you now, after looking at those pictures, if you can remember that person either as Whittaker Chambers or as Carl or as any other individual you have met.

Hiss: May I recall to the committee the testimony I gave in the public session when I was shown another photograph of Mr. Whittaker Chambers, and I had prior to taking the stand tried to get as many newspapers that had photographs of Mr. Chambers as I could. I testified then that I could not swear that I had never seen the man whose picture was shown me. Actually the face has a certain familiarity. I think I also testified to that. . . .

I have written a name on this pad in front of me of a person whom I knew in 1933 and 1934 who not only spent some time in my house but sublet my apartment. That man certainly spent more than a week, not while I was in the same apartment. I do not recognize the photographs as possibly being this man. . . . I want to see Chambers face to face and see if he can be this individual. . . .

The name of the man I brought in—and he may have no relation to this whole nightmare—is a man named George Crosley. I met him when I was working for the Nye Committee.[9] He was a writer. He hoped to sell articles to magazines about the munitions industry.

. . . After we had taken the house on P Street and had the apartment on our hands, he one day in the course of casual conversation said he was going to specialize all summer in getting his articles done here in Washington and was thinking of bringing his family.

I said, "You can have my apartment. It is not terribly cool, but it is up in the air near the Wardman Park." He said he had a wife and little baby. The apartment wasn't very expensive, and I think I let him have it at exact cost. . . .

[Nixon questions Hiss about Crosley's appearance.]

Nixon: How tall was this man, approximately?
   . . . How about his teeth?
Hiss: Very bad teeth. That is one of the things I particularly want to see Chambers about. This man had very bad teeth, did not take care of his teeth. . . .
Nixon: What were the nicknames you and your wife had?
Hiss: My wife, I have always called her "Prossy."
Nixon: What does she call you?
Hiss: Well, at one time she called me quite frequently "Hill." H-i-l-l.
Nixon: What other name?
Hiss: "Hilly," with a "y."
   She called me "Hill" or "Hilly." I called her "Pross" or "Prossy" almost exclusively. I don't think any other nickname.
Nixon: Did you ever call her "Dilly"?
Hiss: No; never. . . .
Nixon: What hobby, if any, do you have, Mr. Hiss?

---

[9]During the early 1930s, Senator Gerald Nye chaired a special committee investigating the role of arms manufacturers in World War I.

Hiss: Tennis and amateur ornithology.

Nixon: Is your wife interested in ornithology?

Hiss: I also like to swim and also like to sail. My wife is interested in ornithology, as I am, through my interest. Maybe I am using too big a word to say an ornithologist because I am pretty amateur, but I have been interested in it since I was in Boston. I think anybody who knows me would know that.

McDowell: Did you ever see a prothonotary warbler?

Hiss: I have right here on the Potomac. Do you know that place?

WHITTAKER CHAMBERS
AND ALGER HISS

Testimony before HUAC

August 17, 1948

The committee went to New York to stage a meeting between Hiss and Chambers.

Nixon: Mr. Hiss, the man standing here is Mr. Whittaker Chambers. I ask you now if you have ever known that man before.

Hiss: May I ask him to speak?

Will you ask him to say something?

Nixon: Yes.

Mr. Chambers, will you tell us your name and your business?

Chambers: My name is Whittaker Chambers.

[At this point, Mr. Hiss walked in the direction of Mr. Chambers.]

Hiss: Would you mind opening your mouth wider?

Chambers: My name is Whittaker Chambers.

Hiss: I said, would you open your mouth?

You know what I am referring to, Mr. Nixon. . . .

I think he is George Crosley, but I would like to hear him talk a little longer. . . .

Are you George Crosley?

Chambers: Not to my knowledge. You are Alger Hiss, I believe. . . .

Hiss: The voice sounds a little less resonant than the voice that I recall of the man I knew as George Crosley. The teeth look to me as though either they have been improved upon or that there has been considerable dental work done since I knew George Crosley, which was some years ago.

I believe that I am not prepared without further checking to take an absolute oath that he must be George Crosley. . . .

Nixon: Mr. Chambers, have you had any dental work since 1934 of a substantial nature?

Chambers: Yes; I have.

Hiss: Did you ever sublet an apartment on Twenty-ninth Street from me?

Chambers: No; I did not.

Hiss: You did not?

Chambers: No.

Hiss: Did you ever spend any time with your wife and child in an apartment on Twenty-ninth Street in Washington when I was not there because I and my family were living on P Street?

Chambers: I most certainly did.

Hiss: You did or did not?

Chambers: I did.

Hiss: Would you tell me how you reconcile your negative answers with this affirmative answer?

Chambers: Very easily, Alger. I was a Communist and you were a Communist.

Hiss: Would you be responsive and continue with your answer? . . .

Chambers: As I have testified before, I came to Washington as a Communist functionary, a functionary of the American Communist Party. I was connected with the underground group of which Mr. Hiss was a member. Mr. Hiss and I became friends. To the best of my knowledge, Mr. Hiss himself suggested that I go there, and I accepted gratefully. . . .

Hiss: Mr. Chairman, I don't need to ask Mr. Whittaker Chambers any more questions. I am now perfectly prepared to identify this man as George Crosley. . . .

McDowell: Mr. Chambers, is this the man, Alger Hiss, who was also a member of the Communist Party at whose home you stayed?

Nixon: According to your testimony.

McDowell: You make the identification positive?

Chambers: Positive identification.

[At this point, Mr. Hiss arose and walked in the direction of Mr. Chambers.]

Hiss: May I say for the record at this point, that I would like to invite Mr. Whittaker Chambers to make those same statements out of the presence of this committee without their being privileged for suit for libel. I challenge you to do it, and I hope you will do it damned quickly.

WHITTAKER CHAMBERS

Statement to the FBI

December 3, 1948

I, Jay David Whittaker Chambers, make the following statement to Floyd L. Jones and Daniel F. X. Callahan, whom I know to be Special Agents of the Federal Bureau of Investigation. I understand that any statement that I make can be used against me in a court of law. No threats or promises have been made to me in connection with this statement. I have been advised that I have a right of counsel, but I have waived same after consulting with my counsel in connection with the making of this statement.

I am presently a defendant in a civil action brought against me by ALGER HISS in Federal Court in Baltimore, Maryland. In connection with a pre-trial deposition being taken at the request of counsel for Mr. Hiss, on November 17, 1948, I produced in evidence 65 typewritten documents and 4 small pieces of white paper on which appeared handwriting that, according to my recollection, is the handwriting of ALGER HISS. The 65 pages of documents were copies or condensations of State Department documents which were turned over to me by ALGER HISS during the latter part of 1937 and early 1938. These documents have been in the possession of NATHAN LEVINE, my wife's nephew, who now resides on Sterling Place in Brooklyn, New York. He is a lawyer and has an office on 42nd Street near Broadway, believed to be in the Newsweek Building. When I gave him these documents shortly after I broke with the Party in 1938, he was living in his mother's house at 260 Rochester Avenue, Brooklyn, New York. When I gave them to him, I asked him to hide them for me and, if anything happened to me, that he should open them and make them public. He didn't know the contents of these documents or where they came from. They were in a brown manila envelope. I got them from him on Sunday, November 14, 1948, at his mother's house in Brooklyn. They were hidden in a dumb waiter shaft in his mother's house. There were also contained in this envelope three cans of undeveloped film and two strips of developed film which I will mention later. I went to LEVINE's house to get the small pieces of paper containing HISS' handwriting and had forgotten about the documents and the film until they were turned over to me.

Also included in this brown envelope were four yellow-lined sheets of paper in the handwriting of HARRY DEXTER WHITE.[10] I had mentioned this handwriting in my deposition on November 17, 1948. The reason I did not introduce the three cans of film at the deposition was because it was undeveloped. I did not introduce the two strips of developed negative film . . . because I wanted to keep all the film together and possibly have the film developed and made readable at a later date.

I did not introduce the handwritten pages turned over to me by HARRY DEXTER WHITE on advice of counsel because they thought it was irrelevant. The handwriting of HARRY DEXTER WHITE described above has been in the possession of my attorneys since November 17, 1948, the date of the pre-trial deposition. The three cans of undeveloped film as well as the two strips of developed negative film were turned over by me to two investigators of the House Committee on Un-American Activities at my home in Westminster, Maryland, on Thursday night, December 2, 1948, in response to a subpoena presented by them to me on that date.[11]

I have no other documents whatever of this nature now.

As far as I can recall, the undeveloped film in the cans described above contained photographs of original documents that came out of the State Department and the Bureau of Standards. The bulk of the documents from the State Department were turned over to me by

[10]Harry Dexter White, a former assistant secretary of the treasury, was the highest-ranking federal official accused of espionage. Named by both Chambers and Elizabeth Bentley, he died of a heart attack a few days after he denied their charges before HUAC in August 1948.

[11]These films became known as the Pumpkin Papers because Chambers had hidden them in a hollowed-out pumpkin on his Maryland farm and then dramatically produced them at the urging of HUAC.

ALGER HISS. Others were turned over to me possibly by JULIAN WADLEIGH.[12] I assume that these were classified Confidential and Strictly Confidential, the same as some of the documents that I presented on November 17, 1948.

The documents that were presented by me at the deposition were copies or condensations of State Department documents. These copies were turned over to me by ALGER HISS during the latter part of 1937 and the first part of 1938 as indicated by the dates on the documents. These documents were given to me for delivery to a Colonel BYKOV, who had previously been introduced to ALGER HISS, at which time ALGER HISS agreed to furnish documents from the State Department to me for delivery to Colonel BYKOV. ALGER HISS was well aware that Colonel BYKOV was the head of a Soviet underground organization. It is possible that some of the 65 documents that I presented at the deposition were photographed and copies of the photographs were turned over to Colonel BYKOV. I didn't destroy the documents because I was preparing to break with the Party in about April, 1938.

Some of the documents supplied by HISS were copied on a typewriter in ALGER HISS's home by him or his wife, and then turned over to me. In other instances, original documents from the State Department were turned over to me by ALGER HISS and taken by me in most instances to photographers to be copied, the original documents then being returned to ALGER HISS the same night to be returned by him to the State Department. . . . ALGER HISS was aware of the fact that the documents were being photographed for delivery to Colonel BYKOV. . . .

. . . Colonel BYKOV wanted to know something about the personnel in the apparatus [the Communist underground] and questioned me very closely about them. He wanted to meet some of them.

The first person that he met in the apparatus was ALGER HISS. In the spring of 1937, I arranged a meeting between ALGER HISS and Colonel BYKOV. HISS went to New York where I met him at place somewhere near the Brooklyn Bridge. We then proceeded to a movie house quite a distance out in Brooklyn. HISS and I waited on a bench in the mezzanine of the theater, and BYKOV emerged from the audience and I introduced him to ALGER HISS. . . .

At the time of the meeting with HISS, after leaving the theater Colonel BYKOV raised the question of procuring documents from the

---

[12]Julian Wadleigh was a former State Department employee who confessed to having given documents to Chambers.

State Department, and ALGER HISS agreed. Following the meeting, ALGER HISS began to supply a consistent flow of material from the State Department, such as the type of documents that I presented at the pre-trial deposition on November 17, 1948. I want to say that as far as I can remember, I have never discussed the existence of the documents that I presented at the pre-trial deposition with anyone. Neither have I told any Governmental agency or Government body concerning the existence of these documents. I have never discussed with anyone the procuring of any documents from Government agencies for transmittal to Colonel BYKOV.

In testifying to various Government agencies over the last ten years, I have had two purposes in mind. The first was to stop the Communist conspiracy. The second was to try to preserve the human elements involved. In this sense, I was shielding these people. For these reasons, I have not previously mentioned the procuring and passing of any documents.

I have read the above statement . . . and to the best of my knowledge and recollection, I declare it is the truth.

Above: FBI Director J. Edgar Hoover describes the nature of the Communist menace in his testimony before HUAC on March 26, 1947.

© Bettmann/Corbis.

Left: Elizabeth Bentley takes an oath on July 30, 1948, prior to telling a congressional investigating committee about her activities as the courier for a Soviet spy ring in the federal government during World War II. Bentley's charges, which were later reinforced by the VENONA decrypts, helped confirm Hoover's conviction that Communists spied.

© Bettmann/Corbis.

Above: At the HUAC hearing of August 25, 1948, Whittaker Chambers repeats his earlier allegations that Alger Hiss was a Communist. Hiss, who will admit later in this session that he once knew Chambers under another name, listens intently in the upper left of the picture.
© Bettmann/Corbis.

Left: Having just been indicted for perjury on December 15, 1948, Alger Hiss denies Whittaker Chambers's charges that he had belonged to a Soviet espionage ring.
© Bettmann/Corbis.

Above: Ethel and Julius Rosenberg return in a patrol van to the Federal House of Detention in New York City on April 5, 1951, after hearing Judge Irving Kaufman sentence them to death for atomic espionage.
© Hulton-Deutsch Collection/Corbis.

6

Atomic Espionage
and the Rosenberg Case

The following documents show how the Soviet Union obtained secret information about the atomic bomb during World War II and how the U.S. government responded to that theft. The most important materials came from Klaus Fuchs and Theodore Hall, two physicists working at the bomb project's main scientific laboratory in Los Alamos, New Mexico. But a New York City engineer and his wife, Julius and Ethel Rosenberg, paid the heaviest price. Significantly, all these people were Communists.

The first document is part of the confession that the German-born Fuchs made to a British intelligence agent shortly before his arrest in February 1950. In that statement, Fuchs discusses the political convictions that led him to give information to the Soviet Union and the nature of his espionage activities.

Fuchs had been captured because of a tip-off from the VENONA project, the top-secret effort to decipher the text of thousands of intercepted wartime telegrams between the KGB's American representatives and their Moscow superiors. By 1948 the U.S. code-breakers could read enough of that correspondence to alert American security

Klaus Fuchs, "Confession to William Skardon," in *Klaus Fuchs: Atom Spy,* ed. Robert Chadwell Williams (Cambridge: Harvard University Press, 1987), 181–84, 186; New York KGB, Telegram to Moscow, November 12, 1944, No. 1585, VENONA files; New York KGB, Telegram to Moscow, November 14, 1944, No. 1600, VENONA files; New York KGB, Telegram to Moscow, November 27, 1944, No. 1657, VENONA files; Office Memorandum on Julius Rosenberg, July 17, 1950, Julius Rosenberg Headquarters File, No. 188; J. Edgar Hoover's memorandum to the Attorney General, July 19, 1950, Rosenberg file, No. 97; Judge Irving Kaufman, "Sentencing of Julius and Ethel Rosenberg," in transcript of record, *Julius Rosenberg and Ethel Rosenberg v. The United States of America,* Supreme Court of the United States, October Term, 1951, 1612–16; correspondence of Julius and Ethel Rosenberg, in Robert and Michael Meeropol, *We Are Your Sons: The Legacy of Julius and Ethel Rosenberg,* 2nd ed. (Urbana: University of Illinois Press, 1986), 89–90, 206–7.

officials to the Soviet penetration of the Manhattan Project, as the program to develop the bomb was called. They could not publicize their findings, however. VENONA remained so highly classified that the government did not release any of its decrypted texts until 1995. When it did, not only did they corroborate the guilt of dozens of accused individuals, but they also made it possible to grasp the scope of the Soviet Union's World War II espionage operations. The following documents — three telegrams — reveal some of those operations. The first reports on Theodore Hall's initial contacts with the KGB. The second describes how Julius Rosenberg recruited his friends to collect military and industrial secrets for the Soviets and how he arranged to have his wife's brother David Greenglass send him information from Los Alamos. The third KGB telegram contains information about Ethel Rosenberg, indicating that, although she supported them, she had not been involved with her husband's espionage activities.

The FBI knew that Ethel Rosenberg was not a spy. Even so, as the next two documents reveal, both the FBI and the Justice Department wanted to prosecute her as a way to make her husband confess. That legal farce turned into tragedy when Judge Irving Kaufman sentenced the couple to death. The next document contains excerpts from his remarks as he imposed that sentence. Kaufman's moralistic tone masked serious improprieties. FBI files indicate that he had been in touch with the prosecution during the trial and knew that FBI and Justice Department officials hoped that the threat of the electric chair would force a confession out of the couple.

It did not. Even in the death house, both Julius and Ethel Rosenberg continued to insist that they were the innocent victims of a "political frame-up." The final two documents contain excerpts from their letters to each other as they waited for a reprieve and struggled to make sense of their fate. Their appeals denied, the Rosenbergs were executed on June 19, 1953.

KLAUS FUCHS

Confession to William Skardon
January 27, 1950

Fuchs was a student in Germany when Hitler came to power.

I had already joined the Communist Party because I felt I had to be in some organization. . . .

I was in the underground until I left Germany. I was sent out by the Party, because they said that I must finish my studies because after the revolution in Germany people would be required with technical knowledge to take part in the building up of the Communist Germany. I went first to France and then to England, where I studied and at the same time I tried to make a serious study of the bases of Marxist philosophy. . . .

I accepted for a long time that what you heard about Russia internally could be deliberate lies. I had my doubts for the first time on acts of foreign policies of Russia; the Russo-German pact was difficult to understand, but in the end I did accept that Russia had done it to gain time, that during that time she was expanding her own influence in the Balkans against the influence of Germany. Finally Germany's attack on Russia seemed to confirm that Russia was not shirking and was prepared to carry out a foreign policy with the risk of war with Germany. . . .

Shortly after my release [from detention as an enemy alien] I was asked to help Professor Peierls[1] in Birmingham, on some war work. I accepted it and I started work without knowing at first what the work was. I doubt whether it would have made any difference to my subsequent actions if I had known the nature of the work beforehand. When I learned the purpose of the work I decided to inform Russia and I established contact through another member of the Communist Party. Since that time I have had continuous contact with persons who were completely unknown to me, except that I knew that they would hand whatever information I gave them to the Russian authorities. At this time I had complete confidence in Russian policy and I believed that

---

[1] Rudolf Peierls was a German refugee physicist in England who worked on the atomic bomb during World War II.

the Western Allies deliberately allowed Russia and Germany to fight each other to the death. I had, therefore, no hesitation in giving all the information I had, even though occasionally I tried to concentrate mainly on giving information about the results of my own work. . . .

There is nobody I know by name who is concerned with collecting information for the Russian authorities. There are people whom I know by sight whom I trusted with my life and who trusted me with theirs and I do not know that I shall be able to do anything that might in the end give them away. They are not inside of the project, but they are the intermediaries between myself and the Russian Government.

At first I thought that all I would do would be to inform the Russian authorities that work upon the atom bomb was going on. They wished to have more details and I agreed to supply them. I concentrated at first mainly on the products of my own work, but in particular at Los Alamos I did what I consider to be the worst I have done, namely to give information about the principles of the design of the plutonium bomb. Later on at Harwell [site of the first British nuclear reactor] I began to sift it, but it is difficult to say exactly when and how I did it because it was a process which went up and down with my inner struggles. The last time I handed over information was in February or March, 1949.

NEW YORK KGB

Telegram to Moscow
November 12, 1944

USSR   Ref. No:

                                        Issued: 25/4/1961

                                        Copy No: 204

DECISION TO MAINTAIN CONTACT
WITH THEODORE HALL (1944)

From: NEW YORK

To: MOSCOW

No: 1585   12 Nov. 44

To VIKTOR.[i]

BEK[ii] visited Theodore HALL [TEODOR KhOLL],[iii] 19 years old, the son of a furrier. He is a graduate of HARVARD University. As a talented physicist he was taken on for government work. He was a GYMNAST [FIZKUL 'TURNIK][iv] and conducted work in the Steel Founders' Union. [a] According to BEK's account HALL has an exceptionally keen mind and a broad outlook, and is politically developed. At the present time H. is in charge of a group at "CAMP-2"[v] (SANTA-FE). H. handed over to BEK a report about the CAMP and named the key personnel employed on ENORMOUS.[vi] He decided to do this on the advice of his colleague Saville SAX [SAVIL SAKS],[vii] a GYMNAST living in TYRE.[viii] SAX's mother is a FELLOW-COUNTRYMAN [ZEMLYaK][ix] and works for RUSSIAN WAR RELIEF. With the aim of hastening a meeting with a competent person, H. on the following day sent a copy of the report by S. to the PLANT[ZAVOD].[x] ALEKSEJ[xi] received S. H. had to leave for CAMP-2 in two days' time. He [b] was compelled to make a decision quickly. Jointly with MAY[MAJ][xii] he gave BEK consent to feel out H., to assure him that everything was in order and to arrange liaison with him. H. left his photograph and came to an understanding with BEK about a place for meeting him. BEK met S. [1 group garbled] our automobile. We consider it expedient to maintain liaison with H. [1 group unidentified] through S. and not to bring in anybody else. MAY has no objection to this. We shall send the details by post.

No. 897   [Signature missing]
11th November

Distribution   [Notes and Comments overleaf]

Notes: [a]   I.e. Trade Union [PROFSOYuZ].

          [b]   I.e. ALEKSEJ.

Comments: [i]   VIKTOR   :   Lt. Gen. P. M. FITIN.

          [ii]   BEK   :   Sergej Nikolaevich KURNAKOV.

          [iii] HALL   :   Theodore Alvin HALL.

          [iv]   GYMNAST   :   Possibly a member of the Young
                                      Communist League.

          [v]   CAMP-2   :   LOS ALAMOS.

          [vi]   ENORMOUS   :   Manhattan Engineering District–
                                      U.S. Atomic Energy Project.

          [vii] SAX

          [viii] TYRE   :   NEW YORK CITY.

          [ix]   FELLOWCOUNTRYMAN :   Member of the
                                      Communist Party.

          [x]   PLANT   :   Soviet Consulate.

          [xi]   ALEKSEJ   :   Anatolij Antonovich YaKOVLEV,
                                      Soviet Vice-Consul in NEW
                                      YORK.

          [xii] MAY   :   Stepan Zakharovich APRESYaN,
                                      Soviet Vice-Consul in NEW
                                      YORK.

NEW YORK KGB

Telegram to Moscow
November 14, 1944

Reissue (T293)

From: NEW YORK

To: MOSCOW

No: 1600

14 November 1944

To VIKTOR [i].

LIBERAL [ii] has safely carried through the contracting of "Kh'YuS" [iii]. Kh'YuS is a good pal of METR's [iv]. We propose to pair them off and get them to photograph their own materials having given a camera for this purpose. Kh'YuS is a good photographer, has a large darkroom [KAMERA] and all the equipment but he does not have a Leica. LIBERAL will receive the films from METR for passing on. Direction of the probationers will be continued through LIBERAL, this will ease the load on him. Details about the contracting are in letter no. 8.

OSA [v] has agreed to cooperate with us in drawing in ShMEL' [vi] (henceforth "KALIBR" — see your no. 5258[a]) with a view to ENORMOUS [ĒNORMOZ] [vii]. On summons from KALIBR she is leaving on 22 November for the Camp 2 area [viii]. KALIBR will have a week's leave. Before OSA's departure LIBERAL will carry out two briefing meetings.

No. 901   ANTON [ix]

Notes: [a]   Not available.
Comments:
　[i]   VIKTOR: Lt. Gen. P. M. FITIN.
　[ii]   LIBERAL: Julius ROSENBERG.
　[iii]   Kh'YuS: i.e. HUGHES, probably Joel BARR or Alfred
　　　SARANT.
　[iv]   METR: i.e. METER, probably either Joel BARR or
　　　Alfred SARANT.
　[v]   OSA: i.e. WASP, Ruth GREENGLASS.
　[vi]   ShMEL'/KALIBR: i.e. BUMBLEBEE/CALIBRE, David
　　　GREENGLASS.
　[vii]   ĒNORMOZ: Atomic Energy Project.
　[viii]   Camp 2: LOS ALAMOS Laboratory, New Mexico.
　[ix]   ANTON: Leonid Romanovich KVASNIKOV.

1 May 1975

NEW YORK KGB

Telegram to Moscow
November 27, 1944

VENONA

Reissue (T9.2)

From: NEW YORK

To: MOSCOW

No: 1657

27 November 1944

To VIKTOR [i].

Your no. 5356 [a]. Information on LIBERAL's [ii] wife [iii]. Surname that of her husband, first name ETHEL, 29 years old. Married five years. Finished secondary school. A FELLOWCOUNTRYMAN [ZEM-LYaK] [iv] since 1938. Sufficiently well developed politically. Knows about her husband's work and the role of METR [v] and NIL [vi]. In view of delicate health does not work. Is characterized positively and as a devoted person.

Notes: [a]   Not available.
Comments:
    [i]   VIKTOR: Lt. Gen. P. M. FITIN.
    [ii]   LIBERAL: Julius Rosenberg.
    [iii]   Ethel ROSENBERG, nee GREENGLASS.
    [iv]   ZEMLYaK: Member of the Communist Party.
    [v]   METR: Probably Joel BARR or Alfred SARANT.
    [vi]   NIL: Unidentified.

A. H. BELMONT

Office Memorandum on Julius Rosenberg

July 17, 1950

To: D. M. LADD

From: A. H. BELMONT

Subject: JULIUS ROSENBERG
              ESPIONAGE–R.

At 1:20 pm, I attempted to reach Mr. James McInerney[2] to furnish him with the summary memorandum dated July 17, 1950, regarding Julius Rosenberg. Mr. McInerney was at lunch. I was successful in reaching him at 2:40 pm, at which time Supervisor Robert Lamphere and I furnished him with the original of the memorandum to the Attorney General and Mr. McInerney copy. Mr. McInerney thoroughly digested the memorandum and rendered the following opinion. . . .

Relative to subject Ethel Rosenberg, Mr. McInerney advised that there is insufficient evidence to issue process against her at this time. He advised that the evidence against her depends upon the statement of Ruth Greenglass that Ethel Rosenberg talked her into going to Albuquerque to see David Greenglass to see if he would cooperate with the Russians in furnishing information. Mr. McInerney requested that any additional information concerning Ethel Rosenberg be furnished the Department. He was of the opinion that it might be possible to utilize her as a lever against her husband.

---

[2]James McInerney was the assistant attorney general in charge of the Criminal Division of the Department of Justice.

J. EDGAR HOOVER

Memorandum to the Attorney General

July 19, 1950

THE ATTORNEY GENERAL

DIRECTOR, FBI

JULIUS ROSENBERG
ESPIONAGE–R   CONFIDENTIAL

In my memorandum to you dated July 17, 1950, I brought to your attention additional information with respect to the espionage activities of David and Ruth Greenglass and Julius and Ethel Rosenberg. I asked for your opinion as to the institution of prosecutive action against Ethel Rosenberg and Ruth Greenglass.

In connection with the above, I desire to bring to your attention the fact that United States Attorney Everett Grantham has expressed the desire to include in the indictment in Santa Fe, New Mexico, both Julius Rosenberg and Ruth Greenglass. It would appear that it might also be possible to proceed against Ethel Rosenberg under such an indictment on the basis of her having urged Ruth Greenglass to approach David Greenglass to act as an espionage agent.

There is no question but that if Julius Rosenberg would furnish the details of his extensive espionage activities it would be possible to proceed against other individuals. In the fact of Rosenberg's refusal I believe that you may desire to seriously consider instituting additional process against him in New Mexico. This might result in a change in his attitude. I also feel that proceeding against his wife might serve as a lever in this matter.

I would like to have your opinion with respect to instituting further process against the Rosenbergs. I would also appreciate having any decision you may reach relative to prosecution of Ruth Greenglass.

JUDGE IRVING KAUFMAN

Sentencing of Julius and Ethel Rosenberg

April 5, 1951

Because of the seriousness of this case and the lack of precedence, I have refrained from asking the Government for a recommendation. The responsibility is so great that I believe that the Court alone should assume this responsibility. . . .

The issue of punishment in this case is presented in a unique framework of history. It is so difficult to make people realize that this country is engaged in a life and death struggle with a completely different system. This struggle is not only manifested externally between these two forces but this case indicates quite clearly that it also involves the employment by the enemy of secret as well as overt outspoken forces among our own people. All of our democratic institutions are, therefore, directly involved in this great conflict. I believe that never at any time in our history were we ever confronted to the same degree that we are today with such a challenge to our very existence. The atom bomb was unknown when the espionage statute was drafted. I emphasize this because we must realize that we are dealing with a missile of destruction which can wipe out millions of Americans.

The competitive advantage held by the United States in superweapons has put a premium on the services of a new school of spies—the homegrown variety that places allegiance to a foreign power before loyalty to the United States. The punishment to be meted out in this case must therefore serve the maximum interest for the preservation of our society against these traitors in our midst.

It is ironic that the very country which these defendants betrayed and sought to destroy placed every safeguard around them for obtaining a fair and impartial trial, a trial which consumed three weeks in this court. I recall the defendant Julius Rosenberg testifying that our American system of jurisprudence met with his approval and was preferred over Russian justice. Even the defendants realize—by this admission—that this type of trial would not have been afforded to them in Russia. Certainly, to a Russian national accused of a conspiracy to destroy Russia not one day would have been consumed in a trial. It is to America's credit that it took the pains and exerted the effort which it did in the trial of these defendants. Yet, they made a choice of devoting themselves to the Russian ideology of denial of God, denial of the sanctity of the individual, and aggression against free men everywhere instead of serving the cause of liberty and freedom.

I consider your crime worse than murder. Plain deliberate contemplated murder is dwarfed in magnitude by comparison with the crime you have committed. In committing the act of murder, the criminal kills only his victim. The immediate family is brought to grief and when justice is meted out the chapter is closed. But in your case, I believe your conduct in putting into the hands of the Russians the A-bomb years before our best scientists predicted Russia would perfect the bomb has already caused, in my opinion, the Communist aggression in Korea, with the resultant casualties exceeding 50,000 and who knows but that millions more of innocent people may pay the price of your treason. Indeed, by your betrayal you undoubtedly have altered the course of history to the disadvantage of our country. No one can say that we do not live in a constant state of tension. We have evidence of your treachery all around us every day—for the civilian defense activities throughout the nation are aimed at preparing us for an atom bomb attack.

Nor can it be said in mitigation of the offense that the power which set the conspiracy in motion and profited from it was not openly hostile to the United States at the time of the conspiracy. If this was your excuse the error of your ways in setting yourselves above our properly constituted authorities and the decision of those authorities not to share the information with Russia must now be obvious.

The evidence indicated quite clearly that Julius Rosenberg was the prime mover in this conspiracy. However, let no mistake be made about the role which his wife, Ethel Rosenberg, played in this conspiracy. Instead of deterring him from pursuing his ignoble cause, she encouraged and assisted the cause. She was a mature woman—almost three years older than her husband and almost seven years older than her younger brother. She was a full-fledged partner in this crime.

Indeed the defendants Julius and Ethel Rosenberg placed their devotion to their cause above their own personal safety and were conscious that they were sacrificing their own children, should their misdeeds be detected—all of which did not deter them from pursuing their course. Love for their cause dominated their lives—it was even greater than their love for their children.

What I am about to say is not easy for me. I have deliberated for hours, days and nights. I have carefully weighed the evidence. Every nerve, every fiber of my body has been taxed. I am just as human as are the people who have given me the power to impose sentence. I am convinced beyond any doubt of your guilt. I have searched the records—I have searched my conscience—to find some reason for mercy—for it is only human to be merciful and it is natural to try to spare lives. I am convinced, however, that I would violate the solemn and sacred trust that the people of this land have placed in my hands were I to show leniency to the defendants Rosenberg.

It is not in my power, Julius and Ethel Rosenberg, to forgive you. Only the Lord can find mercy for what you have done.

The sentence of the Court upon Julius and Ethel Rosenberg is, for the crime for which you have been convicted, you are hereby sentenced to the punishment of death, and it is ordered upon some day within the week beginning with Monday, May 21st, you shall be executed according to law.

ETHEL ROSENBERG

Letter to Julius Rosenberg
February 26, 1952

7:30 A.M. Feb. 26

My dear one,

Last night at 10:00 o'clock, I heard the shocking news.[3] At the present moment, with little or no detail to hand, it is difficult for me to make any comment, beyond an expression of horror at the shameless haste with which the government appears to be pressing for our liquidation. Certainly, it proves that all our contributions in the past regarding the political nature of our case, have been amazingly correct.

My heart aches for the children, unfortunately they are old enough to have heard for themselves, and no matter what amount of control I am able to exercise, my brain reels, picturing their terror. It is for

[3]The Rosenbergs' convictions were upheld by the U.S. Circuit Court of Appeals on February 25, 1952.

them I am most concerned and it is of their reaction I am anxiously awaiting some word. Of course, Manny [Bloch][4] will get here just as soon as he puts in motion proper legal procedure for our continued defense, but meanwhile, my emotions are in storm, as your own must be.

Sweetheart, if only I could truly comfort you, I love you so very dearly.... Courage, darling, there's much to be done.

Your devoted wife,
Ethel

[4]Emmanuel Bloch was the Rosenbergs' lawyer. He handled the custodial arrangements for their children as well as their espionage case.

JULIUS ROSENBERG

Letter to Ethel Rosenberg

May 31, 1953

May 31, 1953

Ethel Darling,

What does one write to his beloved when faced with the very grim reality that in eighteen days, on their 14th wedding anniversary, it is ordered that they be put to death? The approaching darkest hour of our trial and the grave peril that threatened us require every effort on our part to avoid hysteria and false heroics, but only maintain a sober and calm approach to our most crucial problems. . . .

Dearest, over and over again, I have tried to analyze in the most objective manner possible the answers to the position of our government in our case. Everything indicates only one answer—that the wishes of certain madmen are being followed in order to use this case as a coercive bludgeon against all dissenters. However, I still have faith that the more responsible elements in the administration will let sanity be the better part of judgment and save our lives. It seems to me that at this moment it is still touch and go and therefore we must see to it that the maximum is done in our behalf. . . .

Sweetheart, I know that our children and our family are suffering a great deal right now and it is natural that we be concerned for their welfare. However I think we will have to concentrate our strength on ourselves. First, we want to make sure that we stand up under the terrific pressure, and then we ought to try to contribute some share to the fight. To my way of looking at the problem, this is the way we can look out for our children's interests best. . . . All the love I possess is yours—

Julie

7

The Truman Administration Deals with the Communist Menace: The 1947 Loyalty-Security Program

President Truman's Executive Order 9835 of March 21, 1947, set up a loyalty-security program for the executive branch of the federal government. It imposed a political test on federal employees, disqualifying anyone who belonged to the Communist party or had a "sympathetic association" with it or any other allegedly subversive organizations or individuals. The attorney general was to issue a list of such groups (see Document 9). Unfortunately, what constituted a "sympathetic association" with such an organization was left deliberately vague — perhaps because it accorded with the FBI's interest in having the program, which it had essentially designed, reflect its own bureaucratic biases and procedures.

As the case studies in Document 8 reveal, the program's ostensibly fair procedures masked considerable injustice. Although Executive Order 9835 specified that the Civil Service Commission (CSC) would handle most of the program's investigations, within a few months the FBI had muscled the CSC aside. Not only did this mean that the bureau's broadly ideological definition of communism would come to determine what a "sympathetic association" might entail, but it also ensured that the FBI's obsession with secrecy would suffuse the program, making it nearly impossible for employees to discover the basis of the charges against them or successfully appeal their dismissals.

Executive Order 9835, Prescribing Procedures for the Administration of an Employees' Loyalty Program in the Executive Branch of the Government, 12 *Fed. Reg.* 1935. Reprinted in Eleanor Bontecou, *The Federal Loyalty-Security Program* (Ithaca, N.Y.: Cornell University Press, 1953), 275–81.

HARRY S. TRUMAN

Executive Order 9835

March 21, 1947

Part I — Investigation of Applicants

1. There shall be a loyalty investigation of every person entering the civilian employment of any department or agency of the executive branch of the Federal Government.

a. Investigations of persons entering the competitive service shall be conducted by the Civil Service Commission, except in such cases as are covered by a special agreement between the Commission and any given department or agency.

b. Investigations of persons other than those entering the competitive service shall be conducted by the employing department or agency. Departments and agencies without investigative organizations shall utilize the investigative facilities of the Civil Service Commission.

2. The investigations of persons entering the employ of the executive branch may be conducted after any such person enters upon actual employment therein, but in any such case the appointment of such person shall be conditioned upon a favorable determination with respect to his loyalty. . . .

3. An investigation shall be made of all applicants at all available pertinent sources of information and shall include reference to:

a. Federal Bureau of Investigation files.

b. Civil Service Commission files.

c. Military and naval intelligence files.

d. The files of any other appropriate government investigative or intelligence agency.

e. House Committee on Un-American Activities files.

f. Local law-enforcement files at the place of residence and employment of the applicant, including municipal, county, and State law-enforcement files.

g. Schools and colleges attended by applicant.

h. Former employers of applicant.

i. References given by applicant.

j. Any other appropriate source.

4. Whenever derogatory information with respect to loyalty of an applicant is revealed a full field investigation shall be conducted. A full field investigation shall also be conducted of those applicants, or of applicants for particular positions, as may be designated by the head of the employing department or agency, such designations to be based on the determination by any such head of the best interests of national security. . . .

Part II — Investigation of Employees

a. An officer or employee who is charged with being disloyal shall have a right to an administrative hearing before a loyalty board in the employing department or agency. He may appear before such board personally, accompanied by counsel or representative of his own choosing, and present evidence on his own behalf, through witnesses or by affidavit.

b. The officer or employee shall be served with a written notice of such hearing in sufficient time, and shall be informed therein of the nature of the charges against him in sufficient detail, so that he will be enabled to prepare his defense. The charges shall be stated as specifically and completely as, in the discretion of the employing department or agency, security considerations permit. . . .

3. A recommendation of removal by a loyalty board shall be subject to appeal by the officer or employee affected, prior to his removal, to the head of the employing department or agency or to such person or persons as may be designated by such head, under such regulations as may be prescribed by him, and the decision of the department or agency concerned shall be subject to appeal to the Civil Service Commission's Loyalty Review Board, hereinafter provided for, for an advisory recommendation. . . .

Part III — Responsibilities of Civil Service Commission

1. There shall be established in the Civil Service Commission a Loyalty Review Board of not less than three impartial persons, the members of which shall be officers or employees of the Commission. . . .

3. The Loyalty Review Board shall currently be furnished by the Department of Justice the name of each foreign or domestic organization, association, movement, group or combination of persons which the Attorney General, after appropriate investigation and determination,

designates as totalitarian, fascist, communist or subversive, or as having adopted a policy of advocating or approving the commission of acts of force or violence to deny others their rights under the Constitution of the United States, or as seeking to alter the form of government of the United States by unconstitutional means.

a. The Loyalty Review Board shall disseminate such information to all departments and agencies.

Part IV—Security Measures in Investigations

1. At the request of the head of any department or agency of the executive branch an investigative agency shall make available to such head, personally, all investigative material and information collected by the investigative agency concerning any employee or prospective employee of the requesting department or agency, or shall make such material and information available to any officer or officers designated by such head and approved by the investigative agency.

2. Notwithstanding the foregoing requirement, however, the investigative agency may refuse to disclose the names of confidential informants, provided it furnishes sufficient information about such informants on the basis of which the requesting department or agency can make an adequate evaluation of the information furnished by them and provided it advises the requesting department or agency in writing that it is essential to the protection of the informants or to the investigation of other cases that the identity of the informants not be revealed. Investigative agencies shall not use this discretion to decline to reveal sources of information where such action is not essential.

3. Each department and agency of the executive branch should develop and maintain, for the collection and analysis of information relating to the loyalty of its employees and prospective employees, a staff specially trained in security techniques, and an effective security control system for protecting such information generally and for protecting confidential sources of such information particularly.

Part V—Standards

1. The standard for the refusal of employment or the removal from employment in an executive department or agency on grounds relating to loyalty shall be that, on all the evidence, reasonable grounds

exist for belief that the person involved is disloyal to the Government of the United States.

2. Activities and associations of an applicant or employee which may be considered in connection with the determination of disloyalty may include one or more of the following:

a. Sabotage, espionage, or attempts or preparations therefor, or knowingly associating with spies or saboteurs;

b. Treason or sedition or advocacy thereof;

c. Advocacy of revolution or force or violence to alter the constitutional form of government of the United States;

d. Intentional, unauthorized disclosure to any person, under circumstances which may indicate disloyalty to the United States, of documents or information of a confidential or nonpublic character obtained by the person making the disclosure as a result of his employment by the Government of the United States;

e. Performing or attempting to perform his duties, or otherwise acting so as to serve the interests of another government in preference to the interests of the United States;

f. Membership in, affiliation with or sympathetic association with any foreign or domestic organization, association, movement, group or combination of persons, designated by the Attorney General as totalitarian, fascist, communist, or subversive, or as having adopted a policy of advocating or approving the commission of acts of force or violence to deny other persons their rights under the Constitution of the United States, or as seeking to alter the form of government of the United States by unconstitutional means.

Part VI — Miscellaneous

1. Each department and agency of the executive branch, to the extent that it has not already done so, shall submit to the Federal Bureau of Investigation of the Department of Justice, either directly or through the Civil Service Commission, the names (and such other necessary identifying material as the Federal Bureau of Investigation may require) of all of its incumbent employees.

a. The Federal Bureau of Investigation shall check such names against its records of persons concerning whom there is substantial evidence of being within the purview of paragraph 2 of Part V hereof, and shall notify each department and agency of such information.

b. Upon receipt of the above-mentioned information from the Federal Bureau of Investigation, each department and agency shall make, or cause to be made by the Civil Service Commission, such investigation of those employees as the head of the department or agency shall deem advisable. . . .

8

A Political Test for Employment: The Loyalty-Security Program in Operation

The following selection contains excerpts from documents collected during the mid-1950s as part of a foundation-supported study of the federal government's loyalty-security program. Included are samples of the formal charges or "interrogatories" that the employees received as well as selections from the transcripts of their hearings before their agencies' loyalty-security boards. These cases reveal many of the assumptions on which professional security officers based their scrutiny of federal employees.

Because the concept of "sympathetic association" with communism was so vague, the officials who administered the loyalty-security program tended to interpret their mission of judging an individual's political affiliations with considerable latitude. One man almost lost his job because, as the charges against him explained, he "wrote a thesis which was based on material obtained from the Institute of Pacific Relations[1] which has been cited as a Communistic Front organization" by HUAC and the person to whom he subleased his apartment "has had known Communist and Communist Front associations." Another employee was suspended because he was "in close and continuing association with [his] parents," who were under suspicion because they had joined a group on the attorney general's list to buy cheap insurance and a burial plot. Because the main labor union that represented federal employees did have Communist leaders, people could come under suspicion—as the protagonist of the first case did—if

---

[1]The Institute of Pacific Relations was a private research organization that disseminated information about East Asia to scholars and policymakers before World War II. It was attacked during the McCarthy era on the (untrue) grounds that it had served as a conduit for Communist influence over America's China policy.

Adam Yarmolinsky, ed., *Case Studies in Personnel Security* (Washington, D.C.: Bureau of National Affairs, 1955), 142–47, 152, 158–59, 169–74.

they were active in such a union, even if they opposed its left-wing leadership. There were also instances of mistaken identity; the FBI, which handled most of these security investigations, was less than scrupulous about checking its files.

At the hearings before their agencies' security boards, people's political opinions, as well as their associations, came under scrutiny. One civilian Army employee was asked what newspapers and magazines he read, whether he and his wife went to church or "provided any sort of religious training for your children," what he thought about government ownership of public utilities, and whether he had "ever expressed [himself] as being in favor of the abolition of trade marks." These records also reveal considerable apprehension about racial issues on the part of security investigators, who apparently assumed that participation in civil rights activities by African American employees was evidence of disloyalty. An initial clearance did not always end the matter; as the second case indicates, federal employees who had survived one security clearance could face the same charges a few years later.

It is also important to realize that many of the cases about which information is available are those whose protagonists decided to fight the charges against them. These cases, therefore, may well have been among the most outrageous abuses of the loyalty-security program and may not have been completely typical. Many other employees, faced with a set of interrogatories that would have forced them to justify their past political behavior to an unsympathetic audience, probably resigned instead.

The Federal Loyalty-Security Program: Case 1

In late February 1954, the employee was working in a clerical capacity as a substitute postal employee. He performed no supervisory duties. His tasks were routine in nature.

One year prior to the initiation of proceedings, the employee had resigned from his position as an executive officer of a local union whose parent union had been expelled from the CIO in 1949 as Communist dominated. The employee had served as an officer for one year prior to the expulsion, had helped to lead his local out of the expelled parent and back into the CIO, and had thereafter remained in an executive capacity until his resignation in 1953. He resigned from that position upon being appointed a substitute clerk with the United States Post Office in early 1953. . . .

In the last week of February 1954, the employee received notice, by mail, that he was under investigation by the Regional Office of the United States Civil Service Commission. . . .

[The employee immediately answered the first set of charges against him only to be suspended without pay at the end of March on the following charges.]

"3. In January 1948, your name appeared on a general mailing list of the Spanish Refugee Appeal of the Joint Anti-Fascist Refugee Committee.[2]. . .

"5. Your wife . . . was a member of the . . . Club of the Young Communist League.[3]

"6. In 1950, Communist literature was observed in the bookshelves and Communist art was seen on the walls of your residence in ———.

"7. Your signature appeared on a Communist Party nominating petition in the November 1941 Municipal Elections in ———.

"8. You falsely replied 'No' on your Standard Form 60, 'Application for Federal Employment,' in answer to question 16, which is as follows: 'Are you now, or have you ever been, a member of the Communist Party, USA, or any Communist or Fascist organization?' ". . .

The employee had a hearing four months later, in July 1954. The members of the Board were three (3) civilian employees of military installations. None of them were attorneys. The Post Office establishment was represented by an Inspector, who administered the oath to the employee and his witnesses, but did not otherwise participate in the proceedings. There was no attorney-adviser to the Board. There was no testimony by witnesses hostile to the employee, nor was any evidence introduced against him. . . .

. . . Before the employee testified, he submitted a nine-page autobiography to the Hearing Board. . . .

[2]The Joint Anti-Fascist Refugee Committee was a so-called front group that had been organized to help antifascist refugees from the Spanish Civil War. It was on the attorney general's list.

[3]The Young Communist League was the Communist party's youth organization from the 1920s to the 1940s. It was on the attorney general's list.

... The autobiography set forth in some detail the employee's activities as an officer of his local union, and discussed particularly his role therein as an anti-Communist, and his opposition to the pro-Communist policies of the National Organization with which his local was affiliated. The autobiography recited that when his National Union was expelled from the CIO, he and his supporters successfully won a struggle within his local and as a direct result thereof, caused the said local to disaffiliate from the expelled parent, and affiliate with a new organization established within the CIO. The employee's autobiography recited that the aforesaid struggle directly involved the question of Communist domination of the local's parent union, that the victory of the employee and his supporters represented a victory over Communist adherents in the local, and that the employee was the frequent target of threats and slander by the pro-Communist faction of his local. . . .

With respect to the third charge against the employee (that his name had been on a general mailing list of the Spanish Refugee Appeal of the Joint Anti-Fascist Refugee Committee), the employee reiterated his denial of any knowledge concerning it, and his counsel reminded the Board that no Attorney General's list existed in January 1948—the date contained in the charge. The employee testified, further, that he had no recollection of ever having received any mail from the organization involved. . . .

With respect to charge No. 5 against the employee (that his wife had been a member of the Young Communist League), the Chairman of the Hearing Board advised the employee that the date involved was March 1944. The employee testified that he and his wife were married in February 1944, and that the charge was ridiculous. He testified, further, that he had no independent recollection that his wife was ever a member of the said organization. In addition, the employee testified that he had never lived in the neighborhood in which the organization was alleged to have existed, and that he had never heard of said organization. . . .

The Chairman then read charge No. 6 in which it was alleged that Communist literature was observed in the employee's bookshelves at home and Communist art was seen on the walls of his residence in 1950. Immediately following his reading of the charge, the Chairman stated that:

"The Board is at a loss just to what Communist literature they are referring to."

Counsel for the employee then questioned him concerning his courses in college, and the books which he was there required to read for those courses. In this connection, counsel for the employee asked whether books had been recommended as part of study courses by instructors, and whether one of these books had been *Das Kapital* by Karl Marx, and whether the employee had bought *Das Kapital,* following such a recommendation. The employee responded that certain books had been recommended by his instructors, that *Das Kapital* was one, and that he had bought the Modern Library Giant Edition of *Das Kapital. . . .*

Counsel then asked the employee whether, in 1950, he had reproductions of paintings by great painters hanging on the walls of his home, and following the employee's answer in the affirmative, counsel asked him to name some of the artists whose reproductions were hanging upon the walls of the employee's home. The employee named Picasso, Matisse, Renoir, and Moddigliotti [Modigliani?].

Counsel then asked the employee whether pictures by those artists were hanging in museums, including the largest museum in the city in which the employee resides, and following the employee's answer in the affirmative, counsel asked whether there was "any relationship between the art and the Communist Party." The employee responded that he had "no idea of what any relationship there might be that exists there at all."

Thereafter, in response to counsel's question, the employee testified that he had not read *Das Kapital* in its entirety, that he had been required to read "a chapter or two for classwork," and that "he had found it a little dull and tedious.". . .

The Chairman read charge No. 7, in which it was alleged that the employee's signature appeared on a Communist Party nominating petition in 1941 municipal elections in the employee's home city.

The employee had answered this charge by stating that he had signed such a petition; that in 1941, the Communist Party appeared on the initial ballot; that his recollection was that on the cover page of the petition it stated that the signers were not members of the Communist Party, and that prior to 1941 and at all times thereafter, the employee had been registered as a member of one of the two major political parties, and that he had no recollection of voting for any political party other than one of the two major political parties. . . .

Thereafter, counsel for the employee objected to the charge on the ground that the signing of a petition for a party which had a legal place on the ballot in 1941 had no relationship to present security. The Chairman then asked the employee to recall the circumstances in which his signature had been solicited in 1941. The employee responded by stating that, so far as he could recall, someone came down the street and seeing him working on the premises asked him to sign the petition, after explaining the petition to him. In response to a question by a member of the Board, the employee stated that he did not know the person who had solicited his signature, and that he had never seen or heard from him thereafter, nor had he thereafter heard from the Communist Party.

[At the hearing, the employee and his attorney sought unsuccessfully to find out the basis for the final charge against him that he had been in the Communist party or other Communist or fascist organization. In September 1954, the employee was dismissed from his job. He then appealed to the regional director of the Civil Service Commission, who reaffirmed his dismissal. The case then went to the Civil Service Commission in Washington, whose chair upheld the regional director's ruling in February 1955 with the following explanation.]

"A careful study of facts in Mr.———'s case has been completed. It has been established and he has admitted that he signed a petition in November 1941 that the Communist Party be placed on the ballot in the———municipal elections. . . . His name was reported as being on the general mailing list of the Joint Anti-Fascist Refugee Committee. . . . Mrs.———is reported as having been at one time a member of the———Club of Young Communist League.

"Mr.———was an officer of Local———of the [parent union] at the time this organization was expelled from the CIO because of Communist domination. Consideration has been given to information that he was reputed to be one of the leaders of the anti-Communist group which brought Local———back into the CIO as the———. However, it is not felt that this information sufficiently outweighs his reported connections with organizations and individuals whose interests and aims are inimical to those of the United States to the extent that a finding that he is unswervingly loyal to the Government of the United States is warranted and the Commission must regard this record as disqualifying under the purposes and intent of Executive Order 10450. This Executive Order, issued April 1953, requires a positive finding that the employment of each candidate in the Federal Service would be clearly consistent with the interests of the national security."

The Federal Loyalty-Security Program:
Case 2

The employee is a meat inspector for a Federal agency. He has done the same type of work for the same agency in the same community for the past 38 years. He has no access to classified materials. His job involves the inspection of carcasses and meat products. . . .

The employee had been the subject of a previous loyalty proceeding under EO 9835 in 1948–49. This second proceeding was based on identical charges: that he had been a member of the Communist Party from 1943–46 and had falsified his 1944 application to the Civil Service Commission for employment by denying that he had ever been a member of an organization that advocated the overthrow of the government by force and violence. (The charges in the second proceeding added as a ground for the charge of falsification his denial of Party membership in his answer to the 1948 charges and in his answer to the 1954 initial "statement of reasons for suspension.") . . .

At the start of the 1948 hearing one of the agency representatives informed the employee's lawyers that the FBI report on him indicated that he had joined the Communist Party in 1943 and had been issued membership book number————; that he had transferred to another unit in the Party in the same year and had been given a second book with number————; and that in 1945 he had transferred to a third unit in the Party. This representative showed to the employee's lawyers, but would not place in the record, a photostatic copy of his purported second Party membership book, with his name typed in— his first name in abbreviated form and his last name. This representative also said that the Board would put on one witness; the other representative went out of the room to bring the witness in and then returned to announce that he had departed. The representative explained that the Board had no subpoena power and could not compel the witness to appear. The witness was not identified, and the Board did not put on any witnesses in the hearing.

The employee's lawyers put on 12 witnesses. . . .

The substance of the testimony of [the first] ten witnesses was that the employee was an outstanding Christian, family man, and church and community leader; a man of firm religious convictions and outspoken manner. They said that he was devoted to his church work, job, and family, and had always spoken of communism with abhorrence. . . .

The eleventh witness was the employee himself. . . . He said that the only conceivable explanations for the charges were: (1) his struggle within his church in opposition to his pastor, who had been courting left-wing support in his political campaigns, and (2) his membership during 1943–46, while he had worked nights in a defense plant, in a Communist-dominated union which he had been compelled to join to get the job. He said that he had paid his union dues regularly but had never attended a union meeting and had taken no part in union affairs.

He denied emphatically that he had ever been a Communist or had had any connection with them. Under cross-examination he denied that he had ever heard of a half-dozen persons who, the Board said, were Communists and with whom he had allegedly had contacts. He repeatedly challenged the board to bring any person before him to accuse him. . . .

[The employee was reinstated in October 1949. In May 1954, the employee was suspended again on the same charges. He again denied them and was sent a new set of charges, which now included both his 1948 and 1954 denials of party membership. He received a hearing in September 1954 at which the agency lawyer admitted that the case against the employee was "basically the same case" as in 1948. Again, the agency presented no witnesses, largely because its case rested on information from confidential informants whose identity and whereabouts the government's lawyer was not "at liberty to disclose." Fifteen people testified for the employee; his attorneys questioned them about his politics.]

. . . They elicited from the witnesses successively the following samples of statements concerning the employee's political views:

1. "conservative" and "Republican";
2. "normal, both Democratic and Republican";
3. "in the center";
4. "more or less of a Democrat";
5. "a little Republican, but that is about all";
6. "stand-pat Republican";
7. "Democrat";
8. "He is a true man";
9. "Republican";
10. "Not in sympathy with communism";

11. "I don't think his viewpoints are any different than the rest of ours";

12. "I don't know whether he was a Democrat or a Republican."

The second of the employee's witnesses to testify (a retired real estate salesman) spoke of the employee's fight to prevent Communist control of the local branch of the National Association for the Advancement of Colored People (the employee was a Negro). On cross-examination the Department lawyer asked the witness whether some Negroes had joined the Communist Party—"because it represented an avenue to get better conditions for the colored man?" The witness agreed. . . .

Thereafter the agency lawyer asked each witness on cross-examination whether the employee had ever discussed the Negro problem with him; what were the employee's views on pressing for the advancement of Negroes; and, after one witness had testified on direct examination that the employee had spoken unfavorably of Paul Robeson,[4] the agency lawyer asked him what the employee had said, and asked another witness whether the employee had ever spoken to him of Paul Robeson.

On cross-examination of the 12th witness, the employee's superior in meat inspection work, eight pages of the transcript were devoted to the security aspects of meat inspection. Asked by a Board member whether the employee had any access to classified information, the witness said "Well, we don't have any of that type of material in our section or division."

Chairman: "Do you feel that the food could be contaminated without anyone's knowledge by someone if they so desired?"

Witness: "Oh, there is always the possibility of anything like that, yes."

Chairman: "I mean if anyone had such an intent, do you think they could do it without being discovered, or is there too much supervision for that?"

Witness: "Well, it all depends on what they did to contaminate the product. If they put something in there to spoil it, we could know before it goes out."

Chairman: "You would catch it before it goes out?"

---

[4]Paul Robeson was a popular African American singer and actor in the 1940s whose closeness to the Communist party destroyed his career in the 1950s.

Witness: "Yes, if they put bacteria in there to spoil that meat. That meat would become rancid or sour or putrid before it ever left the plant. It would never get out to the public.". . .

Agency Lawyer: "Of course, we are just speculating now as to how the man would do it, but just to point it out, you could walk in there with a needle full of some kind of liquid and stick it into a carcass and it would be contaminated and you would never see it."

Witness: "That is true."

Agency Personnel Security Officer: "In other words, that is the sort of thing I am getting at. In other words, someone in the position of an inspector, if he had an evil design to contaminate a large amount of meat without necessarily being detected until it got out and had done the damage?"

Witness: "That's right. Yes, that is true."

After ascertaining that the employee's job called for him to inspect meat in private packing houses, one of his lawyers asked: "Would it be true that a large number of fifty or a hundred private employees would have the same opportunity that a man in [the employee's] position would have to contaminate the meat?"

Witness: "Certainly."

The employee took the stand and was asked by his lawyer to outline the community activities in which he had engaged and "what their nature has been, as to the Negro Community."

The Employee: "I would like to say to the reporter, to the Representatives from Washington, D.C., and also to the Committee that I have listened to the investigation of 1948 and also at this present time. At the present time it seems as though they are spending more time on the racial situation. . . .

[In summing up the case against the employee, the agency's lawyer made the following assessment.]

"Now, our theory of the case today has been that [the employee] joined the Party because he wanted to. It had a stated purpose which he believed in, and that was to advance the cause of the Negro race. We have, as [the employee's lawyer], speculated as to why his name appears on these records. A logical reason in view of his background to me is that he thought that here was an avenue of attack which he could use to further something which he believed in and which he stood for and which he testified to here, and which was testified to in the earlier hearing, that he wanted to see racial equality, and that is a theory which would make some consistency out of his public life in the community and the membership in the Party."

[The employee's attorney said he was "very much concerned" about the agency lawyer's speculations that the employee had become a Communist because of his desire for racial equality. He also complained about the board's lack of opportunity to "judge the veracity of the unknown informant, who may or may not be reliable, whose identity is something that we still are not aware of."

A week later, the Security Hearing Board notified the agency head that it had cleared the employee. He was reinstated in April 1955.]

Above: Free on bail after being indicted under the 1940 Smith Act for conspiring to advocate the overthrow of the U.S. government by "force and violence," six top Communist leaders leave the federal courthouse in New York City on July 21, 1948. Left to right, William Z. Foster, Benjamin Davis Jr., Eugene Dennis, Henry Winston, John Williamson, and Jacob Stachel.
© Hulton-Deutsch Collection/Corbis.

Top Right: While Eugene Dennis and his co-defendants in the first Smith Act trial were struggling to present the Communist party's case before the unsympathetic judge Harold Medina, who jailed some of the defendants for contempt during the trial, their supporters demonstrated outside the courthouse.
© Bettmann/Corbis.

Bottom Right: By the time he testified before Senator McCarthy's investigating committee in March 1953, Louis Budenz, the former managing editor of the *Daily Worker,* had become the nation's most ubiquitous ex-Communist witness. His "expertise" about the party bolstered the government's case in immigration hearings, congressional investigations, and criminal prosecutions, including the all-important Smith Act trial of Eugene Dennis and the Communist party's top leaders.
© Bettmann/Corbis.

189

9

Guilt by Designation: The Attorney General's List

To facilitate the administration of the federal government's loyalty-security program, President Truman authorized the attorney general to compile a list of those organizations that constituted a threat to the nation's security. Although similar lists had circulated within the Justice Department during World War II, Executive Order 9835 (see Document 7) regularized the process and made it public. In November 1947, the attorney general sent the first list of ninety-three organizations to the Loyalty Review Board. Over the next few years, the Justice Department continued to add new names. The list printed here is the November 1950 version and cites 197 organizations. Some groups, like the Communist party, appear under more than one heading.

The list was out of date from the beginning. Many of the organizations on it were already defunct. Most of the others soon disappeared because the stigma associated with the list usually made it impossible for the groups on it to function. The organizations marked with an asterisk are the only ones that still existed in 1950.

The Attorney General's List of Totalitarian, Fascist, Communist, Subversive, and Other Organizations that have "adopted a policy of advocating or approving the commission of acts of force and violence to deny others their rights under the Constitution of the United States" or "seek to alter the form of government of the United States by unconstitutional means." Reprinted in Eleanor Bontecou, *The Federal Loyalty-Security Program* (Ithaca, N.Y.: Cornell University Press, 1953), 352–58.

The Attorney General's List of Totalitarian, Fascist, Communist, Subversive, and Other Organizations

November 16, 1950

Under the heading "Totalitarian" were twenty-two defunct primarily Japanese organizations, among them such groups as the Black Dragon Society, the Hinomaru Kai (Rising Sun Flag Society, a group of Japanese war veterans), and the Japanese Protective Association. The heading "Fascist" contained twenty-two listings of mainly German, Italian, or fascist groups such as the American National Socialist Party, the German-American Bund, and the Dante Alighieri Society. The National Blue Star Mothers of America was the only group on this section of the list that was extant in 1950.

Communist

Abraham Lincoln Brigade
*Abraham Lincoln School, Chicago, Illinois
Action Committee to Free Spain Now
American Association for Reconstruction in Yugoslavia, Inc.
*American Branch of the Federation of Greek Maritime Unions
American Committee for European Workers' Relief
*American Committee for Protection of Foreign Born
American Committee for Spanish Freedom
American Committee for Yugoslav Relief, Inc.
*American Council for a Democratic Greece, formerly known as the Greek American Council; Greek American Committee for National Unity
*American Council on Soviet Relations
*American Croatian Congress
*American Jewish Labor Council
American League against War and Fascism
American League for Peace and Democracy

*Organizations still in existence in 1950.

191

American Peace Mobilization
*American Polish Labor Council
American Rescue Ship Mission (a project of the United American Spanish Aid Committee)
*American Russian Institute, New York
American Russian Institute, Philadelphia
*American Russian Institute (of San Francisco)
*American Russian Institute of Southern California, Los Angeles
*American Slav Congress
American Youth Congress
American Youth for Democracy
Armenian Progressive League of America
*Boston School for Marxist Studies, Boston, Massachusetts
*California Labor School, Inc., 216 Market Street, San Francisco, California
*Central Council of American Women of Croatian Descent, aka Central Council of American Croatian Women, National Council of Croatian Women
Citizens Committee to Free Earl Browder
Citizens Committee for Harry Bridges
*Civil Rights Congress and its affiliated organizations, including:
— Civil Rights Congress for Texas
— Veterans against Discrimination of Civil Rights Congress of New York
Comite Coordinador Pro Republica Española
*Committee for a Democratic Far Eastern Policy
Commonwealth College, Mena, Arkansas
*Communist Party, U.S.A., its subdivisions, subsidiaries, and affiliates, including:
— Citizens Committee of the Upper West Side (New York City)
— Committee to Aid the Fighting South
— Daily Workers Press Club
— Dennis Defense Committee
— Labor Research Association, Inc.
— Southern Negro Youth Congress
— United May Day Committee
— United Negro and Allied Veterans of America
— Yiddisher Kultur Farband
Communist Political Association, its subdivisions, subsidiaries, and affiliates, including:
— Florida Press and Educational League

—Peoples Educational and Press Association of Texas
—Virginia League for Peoples Education
Connecticut State Youth Conference
Congress of American Revolutionary Writers
*Congress of American Women
*Council on African Affairs
Council for Pan-American Democracy
*Dennis Defense Committee
Detroit Youth Assembly
Emergency Conference to Save Spanish Refugees (founding body of the North American Spanish Aid Committee)
Friends of the Soviet Union
George Washington Carver School, New York City
*Hawaii Civil Liberties Committee
Hollywood Writers Mobilization for Defense
Hungarian-American Council for Democracy
*Independent Socialist League
International Labor Defense
*International Workers Order, its subdivisions, subsidiaries, and affiliates, including:
   —*American-Russian Fraternal Society
   —*Carpatho-Russian Peoples Society
   —*Cervantes Fraternal Society
   —*Croatian Benevolent Fraternity
   —*Finnish-American Mutual Aid Society
   —*Garibaldi American Fraternal Society
   —*Hellenic-American Brotherhood
   —*Hungarian Brotherhood
   —*Jewish Peoples Fraternal Order
   —People's Radio Foundation, Inc.
   —*Polonia Society of the ɪwo
   —*Romanian-American Fraternal Society
   —*Serbian-American Fraternal Society
   —*Slovak Workers Society
   —*Ukrainian-American Fraternal Union
*Jefferson School of Social Science, New York City
*Jewish Peoples Committee
*Joint Anti-Fascist Refugee Committee
*Joseph Weydemeyer School of Social Science, St. Louis, Missouri
*Labor Research Association, Inc.

*Labor Youth League
League of American Writers
Macedonian-American People's League
Michigan Civil Rights Federation
Michigan School of Social Science
National Committee for the Defense of Political Prisoners
National Committee to Win the Peace
National Conference on American Policy in China and the Far East (a Conference called by the Committee for a Democratic Far Eastern Policy)
National Council of Americans of Croatian Descent
*National Council of American-Soviet Friendship
National Federation for Constitutional Liberties
National Negro Congress
Nature Friends of America (since 1935)
Negro Labor Victory Committee
New Committee for Publications
North American Committee to Aid Spanish Democracy
North American Spanish Aid Committee
Ohio School of Social Sciences
Oklahoma Committee to Defend Political Prisoners
*Pacific Northwest Labor School, Seattle, Washington
Partido del Pueblo of Panama (operating in the Canal Zone)
*Peoples Educational Association (incorporated under name Los Angeles Educational Association, Inc.) aka Peoples Educational Center, Peoples University, Peoples School
*Peoples Institute of Applied Religion
Philadelphia School of Social Science and Art
Photo League (New York City)
Progressive German-Americans, aka Progressive German-Americans of Chicago
Proletarian Party of America
Revolutionary Workers League
Samuel Adams School, Boston, Massachusetts
Schappes Defense Committee
Schneiderman-Darcy Defense Committee
*School of Jewish Studies, New York City
*Seattle Labor School, Seattle, Washington
*Serbian Vidovdan Council
*Slovenian-American National Council
Socialist Workers Party, including American Committee for European Workers' Relief

Socialist Youth League
Tom Paine School of Social Science, Philadelphia, Pennsylvania
Tom Paine School of Westchester, New York
*Union of American Croatians
United American Spanish Aid Committee
*United Committee of South Slavic Americans
United Harlem Tenants and Consumers Organization
*Veterans of the Abraham Lincoln Brigade
Walt Whitman School of Social Science, Newark, New Jersey
Washington Bookshop Association
Washington Committee for Democratic Action
Washington Commonwealth Federation
Wisconsin Conference on Social Legislation
Workers Alliance
Workers Party, including Socialist Youth League
Young Communist League

Subversive

*Communist Party, U.S.A., its subdivisions, subsidiaries, and
   affiliates
Communist Political Association, its subdivisions, subsidiaries,
   and affiliates, including:
   — Florida Press and Educational League
   — Peoples Educational and Press Association of Texas
   — Virginia League for Peoples Education
German-American Bund
Independent Socialist League
*Partido del Pueblo of Panama (operating in the Canal Zone)
*Socialist Workers Party
Workers Party
Young Communist League

Organizations which have "adopted a policy of advocating or approving the commission of acts of force and violence to deny others their rights under the Constitution of the United States"

*American Christian Nationalist Party
*Associated Klans of America
*Association of Georgia Klans
Columbians

Knights of the White Camellia
*Ku Klux Klan
*Original Southern Klans, Incorporated
Protestant War Veterans of the U.S., Inc.
Silver Shirt Legion of America

Organizations which "seek to alter the form of government of the United States by unconstitutional means"

*Communist Party, U.S.A., its subdivisions, subsidiaries, and affiliates
Communist Political Association, its subdivisions, subsidiaries, and affiliates, including:
— Florida Press and Educational League
— Peoples Educational and Press Association of Texas
— Virginia League for Peoples Education
Independent Socialist League
*Industrial Workers of the World
*Nationalist Party of Puerto Rico
*Partido del Pueblo of Panama (operating in the Canal Zone)
*Socialist Workers Party
Workers Party
Young Communist League

10

Communism in Court: Excerpts from the 1949 Smith Act Trial of the Communist Party's Eleven Top Leaders

These excerpts from the transcripts of the 1949 Smith Act trial of the Communist party's top leaders reveal something of the bizarre nature of the proceedings. The language of the act, with its prohibition against "teaching and advocating" the overthrow of the government of the United States by "force and violence," compelled the prosecution to focus on the party's literature and educational ventures. Because there was no evidence that the defendants had ever personally advocated revolutionary violence, the government claimed that by subscribing to the doctrines of Marxism-Leninism they were actually calling for the overthrow of the American government. The prosecutors introduced the most violent passages from the writings of Marx, Lenin, and Stalin and brought in FBI informers and ex-Communists to attest to the party's adherence to the offending texts.

The following selections include part of the opening statement by the chief prosecutor, John F. X. McGohey, which outlines the government's case. Note how similar some of his formulations are to those of J. Edgar Hoover in Document 4. Likewise, the excerpts from the opening statement by General Secretary Eugene Dennis recall the rhetoric of William Z. Foster in Document 2.

These selections also contain testimony from the government's most important witness, Louis Budenz, the former managing editor of the *Daily Worker.* Budenz's key contribution was to discount the party's advocacy of peaceful change by explaining that it concealed the party's

Trial testimony in Joint Appendix, *United States of America v. Eugene Dennis et al.,* United States Court of Appeals for the Second Circuit, pp. 3208–09, 3222–23, 3226–29, 3233–34, 3238–40, 3245–48, 3250, 3468–69, 3637–39, 3646, 3656, 3658, 3707, 3729.

support for revolutionary violence by using "Aesopian language" to disguise its real intentions.[1] Finally, these excerpts offer a few examples of the interplay between the defense attorneys and Judge Harold Medina that reveal the contentiousness of the proceedings.

[1]Given the centrality of the concept of "Aesopian language" to the government's case, it is of interest that during the years that the FBI was collecting the evidence on which the government eventually based the prosecution, it could find no evidence that the party was using the term. Many of its undercover agents claimed never even to have heard the phrase.

JOHN F. X. McGOHEY

Opening Statement on Behalf of the Government

March 21, 1949

The charge of conspiracy is set forth in the first paragraph of the indictment, which his Honor has just read to you.

The remaining nine paragraphs of the indictment set forth the details of the indictment. Briefly, these paragraphs charge that these defendants brought about meetings in New York City in June and July of 1945 of the National Committee and the National Board and the National Convention of the Communist Political Association, in order to dissolve that Association and to organize in its stead the Communist Party of the United States of America. They charged that it was a part of the conspiracy that these defendants would assume leadership of the Communist Party of the United States of America; it is further charged that the defendants would organize clubs, district and state units of their party; that they would recruit new members of their party; and that they, the defendants, would publish books, magazines, and newspapers; that they would organize schools and classes, in all of which it was planned that there would be taught and advocated the Marxist-Leninist principles of the duty and necessity of overthrowing and destroying the Government of the United States by force and violence.

Now, that is what we charge. To support that charge we propose to prove by witnesses on that stand, and documents which they will introduce, just what these defendants did, what these defendants said, and what these defendants caused others under their supervision and control to do, and to say what the defendants actually did at that Convention in July 1945, according to their own statements, was to reconstitute the Communist Party of the United States of America; to educate the working class in the course of its day-to-day struggles, for its historic mission, the establishment of Socialism. They based the party upon the principles of Marxism-Leninism. . . .

I ask you ladies and gentlemen to remember that phrase Marxism-Leninism. You will hear it frequently throughout this trial. We propose, we say, that we will establish that it is fundamental in the principles of Marxism-Leninism:

(1) That Socialism cannot be established by peaceful evolution but, on the contrary can be established only by violent revolution; by smashing the machinery of government, and setting up in its stead a dictatorship—a dictatorship of the proletariat.

(2) That this smashing of the machinery of government and setting up of the dictatorship of the proletariat can be accomplished only by the violent and forceful seizure of power by the proletariat under the leadership of the Communist Party.

[McGohey describes the party's schools.]

The revolutionary doctrines of Marx, Lenin, and Stalin are constantly repeated in the lectures and in the discussions, and the thinking of both the teachers and the students is constantly checked against these revolutionary writers. In each of these schools it is reiterated constantly that the students are being trained as professional revolutionaries. Marxism, they are taught, is not merely dogma, it is a guide to action. . . . At the proper time, they are taught—the proper time being a time of national crisis, unrest, disorder brought about by a severe depression or war—at such a time the Party members will be in positions of influence in the key trades in the basic industries, and when the National Board decides that the revolutionary situation is at hand, the Party will lead the proletariat in violent revolution. They teach that this revolution cannot be without violence, for to be successful the entire apparatus of the Government must be smashed. Every vestige of the bourgeois state and class must be wiped out. Only when this has been accomplished can the program of Marxian Socialism be successfully carried out.

Now there are sections in the constitution of the Communist party which was adopted at its convention in July 1945 that purport to urge support of American democracy. These are in that document for legal purposes only, as we will show from witnesses on this stand. We will show that such declarations as I have referred to are mere talk; that they are just empty phrases, that they are inconsistent with the Marxist-Leninist doctrine of the overthrow of the Government by force and violence.

EUGENE DENNIS

Opening Statement on Behalf of the Communist Party

March 21, 1949

In view of the opening statement of the prosecution the defense is obliged to make sure that the jury fully understands just what the indictment charges and what it does not charge. The foreboding-sounding words "overthrow and destruction of the Government of the United States by force and violence" appear five times in the ten paragraphs of the indictment. But I call to your attention that not one of . . . these ten paragraphs charges that we Communist leaders at any time committed a single act, a single overt act of force and violence against the Government of the United States, or that we ever directly or indirectly advocated or attempted its forcible overthrow.

The alleged conspiracy as stated in the indictment limps only on three active verbs—to organize the Communist Party, to teach, and to advocate.

Since no overt criminal act is even alleged there is no X to mark the spot where it was not committed. . . .

The allegation of crime rests on the charge that we Communist leaders used our inalienable American rights of free speech, press, and association, and sought to advance certain general political doctrines which the indictment falsely says teach and advocate the duty and necessity to overthrow the Government of the United States by force and violence. . . .

We 11 defendants will prove that the very time when we allegedly began this menacing conspiracy we were in fact advocating and organizing all-out support to the Government of the United States. . . .

We will prove that all of us . . . taught the duty of upholding the United States Government and of intensifying the anti-Axis war effort . . . and we defendants will put in evidence the honorable war record of the 15,000 American Communists who, in accord with what we taught and advocated, served with the armed forces in the military defense of our country. . . .

We Communist leaders will show that in June and July of 1945 we thought that labor and the people could not rely on the Truman Administration to curb the greedy monopolists. We taught that, on the contrary, the people would have to resist the efforts of the administration and the bipartisan Congress, to scuttle FDR's progressive policies. We will also prove that we did not even consider, let alone teach or advocate, that the Government, headed by President Truman, should therefore be overthrown by force and violence. We will establish that everything we did teach and advocate was in the interests of the American people and in accord with their understanding of achieving a Government of, by, and for the people. . . .

. . . My co-defendants and I will show that we put into practice the real principles of Marxism-Leninism, by teaching that labor and the people should intervene to defend their living standards, their democratic rights, and world peace. . . .

. . . We will show with what peaceful intent we taught and advocated, amongst other things, . . . to oppose American support to the unjust and criminal war against the Chinese people waged by the miserable Chiang Kai-shek, to oppose the civil war against the Greeks, waged by the monarchist-fascist puppet of the American trusts, with the American people footing the bill, to oppose the Anglo-American oil lords against the new State of Israel, and the people of Indonesia, and to oppose the restoration of the German and Japanese monopolies and war potential under the new management of the American cartelists. . . .

. . . I and my co-defendants will show, we will show that we publicly advocated that all peace-loving Americans should unite [and] that the Truman Administration enter into direct negotiations with the U.S.S.R. and respond in good faith to its repeated disarmament and other peace proposals. . . .

And to establish further the record of what we defendants actually have done in the period covered by the indictment, we Communist leaders will show that we have advocated defense of the people's living standards as an inseparable part of the struggle for democracy and peace. . . .

[Dennis then describes Marxism-Leninism as an evolving doctrine that will enable people to "make a better and happier life for themselves."]

... The defense will squarely meet and disprove the prosecution's charge that the principles of scientific socialism teach or imply the duty or the necessity to overthrow the United States Government by force and violence. ...

When the defense puts our Communist Party constitution in evidence, the jury will see that it speaks of the duty to organize and educate the working class, and declares that Socialism should be established, not by force and violence, but "by the free choice of the majority of the American people."

We defendants will prove that we have always taught that capitalism in America or elsewhere cannot be abolished by plots, or conspiracies, or adventures, or by power revolutions. We will put in evidence our teaching that this fundamental change can be brought about only when both of two conditions have been fulfilled, when capitalism has fully outlived its social usefulness and when a majority of the American people—I repeat, a majority—led by labor and the Communists resolve to get rid of a system of social production that has become destructive of their right to life, liberty and the pursuit of happiness. ...

I have already indicated how we American Marxists will prove that we teach that Socialism is not an immediate issue in the United States today, but that the central issues, the central immediate issues confronting our people are peace or war, democracy or fascism. ...

You will see that our Communist Party Constitution acknowledges not only that we learn from Marx and Lenin but that we owe much to and learn from the teachings of men like Thomas Jefferson, Abraham Lincoln, Frederick Douglass, William Sylvis, and Eugene V. Debs.[2] ...

... The prosecution asks this jury for what amounts to a preventative conviction, in order that we Communist leaders may be put under what the Nazis called protective custody. I ask the jury to weigh the prosecution's case against the proof we defendants will offer to establish that we have taught and advocated the duty and necessity to prevent the force and violence of Fascism, imperialists of war and

---

[2] Frederick Douglass was a former slave who was active in the abolitionist movement before the Civil War. William Sylvis was an important American labor leader in the years after the Civil War. Eugene V. Debs was the leading figure in the American Socialist party in the early twentieth century.

lynching and anti-Semitism. I ask you to weigh carefully our sincere offer of proof which demonstrates that we Communists are second to none in our devotion to our people and to our country, and that we teach and advocate and practice a program of peace, of democracy, equality, economic security, and social progress.

LOUIS BUDENZ

Testimony

March 1949

March 24, 1949

McGohey: Mr. Budenz, I show you Government's Exhibit 6 for identification and ask you if that is a copy identical to the copy of the book bearing the same name *Foundations of Leninism* [by Stalin] which you testified yesterday was given to you by Mr. Stachel,[3] the defendant, at or about the time you joined the Communist Party in the fall of 1935?

Budenz: Yes, sir, that is the same edition. . . .

McGohey: And you used this book, did you, in your work as editor of the paper?

Budenz: Yes, sir, constantly. . . .

Crockett:[4] If the Court please, I observe that this book is copyrighted in 1932. I object to its admission in evidence on the ground that the contents in no wise support the charge in the indictment that my client between the period 1945 and 1948 conspired to advocate the overthrow of the United States Government by force and violence.

I object secondly because the use of this document under the circumstances indicated by this is protected so far as my client is concerned by the First Amendment of the United States. . . .

The Court: Objection overruled.

---

[3]Jack Stachel was one of the party's most important policymakers, active in its labor and educational work.

[4]George Crockett, a young African American lawyer from Detroit, was one of the defense attorneys. He later became a judge and served as a member of the House of Representatives from 1980 to 1989.

Gladstein:[5] If your Honor, please, I object on behalf of my clients to the offer in evidence of this book.

...I recognize the book as one somebody once gave me but I won't mention the name of the person who did it because he might get indicted.

The Court: Strike that out. I don't want any more of that impertinence....

March 29, 1949

McGohey: Mr. Budenz, I will read that sentence to you again, "The Communist Party of the United States is the political party of the American working class basing itself upon the principles of scientific socialism, Marxism-Leninism." What did you, in connection with these other Communists that you were working with there, understand that to mean?...

Budenz: This sentence, as is historically meant throughout the Communist movement, is that the Communist Party bases itself upon so-called scientific socialism, the theory and practice of so-called scientific socialism as appears in the writings of Marx, Engels, Lenin, and Stalin, therefore as interpreted by Lenin and Stalin who have specifically interpreted scientific socialism to mean that socialism can only be attained by the violent shattering of the capitalist state, and the setting up of a dictatorship of the proletariat by force and violence in place of that state. In the United States this would mean that the Communist Party of the United States is basically committed to the overthrow of the Government of the United States as set up by the Constitution of the United States....

McGohey: Now, Mr. Budenz, I hand you Government's Exhibit 26, it being the constitution of the Communist Party of the United States ... and again directing your attention to the first sentence of the preamble I call your attention to the fact that it says that "The Communist Party of the United States is the political party of the American working class basing itself upon"—does that language "basing itself upon the principles of scientific socialism, Marxism-Leninism" have any particular meaning with respect to other language which may appear and does appear throughout the constitution?...

---

[5]Richard Gladstein, another defense attorney, was a left-wing labor lawyer from San Francisco.

Budenz: Yes, sir, it implies that those portions of this constitution which are in conflict with Marxism-Leninism are null in effect. They are merely window dressing asserted for protective purposes, the Aesopian language of V. I. Lenin.

McGohey: The what language?

Budenz: The Aesopian language of V. I. Lenin.

McGohey: Will you spell it?

Budenz: A-e-s-o-p-i-a-n. The Aesopian language of V. I. Lenin, that is referred to by V. I. Lenin as Aesopian language; that is, roundabout, protective language based on the well known writer of fables, Aesop. . . .

[McGohey then produces a copy of Lenin's Imperialism: the Highest Stage of Capitalism *and reads a passage from its preface in which Lenin talks about how he had to avoid tsarist censorship and make political observations "with extreme caution by hints in that Aesopian language — in that cursed Aesopian language to which Czarism compelled all revolutionaries to have recourse whenever they took up their pens to write a 'legal' work."]*

McGohey: That first sentence of that sixth paragraph of the Preamble [of the party constitution] reads, does it not, "The Communist Party therefore educates the working class in the course of its day to day struggles for its historic mission, the establishment of Socialism."

Now, can you tell us, Mr. Budenz, what was meant and understood by you and those associated with you, including these defendants, at the time that this Constitution was adopted at the Convention in July 1945? . . .

Budenz: This sentence is well known in Communist circles. It has been stated by Lenin and Stalin, the historical mission of the working class is the establishment of socialism by the violent shattering of the capitalist state, its military and judicial arms. Lenin and Stalin have stated that, and it is well known to be the statements of Lenin and Stalin in the Communist circles. Socialism can only be established through this violent shattering and the setting up of the dictatorship of the proletariat as defined by Lenin and Stalin. . . .

March 30, 1949

The Court: And so everybody will know what it is you are explaining I am going to read this section. This is what it says. And then you are going to tell us what it meant to you under all the circumstances and so on put in the question.

Section 2: "Adherence to and participation in any clique, group, circle, faction, or party which conspires or acts to subvert, undermine, weaken or overthrow any or all institutions of American democracy whereby the majority of the American people can maintain their right to determine their destinies in any degrees shall be punished by immediate expulsion."

Now what did that mean to you?

Budenz: In view of the dedication of the Party in the first sentence [of its constitution] to Marxism-Leninism and the definition that has been given to Marxism-Leninism this was purely Aesopian language for protective purposes to protect the Party in its activities before courts of law in America while it could continue the theory and practice of Marxism-Leninism.

[The government seeks to place a copy of The History of the Communist Party of the Soviet Union *in evidence.]*

Isserman:[6] We are putting a book on trial. . . .

The Court: If the contents of this book and these other pamphlets and documents of one kind or another, that were handed around, and people were told to study them and to teach other people what to do, and how they were to go around and do the things that have been testified to here. I can scarcely believe that it is trying a book. It is trying those persons who used the book and other means to allegedly commit a crime, and that is part of the paraphernalia of the crime.

---

[6]Abraham Isserman, another defense attorney long associated with the Communist party, was disbarred for his efforts in the case and was not able to practice law again until 1961.

11

Outlawing the Communist Party:
The Supreme Court Upholds the Smith Act

On June 4, 1951, the Supreme Court, by a 6–2 majority, affirmed the conviction of the leaders of the Communist party under the Smith Act. The decision, though no surprise, was enormously important. The justices were confronted with the main free-speech case of the cold war—and they knew it. As Justice Felix Frankfurter noted, the Court had dealt with "few questions of comparable import"; and he and his colleagues underlined the seriousness of the case by producing four separate concurring and dissenting opinions in addition to that of Chief Justice Fred Vinson for the majority.

The following selections from Vinson's majority opinion and Justice Hugo Black's dissent reveal the political character of the case. In these excerpts, as well as in the opinions that have not been included, the justices' assessment of the nature of the Communist threat determined the outcome of their deliberations. Most of the Court shared the currently standard view of the Communist party as a highly disciplined organization whose robotlike members "slavishly" followed all party directives and thus might threaten the nation by engaging in espionage or sabotage in the event of a major crisis. While noting that the party was not actually trying to overthrow the government, Frankfurter insisted that "it would be equally wrong to treat it as a seminar in political theory."

National security considerations predominated. The Korean War was raging and the majority of justices felt that the precariousness of the international situation justified the limitations on political freedom. Vinson noted "the context of world crisis after crisis"; Justice Robert Jackson explicitly referred to the 1948 coup in Czechoslovakia; and Frankfurter alluded to atomic spying as testified to by Igor Gouzenko and Klaus Fuchs. The dissenting justices were less fearful about the

---

Dennis et al. v. United States, 341 U.S. 494 (1951).

danger posed by, in William O. Douglas's words, "the best known, the most beset, and the least thriving of any fifth column in history" and more concerned about the First Amendment. As we see in an article by Douglas in Document 22, he feared that the anti-Communist furor might stifle free thought.

CHIEF JUSTICE FRED VINSON

Majority Opinion in Dennis et al. v. United States

June 4, 1951

In the first part of the opinion, Vinson summarizes the results of the trial and agrees with the finding of the lower court that the Communist party did want "to achieve a successful overthrow of the existing order by force and violence." He then tackles the constitutional issues raised by the Smith Act.

II

The obvious purpose of the statute is to protect existing Government, not from change by peaceable, lawful, and constitutional means, but from change by violence, revolution, and terrorism. That it is within the *power* of the Congress to protect the Government of the United States from armed rebellion is a proposition which requires little discussion. Whatever theoretical merit there may be to the argument that there is a "right" to rebellion against dictatorial governments is without force where the existing structure of the government provides for peaceful and orderly change. We reject any principle of governmental helplessness in the face of preparation for revolution, which principle, carried to its logical conclusion, must lead to anarchy. No one could conceive that it is not within the power of Congress to prohibit acts intended to overthrow the Government by force and violence. The question with which we are concerned here is not whether Congress has such *power,* but whether the *means* which it has employed conflict with the First and Fifth Amendments to the Constitution.

One of the bases for the contention that the means which Congress has employed are invalid takes the form of an attack on the face of the statute [the Smith Act] on the grounds that by its terms it prohibits academic discussion of the merits of Marxism-Leninism, that it stifles ideas and is contrary to all concepts of a free speech and a free press. . . .

The very language of the Smith Act negates the interpretation which petitioners would have us impose on that Act. It is directed at advocacy, not discussion. . . . Congress did not intend to eradicate the free discussion of political theories, to destroy the traditional rights of Americans to discuss and evaluate ideas without fear of governmental sanction. Rather Congress was concerned with the very kind of activity in which the evidence showed these petitioners engaged.

III

But although the statute is not directed at the hypothetical cases which petitioners have conjured, its application in this case has resulted in convictions for the teaching and advocacy of the overthrow of the Government by force and violence, which, even though coupled with the intent to accomplish that overthrow, contains an element of speech. For this reason, we must pay special heed to the demands of the First Amendment marking out the boundaries of speech. . . .

[The chief justice then discusses earlier Supreme Court decisions that deal with free speech.]

. . . Speech is not an absolute, above and beyond control by the legislature when its judgment, subject to review here, is that certain kinds of speech are so undesirable as to warrant criminal sanction. . . . To those who would paralyze our Government in the face of impending threat by encasing it in a semantic straitjacket we must reply that all concepts are relative.

In this case we are squarely presented with the application of the "clear and present danger" test, and must decide what that phrase imports. We first note that many of the cases in which this Court has reversed convictions by use of this or similar tests have been based on the fact that the interest which the State was attempting to protect was itself too insubstantial to warrant restriction of speech. . . .

. . . Overthrow of the Government by force and violence is certainly a substantial enough interest for the Government to limit speech.

Indeed, this is the ultimate value of any society, for if a society cannot protect its very structure from armed internal attack, it must follow that no subordinate value can be protected. If, then, this interest may be protected, the literal problem which is presented is what has been meant by the use of the phrase "clear and present danger" of the utterances bringing about the evil within the power of Congress to punish.

Obviously, the words cannot mean that before the Government may act, it must wait until the *putsch* is about to be executed, the plans have been laid and the signal is awaited. If Government is aware that a group aiming at its overthrow is attempting to indoctrinate its members and to commit them to a course whereby they will strike when the leaders feel the circumstances permit, action by the Government is required. The argument that there is no need for Government to concern itself, for Government is strong, it possesses ample powers to put down a rebellion, it may defeat the revolution with ease needs no answer. For that is not the question. Certainly an attempt to overthrow the Government by force, even though doomed from the outset because of inadequate numbers or power of the revolutionists, is a sufficient evil for Congress to prevent. The damage which such attempts create both physically and politically to a nation makes it impossible to measure the validity in terms of the probability of success, or the immediacy of a successful attempt. In the instant case the trial judge charged the jury that they could not convict unless they found that petitioners intended to overthrow the Government "as speedily as circumstances would permit." This does not mean, and could not properly mean, that they would not strike until there was certainty of success. What was meant was that the revolutionists would strike when they thought the time was ripe. We must therefore reject the contention that success or probability of success is the criterion.

The situation with which Justices Holmes and Brandeis were concerned in [their dissent in] *Gitlow* [a 1925 free-speech case] was a comparatively isolated event, bearing little relation in their minds to any substantial threat to the safety of the community. . . . They were not confronted with any situation comparable to the instant one—the development of an apparatus designed and dedicated to the overthrow of the Government, in the context of world crisis after crisis.

Chief Judge Learned Hand, writing for the majority below, interpreted the phrase as follows: "In each case [courts] must ask whether the gravity of the 'evil,' discounted by its improbability, justifies such invasion of free speech as is necessary to avoid the danger." . . . We adopt this statement of the rule. . . .

Likewise, we are in accord with the court below, which affirmed the trial court's finding that the requisite danger existed. The mere fact that from the period 1945 to 1948 petitioners' activities did not result in an attempt to overthrow the Government by force and violence is of course no answer to the fact that there was a group that was ready to make the attempt. The formation by petitioners of such a highly organized conspiracy, with rigidly disciplined members subject to call when the leaders, these petitioners, felt that the time had come for action, coupled with the inflammable nature of world conditions, similar uprisings in other countries, and the touch-and-go nature of our relations with countries with whom petitioners were in the very least ideologically attuned, convince us that their convictions were justified on this score. And this analysis disposes of the contention that a conspiracy to advocate, as distinguished from the advocacy itself, cannot be constitutionally restrained, because it comprises only the preparation. It is the existence of the conspiracy which creates the danger. . . . If the ingredients of the reaction are present, we cannot bind the Government to wait until the catalyst is added. . . .

JUSTICE HUGO BLACK

Dissenting Opinion in Dennis et al. v. United States

June 4, 1951

. . . At the outset I want to emphasize what the crime involved in this case is, and what it is not. These petitioners were not charged with an attempt to overthrow the Government. They were not charged with overt acts of any kind designed to overthrow the Government. They were not even charged with saying anything or writing anything designed to overthrow the Government. The charge was that they agreed to assemble and to talk and publish certain ideas at a later date: The indictment is that they conspired to organize the Communist Party and to use speech or newspapers and other publications in the future to teach and advocate the forcible overthrow of the Government. No matter how it is worded, this is a virulent form of prior censorship of speech and press, which I believe the First Amendment forbids. . . .

But let us assume, contrary to all constitutional ideas of fair criminal procedure, that petitioners although not indicted for the crime of actual advocacy, may be punished for it. Even on this radical assumption, the other opinions in this case show that the only way to affirm these convictions is to repudiate directly or indirectly the established "clear and present danger" rule. This the Court does in a way which greatly restricts the protections afforded by the First Amendment. The opinions for affirmance indicate that the chief reason for jettisoning the rule is the expressed fear that advocacy of Communist doctrine endangers the safety of the Republic. Undoubtedly, a governmental policy of unfettered communication of ideas does entail dangers. To the Founders of this Nation, however, the benefits derived from free expression were worth the risk. . . . I have always believed that the First Amendment is the keystone of our Government, that the freedoms it guarantees provide the best insurance against destruction of all freedom. . . .

So long as this Court exercises the power of judicial review of legislation, I cannot agree that the First Amendment permits us to sustain laws suppressing freedom of speech and press on the basis of Congress' or our own notions of mere "reasonableness." Such a doctrine waters down the First Amendment so that it amounts to little more than an admonition to Congress. The Amendment as so construed is not likely to protect any but those "safe" or orthodox views which rarely need its protection. . . .

Public opinion being what it now is, few will protest the conviction of these Communist petitioners. There is hope, however, that in calmer times, when present pressures, passions, and fears subside, this or some later Court will restore the First Amendment liberties to the high preferred place where they belong in a free society.

Right: With the help of the committee's counsel Robert Stripling, HUAC member Richard Nixon examines microfilms that ex-Communist witness Whittaker Chambers had hidden in a pumpkin on his Maryland farm. The melodramatically staged production of the "Pumpkin Papers" in early December 1948 bolstered Nixon's career, increased HUAC's power, and forced the Justice Department to indict Alger Hiss.
© Bettmann/Corbis.

Above: As the chief sponsor of the Internal Security Act of 1950 and chair of the Senate Judiciary Committee, Nevada Democrat Pat McCarran, shown here shortly before his death in 1954, was the Senate's most powerful anti-Communist. His conduct of the Senate Internal Security Subcommittee's investigation of the Roosevelt and Truman administrations' East Asia policies helped popularize the notion that Communists in the State Department had "lost" China.
© Hulton-Deutsch Collection/Corbis.

Left: At a Senate hearing in April 1950, Johns Hopkins University China expert Owen Lattimore denies Senator McCarthy's charges that he was Russia's top American agent. Two years later Lattimore became the main target of the McCarran Committee's investigation into America's China policy. He spent eleven grueling days on the witness stand and was later indicted for perjury.
© Bettmann/Corbis.

Right: The *Chicago Tribune,* like many of Joe McCarthy's defenders in the Midwest and elsewhere, admired his feistiness and saw him as a champion against the New Deal liberalism that they believed was destroying the country, as this cartoon shows.

Above: After the Supreme Court refused to hear their case, the ten Communist and ex-Communist screenwriters and directors who had refused to cooperate with HUAC in 1947 went to prison for contempt of Congress. Here, some of the Hollywood Ten and their families rally their supporters. Left to right, Edward Dmytryk (holding sign), Lester Cole, Alvah Bessie (with cap), Dalton Trumbo, Albert Maltz (behind child), Ring Lardner Jr., and Herbert Biberman (with glasses and bow tie). Later witnesses would learn from the legal problems of the Ten and would rely on the Fifth Amendment rather than the First Amendment to avoid a contempt citation for not answering the committee's questions.

Courtesy of the Southern California Library for Social Studies and Research.

ARE YOU OR HAVE YOU EVER BEEN A MEMBER OF THE COMMUNIST PARTY?

Left: On the other side of the political spectrum, McCarthyism was so devastating that it became common to exaggerate its threat and claim that anyone could be victimized by the witch-hunt.
© Fred Wright/UE News. Reprinted with the permission of the United Electrical, Radio and Machine Workers of America.

Below: Senator Joseph R. McCarthy gets advice from his counsel Roy Cohn during the televised hearings of the Senate's 1954 special investigation of McCarthy's attempt to obtain special favors from the army for one of his committee's staff members. McCarthy's crudeness and bluster did not play well on the new medium of television, and the Army-McCarthy hearings effectively ended Jolting Joe's career.
© Bettmann/Corbis.

12

A Liberal Opposes
Anti-Communist Legislation:
Truman Vetoes the Internal Security Act
of 1950

The Internal Security Act of 1950, also known as the McCarran Act, was the most important anti-Communist law passed during the cold war. Initially sponsored by HUAC's Richard Nixon and Karl Mundt, the proposed legislation had floated around Congress for several years until the patriotic fervor that accompanied the Korean War brought it to the fore. Truman disliked the measure but could do nothing to prevent its passage once it came under the sponsorship of Pat McCarran, the powerful chair of the Senate Judiciary Committee.

Truman's opposition had little effect. The Democrat-controlled House overrode his veto by a 248–48 margin, the Senate by a 57–10 vote. The veto message, ineffective though it was, does reflect the position that many liberals had adopted by the early 1950s. While not relenting in their hostility to communism, they had developed qualms about what they came to see as the excesses of McCarthyism and its devastating impact on freedom of speech. Truman echoed these concerns. He also questioned the effectiveness of a repressive and probably unconstitutional measure like the McCarran Act and, in an argument that liberals had invoked to oppose the activities of Senator McCarthy, pointed out that the legislation would actually hamper the anti-Communist cause and embarrass the United States overseas.

Internal Security Act, 1950, Veto Message from the President of the United States, 22 Sept. 1950, in *Congressional Record,* 81st Cong., 2nd sess., 15629–32.

HARRY S. TRUMAN

Veto of the Internal Security Act of 1950

September 22, 1950

To the House of Representatives:

I return herewith, without my approval, H.R. 9490, the proposed "Internal Security Act of 1950.". . .

H.R. 9490 would not hurt the Communists. Instead, it would help them. . . .

It would actually weaken our existing internal security measures and would seriously hamper the Federal Bureau of Investigation and our other security agencies.

It would help the Communists in their efforts to create dissension and confusion within our borders.

It would help the Communist propagandists throughout the world who are trying to undermine freedom by discrediting as hypocrisy the efforts of the United States on behalf of freedom. . . .

. . . Fortunately, we already have on the books strong laws which give us most of the protection we need from the real dangers of treason, espionage, sabotage, and actions looking to the overthrow of our Government by force and violence. Most of the provisions of this bill have no relation to these real dangers. . . .

The idea of requiring Communist organizations to divulge information about themselves is a simple and attractive one. But it is about as practical as requiring thieves to register with the sheriff. Obviously, no such organization as the Communist Party is likely to register voluntarily.

Under the provisions of the bill, if an organization which the Attorney General believes should register does not do so, he must request a five-man Subversive Activities Control Board to order the organization to register. The Attorney General would have to produce proof that the organization in question was in fact a Communist-action or a Communist-front organization. To do this he would have to offer evidence relating to every aspect of the organization's activities. The organization could present opposing evidence. Prolonged hearings would be required to allow both sides to present proof and to cross-examine opposing witnesses.

To estimate the duration of such a proceeding involving the Communist Party, we need only recall that on much narrower issues the trial of the eleven Communist leaders under the Smith Act consumed nine months. In a hearing under this bill, the difficulties of proof would be much greater and would take a much longer time. . . .

. . . Under this bill, the Attorney General would have to attempt the difficult task of producing concrete legal evidence that men have particular ideas or opinions. This would inevitably require the disclosure of many of the FBI's confidential sources of information and thus would damage our national security.

If, eventually, the Attorney General should overcome these difficulties and get a favorable decision from the Board, the Board's decision could be appealed to the courts. . . .

All these proceedings would require great effort and much time. It is almost certain that from two to four years would elapse between the Attorney General's decision to go before the Board with a case, and the final disposition of the matter by the courts.[1]

And when all this time and effort had been spent, it is still most likely that no organization would actually register.

The simple fact is that when the courts at long last found that a particular organization was required to register, all the leaders of the organization would have to do to frustrate the law would be to dissolve the organization and establish a new one with a different name and a new roster of nominal officers. . . .

Unfortunately, these provisions are not merely ineffective and unworkable. They represent a clear and present danger to our institutions.

Insofar as the bill would require registration by the Communist Party itself, it does not endanger our traditional liberties. However, the application of the registration requirements to so-called Communist-front organizations can be the greatest danger to freedom of speech, press, and assembly, since the Alien and Sedition Laws of 1798. This danger arises out of the criteria or standards to be applied in determining whether an organization is a Communist-front organization.

There would be no serious problem if the bill required proof that an organization was controlled and financed by the Communist Party. . . . However, recognizing the difficulty of proving those matters, the bill would permit such a determination to be based solely upon the extent to which the positions taken or advanced by it from time to time on matters of policy do not deviate from those of the Communist movement.

---

[1]Truman seriously underestimated the time it took; the process of trying to register the Communist party under the Internal Security Act took fifteen years.

This provision could easily be used to classify as a Communist-front organization any organization which is advocating a single policy or objective which is also being urged by the Communist Party. . . . Thus, an organization which advocates low-cost housing for sincere humanitarian reasons might be classified as a Communist-front organization because the Communists regularly exploit slum conditions as one of their fifth-column techniques.

It is not enough to say that this probably would not be done. The mere fact that it could be done shows clearly how the bill would open a Pandora's box of opportunities for official condemnation of organizations and individuals for perfectly honest opinions which happen to be stated also by Communists.

The basic error of these sections is that they move in the direction of suppressing opinion and belief. This would be a very dangerous course to take, not because we have any sympathy for Communist opinions, but because any governmental stifling of the free expression of opinion is a long step toward totalitarianism. . . .

We can and we will prevent espionage, sabotage, or other actions endangering our national security. But we would betray our finest traditions if we attempted, as this bill would attempt, to curb the simple expression of opinion. This we should never do, no matter how distasteful the opinion may be to the vast majority of our people. The course proposed by this bill would delight the Communists, for it would make a mockery of the Bill of Rights and of our claims to stand for freedom in the world.

And what kind of effect would these provisions have on the normal expression of political views? Obviously, if this law were on the statute books, the part of prudence would be to avoid saying anything that might be construed by someone as not deviating sufficiently from the current Communist propaganda line. And since no one could be sure in advance what views were safe to express, the inevitable tendency would be to express no views on controversial subjects.

The result could only be to reduce the vigor and strength of our political life—an outcome that the Communists would happily welcome, but that free men should abhor. . . .

This is a time when we must marshall all our resources and all the moral strength of our free system in self-defense against the threat of Communist aggression. We will fail in this, and we will destroy all that we seek to preserve, if we sacrifice the liberties of our citizens in a misguided attempt to achieve national security.

13

Purging the Labor Movement:
The CIO Expels Its Left-Wing Unions

Probably no single event dramatized as conclusively the decline of the Communist movement from its pre–cold war position within American society as the expulsion of the left-wing unions from the Congress of Industrial Organizations (CIO) in the fall of 1949. The following document is from the resolution expelling the largest of these unions, the United Electrical, Radio, and Machine Workers of America (UE). As the language of the resolution indicates, the CIO leadership justified the expulsions on the grounds that the unions were under Communist control and were thus by definition undemocratic puppets of the Soviet Union. The leadership did not cite any economic or labor-related reasons for ejecting the UE. The main charges revolved around the UE leaders' opposition to the Truman administration's foreign policy and their support for Henry Wallace's Progressive party in the 1948 presidential election.

Because the UE had stopped paying its per capita dues as a protest against the CIO's refusal to stop other unions from raiding its locals, the CIO convention summarily expelled it and chartered a new union to represent workers in the electrical industry. The convention delegates also voted to bring charges against ten other unions for being under Communist control. After hearings before a trial committee in the spring of 1950, nine were expelled.[1] Again, as with the UE, the CIO claimed that

---

[1]The other nine expelled unions were the American Communications Association; Food, Tobacco, Agricultural, and Allied Workers; International Fishermen and Allied

Resolution on Expulsion of the UERMWA and Withdrawal of Certificate of Affiliation, Report to the 11th Constitutional Convention of the Congress of Industrial Organizations by the Committee on Resolutions [November 1949], copy in the Walter P. Reuther papers, UAW President's Office, box 62, folder 15, Archives of Labor History and Urban Affairs, Wayne State University, Detroit, Michigan.

the unions' positions on such foreign-policy issues as the Marshall Plan and NATO proved that they were under Communist control and were thus unfit for affiliation with the mainstream of American labor.

Workers of America; International Fur and Leather Workers Union; International Long-shoremen's and Warehousemen's Union; International Union of Mine, Mill, and Smelter Workers; National Union of Marine Cooks and Stewards; United Office and Professional Workers of America; and United Public Workers.

Resolution on Expulsion of the United Electrical, Radio, and Machine Workers of America
November 1949

We can no longer tolerate within the family of CIO the Communist Party masquerading as a labor union. The time has come when the CIO must strip the mask from these false leaders whose only purpose is to deceive and betray the workers. So long as the agents of the Communist Party in the labor movement enjoy the benefits of affiliation with the CIO, they will continue to carry on this betrayal under the protection of the good name of the CIO.

The false cry of these mis-leaders of labor for unity and autonomy does not deceive us.

In the name of unity they seek domination.

In the name of autonomy they seek to justify their blind and slavish willingness to act as puppets for the Soviet dictatorship and its foreign policy with all its twists and turns from the Nazi-Soviet Pact to the abuse of the veto in the UN, the Cominform[2] attack upon the Marshall Plan, ECA,[3] the Atlantic Treaty,[4] and arms aid to free nations.

Now that they are at the end of the trail, these Communist agents cry out against "raiding and secession." What they call raiding and secession is simply a movement of workers throwing off their yoke of

---

[2]The Cominform was the Soviet-led international Communist organization set up in 1947.

[3]The Economic Cooperation Administration (ECA) was the multinational organization that administered the Marshall Plan.

[4]The Atlantic Treaty established the North Atlantic Treaty Organization (NATO) in 1949.

domination. These workers seek refuge from a gang of men who are without principle other than a debased loyalty to a foreign power. . . .

The certification of affiliation of the CIO is a symbol of trust, democracy, brotherhood, and loyalty in the never-ending struggle of working men and women for a better life. There is no place in the CIO for any organization whose leaders pervert its certificate of affiliation into an instrument that would betray the American workers into totalitarian bondage.

By the actions of its leadership, by their disloyalty to the CIO, and their dedication to the purposes and program of the Communist Party, contrary to the overwhelming sentiment of the rank and file membership who are loyal Americans and loyal CIO members, the leadership of the United Electrical, Radio, and Machine Workers of America have rendered their union unworthy of and unqualified for this certificate of affiliation.

The UERMWA has been selected by the Communist Party as its labor base from which it can operate to betray the economic, political, and social welfare of the CIO, its affiliates, and the general membership. The program of the UERMWA that has gradually unfolded is but an echo of the Cominform. At the signal of the Cominform, the Communist Party threw off its mask and assumed its true role as a fifth column. Its agents in the labor unions followed the Communist Party line. The UERMWA leadership abandoned any pretense of loyalty to the CIO and its program. The record is clear that wherever the needs of the Communist Party in the Soviet Union dictated, the leadership of the UERMWA was always willing to sacrifice the needs of the workers. The evidence, known to every CIO member, is overwhelming:

1. The CIO along with the American people support the Marshall Plan as a humane policy of physical and human rehabilitation and reconstruction to stop the spread of totalitarianism and strengthen the forces of democracy.

The Soviet Union, the Communist Party, and their highly placed agents in the UERMWA unite in denouncing the Marshall Plan and vilify the CIO and the American people for their humanity.

2. The CIO along with the American people support the Atlantic Pact to prevent any further expansion of the Soviet Union's rule by force and terror.

The Soviet Union, the Communist Party, and the UERMWA leadership attack the Atlantic Pact as warmongering but are eloquently silent about the fact that the Soviet Union has the largest standing army in the world.

3. In the field of political action, the UERMWA leadership, crying aloud for unity and autonomy, joined with Wall Street and other forces of reaction in a desperate attempt to defeat liberalism and democracy in the United States. Against the desire and interests of the American labor movement, the UERMWA leadership joined with the Communist Party in creating the misnamed Progressive Party. In unity with Wall Street they did their utmost to divide the labor and liberal forces in an attempt to elect a reactionary national administration that could ride roughshod over the needs of the American people.

4. In their official organ, the *UE News,* on May 16, 1949, they maliciously charged that the CIO's hard fight to repeal the Taft-Hartley Act[5] was a sell-out. . . .

5. In cynical and outright defiance of the CIO, the UERMWA leadership secretly arranged a merger with the United Farm Equipment and Metal Workers of America [FE]. . . . This merger of FE and UERMWA was the first step in the long-range plans of the Communist Party to establish a Communist-dominated labor federation in America. . . .

We believe that the workers in the electrical and allied industries want and need a union devoted to the principles of the CIO and of our democratic society. Their desire for such a union has been frustrated by the manipulations of the group that has maneuvered the UERMWA into opposition to the CIO on orders of the Communist Party.

NOW THEREFORE BE IT RESOLVED THAT:

1. This Convention finds that the Certificate of Affiliation heretofore granted to the United Electrical, Radio, and Machine Workers of America has fallen into the control of a group devoted primarily to the principles of the Communist Party and opposed to the constitution and democratic objects of the CIO, . . . and, in conformance with the provisions of Article III, Section 6 of our Constitution, this convention hereby expels the United Electrical, Radio, and Machine Workers of America from the Congress of Industrial Organizations and withdraws the said Certificate of Affiliation.

2. This Convention recognizes that the overwhelming majority of the membership of the United Electrical, Radio, and Machine Workers

---

[5]The Taft-Hartley Act, passed in 1947 over President Truman's veto, revised the 1935 Wagner Act to eliminate what its critics felt was the legislation's pro-labor bias. Section 9(h) of the measure required all trade union officials to sign an anti-Communist affidavit.

of America are not members of the Communist Party, and further recognizes the desire of the working men and women in the electrical and allied industries for a free and autonomous union affiliated with the CIO. . . .

3. This Convention hereby authorizes and directs the Executive Board immediately to issue a Certificate of Affiliation to a suitable organization covering electrical and allied workers which will genuinely represent the desires and interests of the men and women in those industries. . . .

We salute the rank and file members of the UERMWA as the way is opened for them to walk out of the shadows of Communist conspiracy, double-talk, division, and betrayal, into the sunlight of democracy to be enjoyed in the CIO and cherished and made equally available to all men and women who prize freedom, honesty, and loyalty to their ideals and their union brothers and sisters.

In this cause and with this faith, we of the family of CIO shall defeat our open and our secret enemies; we shall grow stronger in numbers and in moral stature. Thereby the mission of the CIO, as stated at its founding, shall be realized in happy men and women, secure in their jobs, in their homes, and in their trust in one another.

14

The Dilemma of an Unfriendly Witness: Lillian Hellman Takes the Fifth Amendment

By 1952 when playwright Lillian Hellman received her subpoena from the House Un-American Activities Committee, it had become clear that people who relied on the Fifth Amendment to oppose HUAC's and other committees' activities or avoid naming names would not go to prison for contempt but would probably lose their jobs. Many of these witnesses would have been willing to talk about their own political activities if the committees had not forced them to talk about those of others, but the committees were eager to expose "Fifth Amendment Communists" and would not let their witnesses off the hook.

The following document, the letter Lillian Hellman sent to HUAC two days before her scheduled appearance, is an eloquent statement of the dilemma that faced unfriendly witnesses who, in Hellman's words, did not want "to bring bad trouble" to innocent people. The committee refused Hellman's request and she took the Fifth Amendment. For a fuller description of her ordeal, see *Scoundrel Time* (Boston: Little, Brown, 1976), Hellman's memoir about the blacklist period.

Lillian Hellman, testimony, House Committee on Un-American Activities, *Hearings Regarding Communist Infiltration of the Hollywood Motion-Picture Industry, Part VII*, 82nd Cong., 2nd sess., 21 May 1952.

LILLIAN HELLMAN

Letter to HUAC

May 19, 1952

Dear Mr. Wood:[1]

As you know, I am under subpoena to appear before your committee on May 21, 1952.

I am most willing to answer all questions about myself. I have nothing to hide from your committee and there is nothing in my life of which I am ashamed. I have been advised by counsel that under the fifth amendment I have a constitutional privilege to decline to answer any questions about my political opinions, activities, and associations, on the grounds of self-incrimination. I do not wish to claim this privilege. I am ready and willing to testify before the representatives of our Government as to my own opinions and my own actions, regardless of any risks or consequences to myself.

But I am advised by counsel that if I answer the committee's questions about myself, I must also answer questions about other people and that if I refuse to do so, I can be cited for contempt. My counsel tells me that if I answer questions about myself, I will have waived my rights under the fifth amendment and could be forced legally to answer questions about others. This is very difficult for a layman to understand. But there is one principle that I do understand: I am not willing, now or in the future, to bring bad trouble to people who, in my past association with them, were completely innocent of any talk or any action that was disloyal or subversive. I do not like subversion or disloyalty in any form and if I had ever seen any I would have considered it my duty to have reported it to the proper authorities. But to hurt innocent people whom I knew many years ago in order to save myself is, to me, inhuman and indecent and dishonorable. I cannot and will not cut my conscience to fit this year's fashions, even though I long ago came to the conclusion that I was not a political person and could have no comfortable place in any political group.

I was raised in an old-fashioned American tradition and there were certain homely things that were taught to me: To try to tell the truth, not to bear false witness, not to harm my neighbor, to be loyal to my country, and so on. In general, I respected these ideals of Christian

[1] Representative John Wood, chair of the House Un-American Activities Committee.

honor and did as well with them as I knew how. It is my belief that you will agree with these simple rules of human decency and will not expect me to violate the good American tradition from which they spring. I would, therefore, like to come before you and speak of myself.

I am prepared to waive the privilege against self-incrimination and to tell you everything you wish to know about my views or actions if your committee will agree to refrain from asking me to name other people. If the committee is unwilling to give me this assurance, I will be forced to plead the privilege of the fifth amendment at the hearing.

A reply to this letter would be appreciated.

Sincerely yours,

Lillian Hellman

15

"Are You Now . . . ?":
HUAC Investigates Hollywood

Although HUAC had been investigating communism since the beginning of 1946, it was not until the committee turned to Hollywood in the fall of 1947 that it gained national attention. In its examination of the Communist party's influence within the film industry, the committee subpoenaed a varied group of producers, actors, screenwriters, and directors. Most of the witnesses, like actors Ronald Reagan and Gary Cooper, were friendly. Uniformly deploring communism, they either sought to distance themselves from it or tried to convince the committee that communism had no impact on the films they had made.

Some of the witnesses were not so cooperative. Among them were the Hollywood Ten,[1] a group of screenwriters and directors who refused to answer the committee's questions about their political affiliations. All of them were or had been in the Communist party and many of them, like screenwriter John Howard Lawson, the unofficial dean of the Hollywood left, had been active in the Screen Writers Guild. Unlike later witnesses who relied on the Fifth Amendment's protection against self-incrimination to avoid answering HUAC's questions, the Ten argued with the committee, claiming that it was unconstitutionally violating their freedom of speech and association. They knew that they might be cited for contempt of Congress, but they assumed—and their attorneys did too—that the Supreme Court would eventually acquit them on First Amendment grounds. They

[1]The Ten were Alvah Bessie, Herbert Biberman, Lester Cole, Edward Dmytryk, Ring Lardner Jr., John Howard Lawson, Albert Maltz, Samuel Ornitz, Adrian Scott, and Dalton Trumbo.

John Howard Lawson and Ring Lardner Jr., testimony, House Committee on Un-American Activities, *Hearings Regarding Communist Infiltration of the Hollywood Motion-Picture Industry,* 80th Cong., 1st sess., 27, 28, 30 Oct. 1947.

were wrong. The Supreme Court refused to hear their case in 1950. Not only did they have to serve six-month prison terms for contempt, but, as Document 17 reveals, they were soon blacklisted by the movie studios.

The following selections from some of the Hollywood Ten hearings show how unruly the sessions were. While the committee's chair, J. Parnell Thomas, and its counsel, Robert Stripling, tried to force the unfriendly witnesses to respond to the "$64 Question"[2]—"Are you now or have you ever been a member of the Communist Party?"—the witnesses tried to make political statements. More than once, Thomas had the committee's sergeants at arms physically remove a recalcitrant witness from the stand. After each hostile witness finished testifying, one of the committee's investigators read evidence of his Communist affiliations into the record.

[2]The phrase "$64 Question" came from a popular radio quiz show by that name.

JOHN HOWARD LAWSON

Testimony before HUAC

October 27, 1947

Stripling: What is your occupation, Mr. Lawson?
Lawson: I am a writer.
Stripling: How long have you been a writer?
Lawson: All my life—at least thirty-five years—my adult life.
Stripling: Are you a member of the Screen Writers Guild?
Lawson: The raising of any question here in regard to membership, political beliefs, or affiliation—
Stripling: Mr. Chairman—
Lawson: Is absolutely beyond the powers of this committee.
Stripling: Mr. Chairman—
Lawson: But—

[The chairman pounding gavel.]

Lawson: It is a matter of public record that I am a member of the Screen Writers Guild.

Stripling: I ask—

[Applause.]

Chairman: I want to caution the people in the audience: You are the guests of this committee and you will have to maintain order at all times. I do not care for any applause or any demonstrations of one kind or another.

Stripling: Now, Mr. Chairman, I am also going to request that you instruct the witness to be responsive to the questions.

Chairman: I think the witness will be more responsive to the questions.

Lawson: Mr. Chairman, you permitted—

Chairman [pounding gavel]: Never mind—

Lawson [continuing]: Witnesses in this room to make answers of three or four or five hundred words to questions here.

Chairman: Mr. Lawson, you will please be responsive to these questions and not continue to try to disrupt these hearings.

Lawson: I am not on trial here, Mr. Chairman. This committee is on trial here before the American people. Let us get that straight. . . .

Stripling: Have you ever held any office in the guild?

Lawson: The question of whether I have held office is also a question which is beyond the purview of this committee.

[The chairman pounding gavel.]

Lawson: It is an invasion of the right of association under the Bill of Rights of this country.

Chairman: Please be responsive to the question. . . .

Lawson: I wish to frame my own answers to your questions, Mr. Chairman, and I intend to do so.

Chairman: And you will be responsive to the questions or you will be excused from the witness stand.

Stripling: I repeat the question, Mr. Lawson: Have you ever held any position in the Screen Writers Guild?

Lawson: I stated that it is outside the purview of the rights of this committee to inquire into any form of association—

Chairman: The Chair will determine what is in the purview of this committee.

Lawson: My rights as an American citizen are no less than the responsibilities of this committee of Congress.

Chairman: Now, you are just making a big scene for yourself and getting all "het up." [Laughter.]

Be responsive to the questioning, just the same as all the witnesses have. You are no different from the rest. . . .

Lawson: It is absolutely beyond the power of this committee to inquire into my association in any organization.

Chairman: Mr. Lawson, you will have to stop or you will leave the witness stand. And you will leave the witness stand because you are in contempt. That is why you will leave the witness stand. And if you are just trying to force me to put you in contempt, you won't have to try much harder. You know what has happened to a lot of people that have been in contempt of this committee this year, don't you?

Lawson: I am glad you have made it perfectly clear that you are going to threaten and intimidate the witnesses, Mr. Chairman.

[The chairman pounding gavel.]

Lawson: I am an American and I am not at all easy to intimidate, and don't think I am.

[The chairman pounding gavel.] . . .

Stripling: Mr. Lawson, are you now, or have you ever been a member of the Communist Party of the United States?

Lawson: In framing my answer to that question I must emphasize the points that I have raised before. The question of communism is in no way related to this inquiry, which is an attempt to get control of the screen and to invade the basic rights of American citizens in all fields.

McDowell: Now, I must object—

Stripling: Mr. Chairman—[The chairman pounding gavel.]

Lawson: The question here relates not only to the question of my membership in any political organization, but this committee is attempting to establish the right—

[The chairman pounding gavel.]

Lawson [continuing]: Which has been historically denied to any committee of this sort, to invade the rights and privileges and immunity of American citizens, whether they be Protestant, Methodist, Jewish, or Catholic, whether they be Republicans or Democrats or anything else.

Chairman [pounding gavel]: Mr. Lawson, just quiet down again.

Mr. Lawson, the most pertinent question that we can ask is whether or not you have ever been a member of the Communist Party. Now, do you care to answer that question?

Lawson: You are using the old technique, which was used in Hitler Germany in order to create a scare here—...

Stripling: Mr. Chairman, the witness is not answering the question. ...

Chairman [pounding gavel]: We are going to get the answer to that question if we have to stay here for a week.

Are you a member of the Communist Party, or have you ever been a member of the Communist Party? ...

Lawson: I am framing my answer in the only way in which any American citizen can frame his answer to a question which absolutely invades his rights.

Chairman: Then you refuse to answer that question; is that correct?

Lawson: I have told you that I will offer my beliefs, affiliations, and everything else to the American public, and they will know where I stand.

Chairman [pounding gavel]: Excuse the witness—

Lawson: As they do from what I have written.

Chairman [pounding gavel]: Stand away from the stand—

Lawson: I have written Americanism for many years, and I shall continue to fight for the Bill of Rights, which you are trying to destroy.

Chairman: Officers, take this man away from the stand—

[Applause and boos.]

Chairman [pounding gavel]: There will be no demonstrations. No demonstrations, for or against. Everyone will please be seated.

RING LARDNER JR.

Testimony before HUAC

October 30, 1947

Stripling: Mr. Lardner, are you a member of the Screen Writers Guild?

Lardner: Mr. Stripling, I want to be cooperative about this, but there are certain limits to my cooperation. I don't want to help you divide or smash this particular guild, or to infiltrate the motion-picture business in any way for the purpose which seems to me to be to try to control that business, to control what the American people can see and hear in their motion-picture theaters.

Chairman: Now, Mr. Lardner, don't do like the others, if I were you, or you will never read your statement. I would suggest—

Lardner: Mr. Chairman, let me—

Chairman: You will be responsive to the question. . . .

The question is: Are you a member of the Screen Writers Guild? . . .

[Lardner spars with Thomas about whether he will be able to read his prepared statement.]

Chairman: That is a very simple question. You can answer that "yes" or "no." You don't have to go into a long harangue or speech. If you want to make a speech you know where you can go out there.

Lardner: Well, I am not very good in haranguing, and I won't try it, but it seems to me that if you can make me answer this question, tomorrow you could ask somebody whether he believed in spiritualism.

Chairman: Oh, no; there is no chance of our asking anyone whether they believe in spiritualism, and you know it. That is just plain silly.

Lardner: You might—

Chairman: Now, you haven't learned your lines very well.

Lardner: Well—

Chairman: I want to know whether you can answer the question "yes" or "no."

Lardner: If you did, for instance, ask somebody about that you might ask him—

Chairman: Well, now, never mind what we might ask him. We are asking you now, Are you a member of the Screen Writers Guild?

Lardner: But—

Chairman: You are an American—

Lardner: But that is a question—

Chairman: And Americans should not be afraid to answer that.

Lardner: Yes; but I am also concerned as an American with the question of whether this committee has the right to ask me—

Chairman: Well, we have got the right and until you prove that we haven't got the right then you have to answer that question.

Lardner: As I said, if you ask somebody, say, about spiritualism—

Chairman: You are a witness, aren't you? Aren't you a witness?

Lardner: Mr. Chairman—

Chairman: Aren't you a witness here?

Lardner: Yes; I am.

Chairman: All right, then, a congressional committee is asking you: Are you a member of the Screen Writers Guild? Now you answer it "yes" or "no."

Lardner: Well, I am saying that in order to answer that—

Chairman: All right, put the next question. Go to the $64 question.

Lardner: I haven't—

Chairman: Go to the next question.

Stripling: Mr. Lardner, are you now or have you ever been a member of the Communist Party?

Lardner: Well, I would like to answer that question, too.

Stripling: Mr. Lardner, the charge has been made before this committee that the Screen Writers Guild which, according to the record, you are a member of, whether you admit it or not, has a number of individuals in it who are members of the Communist Party. This committee is seeking to determine the extent of Communist infiltration in the Screen Writers Guild and in other guilds within the motion-picture industry.

Lardner: Yes.

Stripling: And certainly the question of whether or not you are a member of the Communist Party is very pertinent. Now, are you a member or have you ever been a member of the Communist Party?

Lardner: It seems to me you are trying to discredit the Screen Writers Guild through me and the motion-picture industry through the Screen Writers Guild and our whole practice of freedom of expression.

Stripling: If you and others are members of the Communist Party you are the ones who are discrediting the Screen Writers Guild.

Lardner: I am trying to answer the question by stating first what I feel about the purpose of the question which, as I say, is to discredit the whole motion-picture industry.

Chairman: You won't say anything first. You are refusing to answer this question.

Lardner: I am saying my understanding is as an American resident—

Chairman: Never mind your understanding. There is a question: Are you or have you ever been a member of the Communist Party?

Lardner: I could answer exactly the way you want, Mr. Chairman—

Chairman: No—

Lardner [continuing]: But I think that is a—

Chairman: It is not a question of our wanting you to answer that. It is a very simple question. Anybody would be proud to answer it—any real American would be proud to answer the question, "Are you or have you ever been a member of the Communist Party?"—any real American.

Lardner: It depends on the circumstances. I could answer it, but if I did I would hate myself in the morning.

Chairman: Leave the witness chair.

Lardner: It was a question that would—

Chairman: Leave the witness chair.

Lardner: Because it is a question—

Chairman [pounding gavel]: Leave the witness chair.

Lardner: I think I am leaving by force.

Chairman: Sergeant, take the witness away.

[Applause.]

16

"I Have in My Hand . . .": Senator Joseph McCarthy Charges That There Are Communists in the State Department

This document contains the text of Senator Joseph McCarthy's famous speech to the Women's Republican Club of Wheeling, West Virginia, on February 9, 1950. In this version, which McCarthy inserted in the *Congressional Record* on February 20, 1950, he stated that he held in his hand the names of fifty-seven subversives in the State Department; at Wheeling the list reportedly contained 205 names. The significance of the speech, however, is not in its numbers but in the main thrust of its attack: the charge that Communist sympathizers in the State Department had betrayed their country. Like other right-wing Republicans, McCarthy spotlighted the supposed concessions made by the United States to the Soviet Union at the Yalta Conference in 1945 and the "loss" of China to the Communists. Although many of his specific targets were the State Department's China experts such as John Stewart Service, the diplomat who had been implicated in the 1945 *Amerasia* case, McCarthy's real quarry was the Truman administration. As his repeated references to Secretary of State Dean Acheson imply, the Wisconsin senator was accusing the administration of harboring Communist agents at the highest levels.

Such charges may well have been designed to explain to anxious Americans why the United States seemed unable to prevail in the international arena. McCarthy's rhetoric also had a populist strain. His attacks on "the bright young men who are born with silver spoons in their mouths" and "striped pants diplomats with phony British

Senator Joseph McCarthy, speech, *Congressional Record,* Senate, 81st Cong., 2nd sess., 20 Feb. 1950, 1954, 1956–57.

accents" seemed to resonate with the anti-elitist and anti-intellectual appeals of what liberals viewed as the "paranoid tradition" of American politics.

SENATOR JOSEPH McCARTHY

Speech at Wheeling, West Virginia
February 9, 1950

Six years ago, at the time of the first conference to map out the peace—Dumbarton Oaks[1]—there was within the Soviet orbit 180,000,000 people. Lined up on the antitotalitarian side there were in the world at that time roughly 1,625,000,000 people. Today, only six years later, there are 800,000,000 people under the absolute domination of Soviet Russia—an increase of over 400 percent. On our side, the figure has shrunk to around 500,000,000. In other words, in less than six years the odds have changed from nine to one in our favor to eight to five against us. This indicates the swiftness of the tempo of Communist victories and American defeats in the cold war. As one of our outstanding historical figures once said, "When a great democracy is destroyed, it will not be because of enemies from without, but rather because of enemies from within."

The truth of this statement is becoming terrifyingly clear as we see this country each day losing on every front.

At war's end we were physically the strongest nation on earth and, at least potentially, the most powerful intellectually and morally. Ours could have been the honor of being a beacon in the desert of destruction, a shining living proof that civilization was not yet ready to destroy itself. Unfortunately, we have failed miserably and tragically to arise to the opportunity.

The reason why we find ourselves in a position of impotency is not because our only powerful potential enemy has sent men to invade our shores, but rather because of the traitorous actions of those who have been treated so well by this Nation. It has not been the less for-

---

[1]Dumbarton Oaks, an estate in Washington, D.C., was the scene of a 1944 conference at which the United States, Great Britain, China, and the Soviet Union agreed to create the United Nations.

tunate or members of minority groups who have been selling this Nation out, but rather those who have had all the benefits that the wealthiest nation on earth has had to offer—the finest homes, the finest college education, and the finest jobs in Government we can give.

This is glaringly true in the State Department. There the bright young men who are born with silver spoons in their mouths are the ones who have been worst.

Now I know it is very easy for anyone to condemn a particular bureau or department in general terms. Therefore, I would like to cite one rather unusual case—the case of a man who has done much to shape our foreign policy.

When Chiang Kai-shek was fighting our war,[2] the State Department had in China a young man named John S. Service. His task, obviously, was not to work for the communization of China. Strangely, however, he sent official reports back to the State Department urging that we torpedo our ally Chiang Kai-shek and stating, in effect, that communism was the best hope of China.

Later, this man—John Service—was picked up by the Federal Bureau of Investigation for turning over to the Communists secret State Department information. Strangely, however, he was never prosecuted. However, Joseph Grew, the Under Secretary of State, who insisted on his prosecution, was forced to resign. Two days after Grew's successor, Dean Acheson, took over as Under Secretary of State, this man—John Service—who had been picked up by the FBI and who had previously urged that communism was the best hope of China, was not only reinstated in the State Department but promoted. And finally, under Acheson, placed in charge of all placements and promotions.

Today, ladies and gentlemen, this man Service is on his way to represent the State Department and Acheson in Calcutta—by far and away the most important listening post in the Far East. . . .

Another interesting case was that of Julian H. Wadleigh,[3] economist in the Trade Agreements Section of the State Department for 11 years [who] was sent to Turkey and Italy and other countries as United States representative. After the statute of limitations had run so he

---

[2]Chiang Kai-shek was the leader of the Chinese Nationalist government who was driven from power by the Communists under Mao Tse-tung in 1949.

[3]Julian Wadleigh was a former State Department official who confessed to having given documents to Whittaker Chambers.

could not be prosecuted for treason, he openly and brazenly not only admitted but proclaimed that he had been a member of the Communist Party, . . . that while working for the State Department he stole a vast number of secret documents . . . and furnished these documents to the Russian spy ring of which he was a part.

This, ladies and gentlemen, gives you somewhat of a picture of the type of individuals who have been helping to shape our foreign policy. In my opinion the State Department, which is one of the most important government departments, is thoroughly infested with Communists.

I have in my hand fifty-seven cases of individuals who would appear to be either card carrying members or certainly loyal to the Communist Party, but who nevertheless are still helping to shape our foreign policy.

One thing to remember in discussing the Communists in our Government is that we are not dealing with spies who get thirty pieces of silver to steal the blueprints of a new weapon. We are dealing with a far more sinister type of activity because it permits the enemy to guide and shape our policy. . . .

This brings us down to the case of one Alger Hiss who is important not as an individual any more, but rather because he is so representative of a group in the State Department. It is unnecessary to go over the sordid events showing how he sold out the Nation which had given him so much. Those are rather fresh in all of our minds.

However, it should be remembered that the facts in regard to his connection with this international Communist spy ring were made known to the then Under Secretary of State Berle three days after Hitler and Stalin signed the Russo-German alliance pact. . . .

Under Secretary Berle promptly contacted Dean Acheson and received word in return that Acheson (and I quote) "could vouch for Hiss absolutely"—at which time the matter was dropped. . . .

Again in 1943, the FBI had occasion to investigate the facts surrounding Hiss' contacts with the Russian spy ring. But even after that FBI report was submitted, nothing was done.

Then late in 1948—on August 5—when the Un-American Activities Committee called Alger Hiss to give an accounting, President Truman at once issued a Presidential directive ordering all Government agencies to refuse to turn over any information whatsoever in regard to the Communist activities of any Government employee to a congressional committee. . . .

If time permitted, it might be well to go into detail about the fact that Hiss was Roosevelt's chief adviser at Yalta when Roosevelt was admittedly in ill health and tired physically and mentally . . . and when, according to the Secretary of State, Hiss and Gromyko[4] drafted the report on the conference . . .

Of the results of this conference, Arthur Bliss Lane of the State Department had this to say: "As I glanced over the document, I could not believe my eyes. To me, almost every line spoke of a surrender to Stalin."

As you hear this story of high treason, I know that you are saying to yourself, "Well, why doesn't the Congress do something about it?" Actually, ladies and gentlemen, one of the important reasons for the graft, the corruption, the dishonesty, the disloyalty, the treason in high Government positions—one of the most important reasons why this continues is a lack of moral uprising on the part of the 140,000,000 American people. . . .

As you know, very recently the Secretary of State proclaimed his loyalty to a man guilty of what has always been considered as the most abominable of all crimes—of being a traitor to the people who gave him a position of great trust. The Secretary of State in attempting to justify his continued devotion to the man who sold out the Christian world to the atheistic world, referred to Christ's Sermon on the Mount as a justification and reason therefor, and the reaction of the American people to this would have made the heart of Abraham Lincoln happy.

When this pompous diplomat in striped pants, with a phony British accent, proclaimed to the American people that Christ on the Mount endorsed communism, high treason, and betrayal of a sacred trust, the blasphemy was so great that it awakened the dormant indignation of the American people.

He has lighted the spark which is resulting in a moral uprising and will end only when the whole sorry mess of twisted, warped thinkers are swept from the national scene so that we may have a new birth of national honesty and decency in Government.

---

[4]Andrei Gromyko was a Soviet diplomat and longtime foreign minister.

17
The Hollywood Blacklist Begins:
Studio Heads Fire the Hollywood Ten

The initial reaction to HUAC's October 1947 investigation of Communists in the film industry was mixed. The hearings, as Document 15 reveals, were tumultuous, and the press seemed equally hostile to both the committee and its unfriendly witnesses. The Hollywood studios' response was muted. Eric Johnston, president of the Motion Picture Association of America and the film industry's official spokesperson, pledged that Hollywood would cooperate with the investigation at the same time as he insisted that there would be no blacklist. Once it was clear that the Ten would be cited for contempt, however, the situation changed. Meeting in New York at the Waldorf-Astoria Hotel on November 24–25, 1947, the major producers decided to fire the unfriendly witnesses. The producers' statement, released publicly on December 3, announced a policy of refusing to hire Communists. The blacklist had begun.

The Waldorf Statement, 3 Dec. 1947, in Larry Ceplair and Steven Englund, *The Inquisition in Hollywood: Politics in the Film Community, 1930–1960* (Garden City, N.Y.: Anchor Press/Doubleday, 1980), 445.

The Waldorf Statement

December 3, 1947

Members of the Association of Motion Picture Producers deplore the action of the ten Hollywood men who have been cited for contempt. We do not desire to prejudge their legal rights, but their actions have been a disservice to their employers and have impaired their usefulness to the industry.

We will forthwith discharge or suspend without compensation those in our employ and we will not re-employ any of the ten until such time as he is acquitted or has purged himself of contempt and declares under oath that he is not a Communist.

On the broader issues of alleged subversive and disloyal elements in Hollywood, our members are likewise prepared to take positive action.

We will not knowingly employ a Communist or a member of any party or group which advocates the overthrow of the Government of the United States by force or by illegal or unconstitutional methods. In pursuing this policy, we are not going to be swayed by hysteria or intimidation from any source. We are frank to recognize that such a policy involves dangers and risks. There is the danger of hurting innocent people. There is the risk of creating an atmosphere of fear. Creative work at its best cannot be carried on in an atmosphere of fear. We will guard against this danger, this risk, this fear. To this end we will invite the Hollywood talent guilds to work with us to eliminate any subversives, to protect the innocent, and to safeguard free speech and a free screen wherever threatened.

18

The Blacklisters' Bible:
Red Channels

If there was an official blacklist in the entertainment industry, *Red Channels* was it. Issued on June 22, 1950, just three days before the outbreak of the Korean War, it was a compilation of the allegedly subversive affiliations of 151 writers, directors, and performers.[1] Its

[1]Those listed were Larry Adler, Luther Adler, Stella Adler, Edith Atwater, Howard Bay, Ralph Bell, Leonard Bernstein, Walter Bernstein, Michael Blankfort, Marc Blitzstein, True Boardman, Millen Brand, Oscar Brand, J. Edward Bromberg, Himan Brown, John Brown, Abe Burrows, Morris Carnovsky, Vera Caspary, Edward Chodorov, Jerome Chodorov, Mady Christians, Lee J. Cobb, Marc Connelly, Aaron Copeland, Norman Corwin, Howard Da Silva, Roger De Koven, Dean Dixon, Olin Downes, Alfred Drake, Paul Draper, Howard Duff, Clifford J. Durr, Richard Dyer-Bennett, José Ferrer, Louise Fitch, Martin Gabel, Arthur Gaeth, William S. Gailmor, John Garfield, Will Geer, Jack Gilford, Tom Glazer, Ruth Gordon, Lloyd Gough, Morton Gould, Shirley Graham, Ben Grauer, Mitchell Grayson, Horace Grenell, Uta Hagen, Dashiell Hammett, E. Y. ("Yip") Harburg, Robert P. Heller, Lillian Hellman, Nat Hiken, Rose Hobart, Judy Holliday, Roderick B. Holmgren, Lena Horne, Langston Hughes, Marsha Hunt, Leo Hurwitz, Charles Irving, Burl Ives, Sam Jaffe, Leon Janney, Joe Julian, Garson Kanin, George Keane, Donna Keath, Pert Kelton, Alexander Kendrick, Adelaide Klein, Felix Knight, Howard Koch, Tony Kraber, Millard Lampell, John La Touche, Arthur Laurents, Gypsy Rose Lee, Madeline Lee, Ray Lev, Philip Loeb, Ella Logan, Alan Lomax, Avon Long, Joseph Losey, Peter Lyon, Aline MacMahon, Paul Mann, Margo, Myron McCormick, Paul McGrath, Burgess Meredith, Ben Myers, Arthur Miller, Henry Morgan, Zero Mostel, Jean Muir, Meg Mundy, Lynn Murray, Dorothy Parker, Arnold Perl, Minerva Pious, Samson Raphaelson, Bernard Reis, Anne Revere, Kenneth Roberts, Earl Robinson, Edward G. Robinson, William N. Robson, Harold Rome, Norman Rosten, Selena Royle, Coby Ruskin, Robert St. John, Hazel Scott, Pete Seeger, Lisa Sergio, Artie Shaw, Irwin Shaw, Robert Lewis Shayon, Ann Shepherd, William L. Shirer, Allan Sloane, Howard K. Smith, Gale Sondergaard, Hester Sondergaard, Lionel Stander, Johannes Steel, Paul Stewart, Elliot Sullivan, William Sweets, Helen Tamiris, Betty Todd, Louis Untermeyer, Hilda Vaughn, J. Raymond Walsh, Sam Wanamaker, Theodore Ward, Fredi Washington, Margaret Webster, Orson Welles, Josh White, Irene Wicker, Betty Winkler, Martin Wolfson, Lesley Woods, Richard Yaffe.

Red Channels, American Business Consultants, New York, 22 June 1950, 16–17, 75–77, 79–80, 90, 110–13, 155–56.

authors—three former FBI agents and an aspiring television producer named Vincent Hartnett—drew their citations from a miscellaneous potpourri of left-wing letterheads, clippings from the Communist party's *Daily Worker,* and the publications of HUAC and other investigating committees.

Each individual entry contained from one to forty-one citations, annotated to indicate the source of the incriminating information. Some of the allegedly Communist groups cited in *Red Channels* were, like Consumers Union, the publisher of *Consumer Reports,* politically innocuous. Most, however, were the so-called front groups, organizations like those on the attorney general's list (see Document 9) that had close ties to the Communist party. Although party members belonged to these groups, so too did non-Communists. In addition, *Red Channels* treated the 1948 presidential campaign of Henry Wallace and the Progressive party as a questionable activity, as it also did any sign of public opposition to the anti-Communist purges.

Many of the individual entries were simply wrong—cases of mistaken identity or erroneous listings and false reports in the Communist press. Others ignored history and treated as suspect the willingness of many American entertainers to rally support for the Soviet Union as part of the U.S. war effort. Of the two citations that derailed actor Joe Julian's career, one was for an innocuous public appearance during World War II and the other for a meeting that he walked out of when he discovered its sponsors had Communist ties. Lena Horne, like many African American entertainers, got into *Red Channels* because of her support for left-wing civil rights groups.

The following selections are representative. They show the types of affiliations that *Red Channels'* compilers considered subversive as well as the sources of information they used. What they do not show is the damage the booklet inflicted. It temporarily (and sometimes permanently) ruined the careers of almost every entertainer whose name appeared in it. "Nobody has to tell me not to use anybody listed in *Red Channels,*" an account executive in an advertising agency explained at the time. "I just know not to."

Red Channels:
The Report of Communist Influence in Radio and Television
1950

Lillian Hellman

PLAYWRIGHT, AUTHOR

REPORTED AS:

Independent Citizens Committee of the Arts, Sciences, and Professions	Speaker, Theatre Panel, Conference of the Arts, Sciences, and Professions, 6/22, 23/45. *Daily Worker,* 6/10/45, p. 14.
Progressive Citizens of America, National Arts, Sciences, and Professions Council	Participant, Cultural Freedom Conference, 10/25, 26/47. *Daily Worker,* 10/27/47, p. 2.
National Council of American-Soviet Friendship	Signer. Women's Committee. Greetings to women of Soviet Union in celebration of International Women's Day. *Daily Worker,* 3/9/48, p. 5.
National Wallace for President Committee	Member. *Daily Worker,* 3/26/48, p. 7.
Harlem Women for Wallace	Speaker, 6/9/48; gave forceful tribute to Wallace. *Daily Worker,* 6/10/48, p. 6.
"New Party" (Wallace)	Member, Platform Committee, 7/23/48. *Daily Worker,* 7/19/48, p. 5.
Writers for Wallace	Member, Initiating Committee. *Daily Worker,* 9/21/48, p. 7.
Moscow Art Theatre	Sent greetings to directors and members. Celebration of Moscow Art Theatre's 50th Anniversary. *Daily Worker,* 11/1/48, p. 13.
Progressive Party	Attended three-day conference. *Daily Worker,* 11/16/48, p. 5.
National Council of the Arts, Sciences, and Professions	Signer. Statement calling for abolition of House Committee on Un-American Activities. *Daily Worker,* 12/29/48, p. 2.

Scientific and Cultural Conference for World Peace	Signer. Invitation to conference. *Daily Worker,* 1/10/49, p. 11. Member, Program Committee. *Daily Worker,* 2/28/49, p. 9.
Amicus Curiae Brief	Signer. Petition to Supreme Court to review the conviction of [John Howard] Lawson and [Dalton] Trumbo.
Moscow Theaters	Plays, "The Watch on the Rhine," "The Little Foxes," performed in Moscow theaters. *Soviet Russia Today,* 10/45, p. 32.
American Committee for Democracy and Intellectual Freedom	Signer. Petition to discontinue Dies Committee. *House Un-Am. Act. Com., Appendix 9,* p. 331.
American Committee to Save Refugees; Exiled Writers Committee of the League of American Writers; United American Spanish Aid Committee	Chairman, "Europe Today" dinner forum, 10/9/41. *House Un-Am. Act. Com., Appendix 9,* p. 357.
American League for Peace and Democracy	Sponsor, Refugee Scholarship and Peace Campaign, 8/3/39. *House Un-Am. Act. Com., Appendix 9,* p. 410.
Russian War Relief, Inc.	Signer. Advertisement asking for help on behalf of the Russian people, 10/10/41. *House Un-Am. Act. Com., Appendix 9,* p. 475.
Artists' Front to Win the War	Participant. Meeting, 10/16/42. *House Un-Am. Act. Com., Appendix 9,* p. 575.
Citizens Committee for Harry Bridges	Member and sponsor, 1941. *House Un-Am. Act. Com., Appendix 9,* p. 599.
Equality	Member, Editorial Council, 12/39. *House Un-Am. Act. Com., Appendix 9,* p. 698.
Friends of the Abraham Lincoln Brigade	Sponsor, 6/11/38. *House Un-Am. Act. Com., Appendix 9,* pp. 753–56. Sponsor. Disabled Veterans Fund, 3/22/39. *House Un-Am. Act. Com., Appendix 9,* p. 753.

Joint Anti-Fascist Refugee Committee	Sponsor. Dinner, 10/27/43. *House Un-Am. Act. Com., Appendix 9,* p. 941.
The League of Women Shoppers, Inc.	Vice-president. *House Un-Am. Act. Com., Appendix 9,* pp. 1007–10.
National Emergency Conference for Democratic Rights	Signer. "Open Letter to the United States Senate." *House Un-Am. Act. Com., Appendix 9,* p. 1212.
Progressive Committee to Rebuild the American Labor Party	Member, Executive Committee. *House Un-Am. Act. Com., Appendix 9,* p. 1500.
Statement by American Progressives on the Moscow Trials	Signer, 5/3/38. *House Un-Am. Act. Com., Appendix 9,* p. 1617.
Theatre Arts Committee	Member, Executive Board. *House Un-Am. Act. Com., Appendix 9,* p. 1626.
Frontier Films	Member, Advisory Board, 4/6/37. *Un-Am. Act. in California, 1948,* p. 96.

Lena Horne

SINGER—STAGE, SCREEN, RADIO

REPORTED AS:

American Committee for Protection of Foreign Born	Speaker. Mass Rally. *Daily Worker,* 3/3/48, p. 7.
Civil Rights Congress	Speaker. *Daily Worker,* 10/6/47, pp. 5, 8. Speaker. Civil Rights Congress of N.Y. Conference, Manhattan Center, 10/11/47. Program.
Citizens Non-Partisan Committee for Re-election of Benjamin J. Davis[2] to the City Council	Supporter. *Daily Worker,* 9/25/45, p. 12.

[2]Benjamin Davis was a leading African American Communist who served on the New York City Council in the early 1940s and was convicted under the Smith Act in 1949 along with the Communist party's other top leaders.

New Masses	Received award from New Masses Dinner Committee. *New Masses,* 1/23/45, p. 32. Contributor. *New Masses,* 9/16/47, p. 16.
People's Songs	Sponsor. *Bulletin of People's Songs,* 5/47.
Council on African Affairs	Sponsor, South African Famine Relief. Letterhead, 5/4/46.
United Electrical, Radio, and Machine Workers of America	Participant. Radio program, "Fighters for Liberty." *Daily Worker,* 2/9/48, p. 13.
Southern Conference for Human Welfare	Fund raiser. *People's Daily World,* 5/25/48, p. 5.
United Negro and Allied Veterans of America, Inc.	Affiliated. *Daily Worker,* 7/2/47, p. 4. Member, National Advisory Board. Letterhead.
Outstanding women who received praise of Elizabeth Gurley Flynn	Listed. *The Worker,* 3/9/47, p. 7.
Communist Party celebration in honor of Benjamin J. Davis	Announced as performer by Communist Party State Committee, 5/6/45, Golden Gate Ballroom, NYC. *U.S. Senate Hearings on S1832,* p. 593.

Joe Julian

ACTOR—RADIO

REPORTED AS:

Artists' Front to Win the War	Speaker. Meeting, 10/16/42. *House Un-Am. Act. Com., Appendix 9,* p. 575.
National Council of the Arts, Sciences, and Professions	Attended meeting to abolish House Un-American Activities Committee, Hotel Commodore, NYC, 1/9/49. *NY Journal-American,* 12/30/48.

19

The Blacklist in Operation: Testimony from the John Henry Faulk Trial

By the mid-1950s, the entertainment industry's blacklist had become so powerful that simply taking a strong stand against blacklisting could destroy someone's career. This is what happened to John Henry Faulk, a homespun radio raconteur whose burgeoning career as a talk show host was permanently derailed after he and a group of colleagues tried to mobilize the broadcast industry's talent union, the American Federation of Radio and Television Artists (AFTRA), against the blacklist. After Faulk's "Middle of the Road" slate won temporary control of AFTRA in 1955, the professional blacklisters attacked Faulk and got him fired from CBS.

Faulk fought back. He sued the main blacklisters: AWARE, Incorporated, an anti-Communist organization within the broadcast industry that mobilized support for the blacklist and published charges against Faulk and his allies in its bulletin; Laurence Johnson, a Syracuse supermarket owner who threatened sponsors that he would boycott their products if they hired tainted talent; and Vincent Hartnett, a professional anti-Communist who helped compile *Red Channels* (see Document 18) and then went into business shepherding blacklisted entertainers through the convoluted procedure required to clear them of the charges he and his allies had made.

When the case finally came to trial in 1962, witnesses for Faulk explained how the blacklist operated. Producers David Susskind and Mark Goodson described the procedures used to screen entertainers. Actors Kim Hunter and Everett Sloan testified about what they did to

Testimony, *John Henry Faulk v. AWARE, Inc. et al.,* in John Henry Faulk, *Fear on Trial,* 2nd ed. (Austin: University of Texas Press, 1983), 91–97, 135–40, 149–52, 157–62.

get cleared. After Faulk won his case, the blacklist began to wane. Still, many of the performers it had affected—including John Henry Faulk—were never able to recoup their careers.

DAVID SUSSKIND

Testimony in Faulk v. AWARE

1962

[Faulk's attorney, Louis] Nizer: Now, did you when you selected various actors and actresses and even the names of technicians or the director or the assistant director, did you submit those names to anyone?

Susskind: Yes, sir, I had to submit the names of everybody on every show in every category to an executive of Young & Rubicam, and nobody could be engaged by me finally or a deal made and consummated, before a clearance or acceptance came back from Young & Rubicam. . . .

. . . When I sold the program to the advertising agency, Young & Rubicam, for Lorillard cigarettes, the condition of the sale was that all names of all personnel in all categories on every program were to be submitted for political clearance by Young & Rubicam, and nobody was to be hired until they approved and said, "All right, hire such a person.". . . It generally took forty-eight hours. I was told that I should always anticipate a forty-eight-hour delay on the approval or rejection of any name.

Nizer: Can you estimate how many names on this one program over the year that it ran that you submitted in this way for political approval?

Susskind: I must have submitted over the period of time about five thousand names, I would guess. . . .

. . . I would telephone the executive at Young & Rubicam. I would have had previously made tentative commitments to actors, writers, producers, directors, everybody on the program. . . . I would then call the advertising agency executive. I would submit the names. He would, as I say, reject or approve them in terms of their political acceptability. . . .

... I said to Mr. Levy [advertising executive] that it is extraordinarily difficult to find the right actors for the right parts, the right writers for the right scripts, and the right directors for the right stories, that his rejections were making the program almost unworkable and impossible artistically, and that I could not accept the responsibility for the steady deterioration of the program when this practice was in vogue. ...

... [I said,] "I know a great number of the people you have rejected. I know them socially and professionally and there is no question about their political reliability or their good citizenship or their loyalty to this country, and on all these grounds I beg you to let me confront these people with whatever you have on them and let them answer and you will find that they will be all right and you will have a much better show." And he (Mr. Levy) said, "I am helpless. We are helpless. This is the practice. We have no choice, and we have to pay five dollars for every clearance and two dollars for every recheck. Do you think we like it? It's costing us a bloody fortune." And I believe he said, "Cut down the number of actors you submit, cut down the number of directors and the number of writers, because you are breaking us. It's five dollars a throw, and two dollars a throw, and you give us eight actors for each role and then you give us three writers for each script, and then you give us four directors for each show. Somebody is getting rich. We're growing broke. Stop it. Narrow it down."

I said, "I can't narrow it down, because I have learned that your percentage of rejections is so high I have to have alternative choices to be prepared when you reject them politically.". . .

Nizer: When these names came back not approved, rejected for political reasons, what was your practice in dealing with the actors and actresses or director who was not approved? . . .

Susskind: . . . When they came back rejected, as part of my instruction at the beginning of the program when I made the sale of "Appointment with Adventure" and subsequently "Justice" and many other programs, it was stipulated that I was never to tell any rejectee why he was rejected. . . .

Nizer: Did you also submit the names even of children on this program? Could you put a child on without getting clearance?

Susskind: Even children. . . .

. . . In the course of "Appointment with Adventure," sponsored by Lorillard at Young & Rubicam Agency, we required the services of a, I believe, at least a seven- or eight-year-old girl actress, child actress. It was a backbreaking assignment to find a child who could act well enough to be in a professional program coast to coast. We went to all the established sources, the talent agencies. They did not represent children. . . .

It was an extraordinarily difficult search involving going to the public schools system, the United Nations schools. We finally found a child, an American child eight years old, female. I put her name in along with some other names. That child's name came back unacceptable, politically unreliable.

MARK GOODSON

Testimony in Faulk v. AWARE

1962

[Faulk's attorney, Louis] Nizer: Can you state with reasonable certainty whether, if a performer becomes controversial in the sense of his or her patriotism being involved, such performer—can you state with reasonable certainty the general practice as to whether such performer can obtain employment in the television and radio industry, generally, as a trade practice.

Goodson: Yes, I would say in general that nonclearability meant unemployability.

Nizer: Does it matter, in giving your answer—can you state with reasonable certainty what the practice was whether the innocence or guilt of that performer were established or not?

Goodson: Well, the innocence or guilt was never brought up, Mr. Nizer, because the facts of the matter were never discussed. . . .

. . . A sponsor is in business to sell his goods. He has no interest in being involved in causes. He does not want controversy. . . .

. . . The favorite slogan along Madison Avenue is "Why buy yourself a headache?" The advertising agency's job is to see to it that the products are sold but that the sponsor keeps out of trouble, and an advertising agency can lose a great deal, it can lose the account. The sponsor can lose a little bit of business, but he still can recoup it. The agency can lose the account and I would say that a great portion of an agency's job is concerned with the pleasing and taking care and serving a client.

So I think in many instances, the clients were perhaps even less aware of all this than the advertising agency, which considered one of its principal jobs keeping out of trouble, just keep out of trouble. I don't think that they took a political position. I think it was apolitical. It was just anticontroversial.

Given the choice between performer A who is noncontroversial, and performer B, about whom there is any kind of a cloud whatsoever, the natural instinct on a commonsense business basis is to use the noncontroversial personality. Again, a favorite saying is "There are a lot of other actors, a lot of other performers. Why bother with this one? Why buy this headache?"....

[Goodson discusses why people were put on the blacklist.]

Goodson: ...All I can say is there were no differentiations made between Communists, Communist sympathizers, those who had lunch with Communist sympathizers, those who knew somebody who had lunch with Communist sympathizers, and so forth, but there was one overall list and the differentiation was not made for us....

...Sponsors and their agencies wanted to keep out of trouble with the public and, therefore, wanted to eliminate anybody that might be accused of anything which could involve the sponsor in controversy....

It [the reasons for blacklisting] also included various forms of associations that were much narrower, much further apart than that [association with the Communist party]. It included general controversy of any kind and in certain cases it even—I'm ashamed to say—included the elimination of people from shows because they had the same name as members of the Communist Party.

KIM HUNTER

Testimony in Faulk v. AWARE

1962

Hunter explains that it took several years before she became aware that she was being blacklisted. Finally, in 1953, Arthur P. Jacobs, Hunter's public relations adviser, contacted Vincent Hartnett, one of the defen-

dants. Hartnett offered to investigate Hunter for a fee of two hundred dollars. Nizer asked Hunter about the incident.

Hunter: ... Mr. Jacobs called me on the telephone. We had a phone conversation in which he ... asked if I were willing to pay the two hundred dollars for information from Mr. Hartnett. I said that I would not, that my life is absolutely an open book, and I did not feel I needed Mr. Hartnett's information or investigation and I certainly wasn't going to pay two hundred dollars for it. ...
... And I did not. However, Mr. Jacobs said "Please—"

[Nizer reads into the record a letter from Hartnett to Geraldine B. Zorbaugh, general counsel for the American Broadcasting Company.]

Nizer [reading]: "Dear Gerry, On October 2 (1953), I received from you the enclosed list of names for the purpose of evaluation. To keep my own records straight I note that on the list appeared the following names ... and one of these names is Kim Hunter. ... In my opinion, finally, you would run a serious risk of adverse public opinion by featuring on your network Kim Hunter."

[Hunter is then asked about a telephone conversation with Hartnett about the antiblacklist fight within AFTRA.]

Hunter: The substance of it was that he said to show—kind of show my good faith, that I was truly a loyal American and not pro-Communist, that affidavits were not sufficient, that I should by all rights do something actively anti-Communist and did I object to do any such thing, and I said, "No, certainly not."

He asked me then if I knew about the AWARE resolution, the resolution to condemn AWARE that was pending within our television union at AFTRA, and I said yes, I know about it.

And he said, well one way that I could show a strong anti-Communist stand would be to go to that meeting and speak up in support of AWARE, publicly, in front of everybody.

I said, "Mr. Hartnett, it would be very difficult for me to speak in support of AWARE because I am not in support of AWARE, Incorporated."

He said, "Well, it wouldn't be necessary to support AWARE, Incorporated, as such, and, in fact, it wouldn't even really be necessary for you to go to the meeting, if you would be willing to send a telegram that could be read before the meeting publicly, speaking, saying in so many words that you are against this resolution to condemn AWARE."

I said, "Mr. Hartnett, I will do my best to form a telegram.". . .

[Nizer reads into the record the text of Hunter's telegram and an attached note to Hartnett.]

Nizer [reading]: "To the membership: For your union to condemn AWARE, Inc. shouldn't it also bring suit against AWARE for libel and defamation of character? Is AFTRA prepared to follow this through to its logical conclusion? And what earthly good do we hope to accomplish for the union or its members by passing this resolution?

"I'm neither a member of AWARE, Inc. nor a friend, nor am I in sympathy with any of its methods, but I urge you all to think very carefully indeed before voting for this resolution. The individuals hurt by Bulletin No. 12 have recourse to right any wrong that may have been committed, but AFTRA will have no recourse whatsoever if it places itself on record as protesting and aiding the Communist conspiracy, even if this action is taken in the noble desire to aid and protect the innocent. Signed, Kim Hunter."

And annexed to it, this is from Mr. Hartnett's files, May 25, 1955: "Dear Mr. Hartnett. Enclosed is a copy of the wire I sent to the AFTRA membership meeting last night. I was unable to attend the meeting so I have no idea whether it was read or not. Signed, Kim Hunter."

Nizer: After this date, did you get television appearances? . . .
Hunter: Yes, Mr. Nizer, I worked. . . .
. . . I worked quite frequently after that and to the present date.

EVERETT SLOAN

Testimony in Faulk v. AWARE

1962

Sloan describes his inability to find work after 1952 because he had been confused with Alan Sloane, whose name appeared in Red Channels.

Sloan: I found out by inquiring that if you work for the UN Radio more
than twice, that the third time you work for them you are required
to obtain the same status as a permanent employee, and that
included submitting to an FBI check. . . .

   . . . And so, having already worked for the UN Radio twice, I
sought a third employment from them, which I received. . . .

*[Sloan was cleared by the FBI but was still unemployable, so he met with
Paul Milton, whom a friend had recommended he consult.]*

Sloan: [Milton said] "Well, I take this with a grain of salt." Then I said,
"What do you mean by that?" He said, "Well, we don't put much
stock in it." And I said, "Who is we?" He said, "AWARE, Incorporated." And that was the first time that he represented AWARE in
any way. I said, "I wasn't aware of the fact you were a member or a
director of AWARE or represented them in any way." I said, "If I
had known that, I certainly wouldn't have come to see you." I said,
"But aside from that, what is your objection to this document [an
FBI clearance], now that you have seen it?" He said, "Well, we at
AWARE had different standards of clearance than the United States
Government's agencies. We are a little more stringent. We feel they
are a little too lenient." And I said, "You mean to say that you set
yourselves up as opposed to the United States Government in the
matter of loyalty, which is, indeed, I would say, their province?" He
said, "Yes, we do." I said, "Well, what would AWARE, Inc. suggest
that I do, then, in view of the fact that this document doesn't seem
to mean much to them?"

   And he said, "I suggest that you let me arrange a meeting for
you with Mr. Hartnett, at which meeting perhaps you and he can
evolve some statement that you can make that will be satisfactory
to Mr. Hartnett and will also prove satisfactory to, perhaps, the
people who are not presently hiring you.". . .

   . . . I said, "Go fly a kite." I told Mr. Milton that as far as I was
concerned I was much more interested in the opinion of the United
States Government than of Mr. Milton of AWARE or of Vincent
Hartnett, and that as far as I was concerned both their purpose and
methods as I could gather were immoral and illegal and that I
would have nothing to do with them whatsoever.

   . . . I hoped that very soon the fact that they were conducting
their business in a way that I considered immoral and illegal would
be proven and come to light, and I walked out of the restaurant.

20

Unfriendly Witnesses and Their Lawyers: The HUAC Testimony of Robert Treuhaft

The difficulty that Bay Area attorney Robert Treuhaft had in finding a member of the bar to represent him before HUAC was experienced by many witnesses. The difficulty was compounded for those who, like Treuhaft, did not plan to cooperate with the committee and did not want to be represented by an attorney who was, as Treuhaft himself was, openly identified with the left. In this selection, which was a prepared statement Treuhaft read to the committee before he took the Fifth Amendment, Treuhaft describes his own quest for a lawyer.

For further information on Treuhaft's activities in the Communist party during the 1940s and 1950s, see the amusing memoir of his wife, Jessica Mitford, *A Fine Old Conflict* (New York: Knopf, 1977).

Robert Treuhaft, testimony, House Committee on Un-American Activities, *Investigation of Communist Activities in the San Francisco Area,* Part 3, 83rd Cong., 1st sess., 3 Dec. 1953, San Francisco.

ROBERT TREUHAFT

Testimony before HUAC

December 3, 1953

I am obliged to appear before this committee without assistance of
counsel, Mr. Tavenner, because of the fact that the repressive activities of this committee have made it impossible for me to secure the
assistance of attorneys of my choice. This is a serious charge for a
lawyer to make. I am compelled, however, to make it because the state
of affairs that I have found to exist in this regard is truly shocking.

A month ago I received a subpoena calling for my appearance
before this committee. My law partner and I have been, for many
years, and are now, general counsel for the East Bay Division of Ware-
house Union Local 6, ILWU,[1] a labor organization which is one of the
principal targets under attack by this committee. In fact, I am sure this
was well known to the committee's investigators, and I cannot down
the suspicion that my representation of this union had something to
do with the fact that my law partner and I are the only East Bay
lawyers subpoenaed before the committee at these hearings so far as I
know.

I readily agreed to represent four East Bay members of this union
as their attorney, who likewise were subpoenaed, despite the fact that
I, myself, had been subpoenaed as a witness.

Upon receipt of my subpoena I immediately began to make diligent
efforts to secure counsel to represent me. I compiled a list of the
seven leading East Bay lawyers whom I would want to represent me
because of their known ability in their profession and because all of
them had from time to time, shown themselves to be champions of the
right of advocacy. All had a sound understanding of due process of law
and of the other constitutional rights and immunities which are daily
trampled upon by this committee. . . .

The first lawyer, whom I will call lawyer No. 1, holds high office in
the Alameda County Bar Association. When I first approached this

---

[1]The International Longshoremen's and Warehousemen's Union (ILWU) was one
of the left-wing unions expelled by the CIO in 1950 (see Document 13). The union's
Australian-born leader Harry Bridges was repeatedly threatened with deportation by
the federal government.

lawyer, he told me that he could see no reason why he could not represent me. The next day, however, he informed me that he felt that he could not do so because of the controversial nature and the publicity attendant upon hearings before this committee and because of his position in the county bar association.

The second lawyer I consulted out of this list, lawyer No. 2, is a former judge who has an active practice on both sides of the bay. I discussed with him the position which I intended to take before this committee; that is, to uphold the Constitution and to rely upon the First and Fifth Amendments to the Constitution as they might apply to every question that this committee might put to me.

This attorney, who is highly placed in the bar, agreed fully with me in principle and stated that it was his opinion that my decision was sound and wise. He told me that he would like to represent me.

After conferring with his associates, however, he called me in again, and he said that he was very sorry that he could not because representing me with the attendant publicity or representing any witness before this committee would involve financial hardship. He said that he regretted very much to give me this answer because we have been on friendly terms. He said to me, although he is a well-established lawyer, and older than I am, "Why don't you find some older lawyer, someone who is in a better financial position, to take this risk?"

The third lawyer I went to see and offered a retainer to represent me before these hearings was an older lawyer; and he was a better financially established lawyer so far as I know. He formerly held high office in the American Bar Association, and he, too, has been a champion of the right of advocacy. He told me, "Try to find a younger lawyer. The activities before this committee would be too strenuous," he thought the publicity would be harmful.

The fourth lawyer I went to is a leading criminal lawyer in the East Bay. We have been on very friendly terms, and he readily agreed to represent me without any hesitation at all. When I offered him a retainer, he said that he would not accept a retainer from a fellow lawyer. He took the subpoena, and we proceeded to discuss the position I was going to take, and he agreed with me fully that anybody who had represented unpopular causes as a lawyer, as I have, would face grave dangers in answering any questions put by this committee. Three days ago I—I consulted him two weeks ago—three days ago, the day before—three days before I was supposed to come here, he called me, and told me that his partner had just returned from out of town and had learned that he had undertaken to represent me. He said that his partner represented a bank, and that his partner felt that the attendant publicity would be so harmful to them that he insisted that they could not represent a witness before this committee. . . .

Lawyer No. 5 is one of the most distinguished members of the bar of Contra Costa County. He has held high office in the bar association there, and he is a leading lawyer in every sense of the word. He has also been a fighter for the right of advocacy. He told me with very great regret that he had discussed with some of his corporate clients the advisability of his intention to represent a witness before this committee. These clients told him that they would consider it an unfriendly act if he were to represent a witness before this committee. He said that although he was well established, he had very high overhead and that he didn't want to subject his organization to the financial hardship and risk of losing clients that would be involved in representing anyone before this committee. I told him that I intended to take this matter up with the bar association and also to make a statement to this committee on my experiences in attempting to obtain counsel, and that I intended to keep the names of the individuals that I had consulted confidential. He said, "Bob, a fact is a fact. I feel rotten about telling you what I have to tell you, but a fact is a fact; you state the facts, and I authorize you to use my name and to give the reasons that I have given you."

This man had real courage.

21

Heresy and Conspiracy:
A Cold War Liberal View
of the Communist Threat

During the height of the cold war, American intellectuals were deeply divided about McCarthyism. On one side were civil libertarians who, like Supreme Court Justice William O. Douglas (see Document 22), argued that the anti-Communist crusade threatened basic American freedoms. On the other side were the cold war liberals like Sidney Hook, Irving Kristol,[1] and Arthur Schlesinger Jr., who deplored the excesses of that crusade but supported its underlying goals. Neither group sympathized with the Communist party, but the latter, many of whose members had once been in or near the party, claimed to have a more realistic approach to dealing with it. Their writings constituted the McCarthy era's most authoritative intellectual justification for invoking sanctions against Communists and their allies.

In his influential article reproduced here, Hook, then a philosophy professor at New York University, sought to explain why liberals did not have to defend the civil liberties of Communists. Like J. Edgar Hoover and the prosecution in the *Dennis* case (see Documents 4 and 10), Hook relied heavily on Lenin's writings to show how communism endangered the United States. Hook criticized the right's inability to distinguish between legitimate dissent and illegal conspiracy, but he claimed that liberal institutions could keep the reactionaries at bay by doing their own housecleaning, just as the CIO had done when it elimi-

---

[1]Kristol, a leading neoconservative intellectual, refused to grant permission for the publication in this volume of excerpts from his important essay "'Civil Liberties, 1952': A Study in Confusion," *Commentary* (March 1952).

Sidney Hook, "Heresy, Yes—But Conspiracy, No," *New York Times Magazine,* 9 July 1950, 12, 38–39.

nated its left-wing unions (see Document 13). Like many cold war liberals, Hook emphasized the need for toughness and denounced the "ritualistic liberals" (Schlesinger calls them "doughfaces")[2] who allegedly underestimated the threat of the Communist conspiracy and exaggerated the dangers of the campaign against it.

There is considerable irony in Hook's emphasis on the dishonesty and conspiratorial tactics of the Communist movement, for during the 1950s, along with Schlesinger, Kristol, and other leading intellectuals, he was active in the Congress for Cultural Freedom (CCF), an anti-Communist organization secretly subsidized by the CIA to win support for American foreign policy.

[2]This unflattering characterization of the left-wing remnants of the Popular Front is in Schlesinger's influential 1949 book *The Vital Center.* Later cold war liberals and neo-conservatives coined the term "anti-anti-Communists" for the same group.

SIDNEY HOOK

Heresy, Yes—But Conspiracy, No

July 9, 1950

The "hot war" in Korea makes it even more urgent that we clarify our thinking on the "cold war" of ideologies. At the heart of the matter are basic philosophical issues which in more settled times would have been dismissed as of no practical concern. One of them is the meaning of "liberalism," which becomes important because communism invokes the freedom of a liberal society in order to destroy that society. Many proposals have been made to cope with this problem. All of them must face the question whether in advocating such measures the principles of liberalism are themselves being consistently applied or compromised.

It is easier to say what liberalism is not than what it is. It is not belief in laissez-faire or free enterprise in economics—the temper of Great Britain has remained liberal despite the shifting economic programs and institutions of the last century. Neither is liberalism the philosophy of invariable compromise or the comforting notion that it is always possible to find a middle ground—if a man demands my purse, to grant him half of it is not a liberal solution. Nor can liberalism be identified with the traditional belief in absolute or inalienable rights—every right is, in fact, evaluated in terms of its consequences for society, and is, therefore, subject to modification if it endangers other rights of equal or greater validity.

When one right limits another, the final adjudication of their conflict, in a liberal society, is made in the reflective light of the total situation and of that set of rationally preferred freedoms whose preservation may require the temporary abridgment of some specific freedom. To say that we cannot preserve our freedoms by sacrificing them is, therefore, an empty piece of rhetoric. Our common experience brings home to us the necessity of sacrificing some particular freedom to preserve other freedoms just as we must sometimes surrender a genuine good for the sake of other and better goods. Here the readiness to reflect is all.

This provides a key to the abiding meaning of the liberal tradition from Socrates to John Dewey and Justice Holmes.

Liberalism is, in the memorable words of Justice Holmes, the belief "in the free trade of ideas—that the test of truth is the power of thought to get itself accepted in the competition of the market."

There are at least two presuppositions of this belief in the free market of ideas. One of them, explicitly drawn by Justice Holmes, is that the free expression and circulation of ideas may be checked wherever their likely effects constitute a clear and present danger to public peace or the security of the country. The second presupposition is that in the free market of ideas the competition will be honestly and openly conducted. What the liberal fears is the systematic corruption of the free market of ideas by activities which make intelligent choice impossible. In short, what he fears is not heresy but conspiracy.

The failure to recognize the distinction between heresy and conspiracy is fatal to a liberal civilization, for the inescapable consequence of their identification is either self-destruction, when heresies are punished as conspiracies, or destruction at the hands of their enemies, when conspiracies are tolerated as heresies.

A heresy is a set of unpopular ideas or opinions on matters of grave concern to the community. The right to profess and advocate heresy of any character, including communism, is an essential element of a liberal society. The liberal stands ready to defend the honest heretic no matter what his views against any attempt to curb him. It is enough that the heretic pays the price of unpopularity which he cannot avoid and from which he cannot reasonably plead exemption, or use as a pretext for conspiracy. In some respects each of us is a heretic, but a liberal society can impose no official orthodoxies of belief, disagreement with which entails legal sanctions of any kind.

A conspiracy, as distinct from a heresy, is a secret or underground movement which seeks to attain its ends not by normal political or educational process but by playing outside the rules of the game. Because it undermines the conditions which are required in order that doctrines may freely compete for acceptance, because where successful it ruthlessly destroys all heretics and dissenters, conspiracies cannot be tolerated without self-stultification in a liberal society.

A heresy does not shrink from publicity. It welcomes it. Not so a conspiracy. The signs of a conspiracy are secrecy, anonymity, the use of false labels, and the calculated lie. It does not offer its wares openly but by systematic infiltration into all organizations of cultural life, it seeks to capture strategic posts to carry out a policy alien to the purposes of the organizations. There is political conspiracy which is the concern of the state. But there may also be a conspiracy against a labor union, a cultural or professional association, or an educational institution which is not primarily the concern of the state but of its own members. In general, whoever subverts the rules of a democratic organization and seeks to win by chicanery what cannot be fairly won in the processes of free discussion is a conspirator.

This suggests what the guiding principle of liberalism should be toward communism. Communist ideas are heresies, and liberals need have no fear of them where they are freely and openly expressed. The Communist movement, however, is something much more than a heresy, for wherever it exists it operates along the lines laid down by Lenin as guides to Communists of all countries, and perfected in all details since then.

"It is necessary," so Lenin instructs all Communists, "to agree to any and every sacrifice and even—if need be—resort to all sorts of stratagems, maneuvers, and illegal methods, to evasions and subterfuges . . . in order to carry on Communist work." Further: "In all organizations without exception . . . (political, industrial, military, cooperative, educational, sports), groups or nuclei of Communists should be formed . . . mainly [in] open groups but also secret groups."

There are no exceptions: "In all countries, even the freest, 'legal' and 'peaceful' in the sense that the class struggle is least acute in them, the time has fully matured when it is absolutely necessary for every Communist party systematically to combine legal with illegal work, legal and illegal organizations. . . . Illegal work is particularly necessary in the Army, the Navy, and police."

Under present conditions of political and military warfare it is not hard to see what immense dangers to the security of liberal institutions is implicit in this strategy of infiltration and deceit. Even a few men in sensitive posts can do incalculable harm. These instructions, combined with explicit directives to Communists to transform any war in which their country is involved, except one approved by the Soviet Union, into a civil war against their own Government, indicate that members of the Communist party are not so much heretics as conspirators, and regard themselves as such.

There may be some justification for conspiratorial activity in undemocratic countries where heresies are proscribed, but Lenin, as we have seen, makes no exceptions.

How faithfully the Communist movement pursues the pattern laid down by its authoritative leaders in the political sphere is a matter of historical record. But unfortunately for the peace of mind of liberals the same tactics are followed in other areas of social and cultural life. The history of American labor is replete with illustrations.

Every large labor organization in the United States has been compelled to take disciplinary action against Communist party elements, not because of their beliefs—their heresies—but because their pattern of conduct made the Communist party, and ultimately the Kremlin, the decisive power in the life of the union, and not the needs and wishes of the membership.

President Philip Murray of the CIO, in the recent expulsion of the Mine, Mill and Smelter Workers Union, exposed the technique in detail. In all these situations it is not fear of Communist ideas which has led to disciplinary action. The charge against the Communists is that it is they who fear the open and honest confrontation of ideas. They operate through "fronts," the charge continues, because they fear that if the membership is given a free choice of honestly labeled alternatives they will be rejected; and once they slip into power they consolidate their position by terrorizing any opposition.

By now it should be apparent that liberals in the twentieth century are confronted by a situation quite unfamiliar to their forebears. For they must contend, not with fearless heretics—indigenous elements of the community—who like the Abolitionists and revolutionists of old scorn concealment, and who make no bones about their hostility to the principles of liberalism. They find themselves in a unique historical predicament of dealing with native elements who by secrecy and stratagem serve the interests of a foreign power which believes itself entitled to speak for all mankind, and whose victory spells the end of all liberal civilization and with it the right to heresy.

The problems this creates for a liberal society are of tremendous magnitude. They cannot be dismissed by a quotation from Jefferson. Nor can they be solved by placing the Communist movement and its entire periphery outside the law by special legislation. They require constructive intelligence, the discovery and application of techniques in each field which will meet the conspiratorial threats to the proper functioning of liberal institutions without creating still greater ones.

Failure to take this approach is characteristic of some current wholesale responses to the problem. The first is that of frightened reactionaries who cannot distinguish between heresy and conspiracy, and in addition, identify communism with any decent thing they wish to destroy. By making reckless charges of conspiracy where there is only honest heresy, they prevent intelligent choice. And by labeling all progressive ideas as communistic they help the Communist strategy. If this reactionary movement gains momentum it will petrify the status quo and destroy the possibilities of peaceful social change.

Then there is a small but influential group of men who believe that they can check Communist conspiracy merely by passing laws against it and that they can protect institutions from subversives by requiring all individuals, particularly teachers, to take loyalty oaths. As if any member of the Communist party regarded any oath except one to the Communist party and the Soviet Union as binding!

A third group consists of those whom we may call ritualistic, as distinct from realistic, liberals. They ignore or blithely dismiss the mass of evidence concerning the conspiratorial character of the Communist movement in all institutions in which it is active. They regard communism merely as an unpleasant heresy, just a little worse than a crotchety theory of disease or finance. They sometimes characterize a prosecution of a conspirator for espionage or perjury as a persecution of heresy. This gives a new lease of life to the reactionaries who now tend to regard the ritualistic liberals as the dupes or accomplices of the Communists, thus confirming in turn the illusions of these liberals that there really is no problem of Communist conspiracy.

Ritualistic liberals legitimately criticize the dangerous nonsense of those who proscribe heresy. But they carry their criticism to a point where they give the impression that the country is in the grip of a reign of terror or hysteria much more dangerous than Communist expansion from without and infiltration from within.

Because some security regulations in government are questionable and because some blunders have been made, the ritualistic liberals intimate that no security regulations are necessary and that the existing laws against treason and criminal conspiracy are sufficient for all purposes. By artfully collecting instances of foolishness from the press and blowing up their significance, and by disregarding counter-instances of equal or greater significance, they paint a very misleading picture of the actual state of American civil liberties comparable to an account of American business composed only of bankruptcies, or an account of public order that featured only crime stories.

David Lilienthal,[3] a realistic not a ritualistic liberal, has warned us against the "Scare-the-dopes!" method of discussing nuclear energy. There is also a "Scare-the-dopes" method of discussion of the problem of Communist conspiracy. It is used by those who with scandalous looseness employ the term Communist for any economic or political heresy, and who shout conspiracy where there is only heresy. It is also used by those who do not tell us how to meet the real dangers of Communist conspiracy but shout, "Hysteria" and "Fascism" or "Police State" when the first faltering efforts are made to cope with dangers hitherto unprecedented.

The position of realistic liberalism in three troubled centers of American life in which overt conspiratorial activity of a criminal nature is not involved may be briefly indicated.

Where government service is concerned, the operating maxim for every sensitive and policymaking post should be a principle enunciated by Roger Baldwin, former head of the American Civil Liberties Union: "A superior loyalty to a foreign Government disqualifies a citizen for service to our own." The difficulty is to determine what constitutes sufficient evidence to warrant the inference that a particular individual is unsafe. No hard and fast rules can be laid down in advance, for in some cases even past membership in subversive organizations is not conclusive. The criterion for establishing unreliability obviously must be less stringent than those which lead us to deprive an individual of freedom. The main problem is not punitive but preventive.

In labor organizations the existence of Communist party leaderships is extremely dangerous because of the Communists' unfailing use of the strike as a political instrument at the behest of the Kremlin.

---

[3] David Lilienthal was the first chair of the Atomic Energy Commission.

The history of Communist-led trade unions here and abroad is instructive enough. The most effective way of meeting this situation, however, is not by requiring non-Communist oaths on the part of union officers, for this can be circumvented by delegating office to individuals who are faithful non–card holding Communists. The most intelligent procedure here is to let labor clean its own house. Free and independent trade unions which are essential to a democracy cannot be liberated from the organizational stranglehold of the Communist party by government intervention. Only an aroused membership can do it.

The question of freedom and control in the schools is not political. It does not involve civil rights but the ethics of professional conduct. Heresy in the schools, whether in science, economics, or politics, must be protected against any agency which seeks to impose orthodoxy. For the scholar there are no subversive doctrines but only those that are valid or invalid or not proved in the light of evidence. The primary commitment of the teacher is to the ethics and logic of inquiry. It is not his beliefs, right or wrong; it is not his heresies, which disqualify the Communist party teacher but his declaration of intention, as evidenced by official statements of his party, to practice educational fraud.

The common sense of the matter is clear and independent of the issue of communism. An individual joins an organization which explicitly instructs him that his duty is to sabotage the purposes of the institution in which he works and which provides him with his livelihood. Is it necessary to apprehend him in the act of carrying out these instructions in order to forestall the sabotage? Does not his voluntary and continuous act of membership in such an organization constitute prima facie evidence of unfitness?

This is a matter of ethical hygiene, not of politics or of persecution. And because it is, the enforcement of the proper professional standards should rest with the teachers themselves and not with the state or Regents or even boards of trustees. The actual techniques of handling such issues must be worked out but the problem should not be confused with the issue of heresy.

Liberalism in the twentieth century must toughen its fiber for it is engaged in a fight on many different fronts. Liberalism must defend the free market in ideas against the racists, the professional patrioteer, and those spokesmen of the status quo who would freeze the existing inequalities of opportunity and economic power by choking off criticism.

Liberalism must also defend freedom of ideas against those agents and apologists of Communist totalitarianism who, instead of honestly defending their heresies, resort to conspiratorial methods of anonymity and other techniques of fifth columnists. It will not be taken in by labels like "left" and "right." These terms came into use after the French Revolution but the legacy of the men who then called themselves "left"—the strategic freedoms of the Bill of Rights— is everywhere repudiated by those who today are sometimes euphemistically referred to as "leftists" but who are actually Communists more reactionary than many parties conventionally called "right."

Realistic liberalism recognizes that to survive we must solve many hard problems, and that they can be solved only by intelligence and not by pious rhetoric. It recognizes that our greatest danger today is not fear of ideas but absence of ideas—specific ideas, addressed to concrete problems here and now, problems of such complexity that only the ignorant can be cocksure or dogmatic about the answers to them.

Finally, liberalism conceives of life not in terms of bare survival or peace at any price but in the light of ideals upon which it is prepared to stake everything. Among these ideals are the strategic freedoms of the liberal American tradition which make the continuous use of intelligence possible.

22

A Liberal Deplores the Witch-Hunt: Supreme Court Justice William O. Douglas on "The Black Silence of Fear"

By the early 1950s, a number of distinguished citizens were beginning to speak out against McCarthyism. The following selection comes from one of the most influential of such statements, an article by Supreme Court Justice William O. Douglas in the *New York Times Magazine* in January 1952. The essay was similar to Truman's veto of the McCarran Act (see Document 12) and other liberal attacks on McCarthyism; in it Douglas criticizes the growing drift toward political conformity and worries that it would weaken the United States's position in the world.

WILLIAM O. DOUGLAS

The Black Silence of Fear

January 13, 1952

There is an ominous trend in this nation. We are developing tolerance only for the orthodox point of view on world affairs, intolerance for new or different approaches....

... We have over the years swung from tolerance to intolerance and back again. There have been years of intolerance when the views of

William O. Douglas, "The Black Silence of Fear," *New York Times Magazine,* 13 Jan. 1952, 7, 37–38.

minorities have been suppressed. But there probably has not been a period of greater intolerance than we witness today.

To understand this, I think one has to leave the country, go into the back regions of the world, lose himself there, and become absorbed in the problems of the peoples of different civilizations. When he returns to America after a few months he probably will be shocked. He will be shocked not at the intentions or purposes or ideals of the American people. He will be shocked at the arrogance and intolerance of great segments of the American press, at the arrogance and intolerance of many leaders in public office, at the arrogance and intolerance reflected in many of our attitudes toward Asia. He will find that thought is being standardized, that the permissible area for calm discussion is being narrowed, that the range of ideas is being limited, that many minds are closed. . . .

This is alarming to one who loves his country. It means that the philosophy of strength through free speech is being forsaken for the philosophy of fear through repression.

That choice in Russia is conscious. Under Lenin the ministers and officials were encouraged to debate, to advance new ideas and criticisms. Once the debate was over, however, no dissension or disagreement was permitted. But even that small degree of tolerance for free discussion that Lenin permitted disappeared under Stalin. Stalin maintains a tight system of control, permitting no free speech, no real clash in ideas, even in the inner circle. We are, of course, not emulating either Lenin or Stalin. But we are drifting in the direction of repression, drifting dangerously fast. . . .

The drift goes back, I think, to the fact that we carried over to days of peace the military approach to world affairs. . . .

. . . Today in Asia we are identified not with ideas of freedom, but with guns. Today at home we are thinking less and less in terms of defeating communism with ideas, more and more in terms of defeating communism with military might.

The concentration on military means has helped to breed fear. It has bred fear and insecurity partly because of the horror of atomic war. But the real reason strikes deeper. In spite of our enormous expenditures, we see that Soviet imperialism continues to expand and that the expansion proceeds without the Soviets firing a shot. The free world continues to contract without a battle for its survival having been fought. It becomes apparent, as country after country falls to Soviet imperialistic ambitions, that military policy alone is a weak one, that military policy alone will end in political bankruptcy and futility. Thus fear mounts.

Fear has many manifestations. The Communist threat inside the country has been magnified and exalted far beyond its realities. Irresponsible talk by irresponsible people has fanned the flames of fear. Accusations have been loosely made. Character assassinations have become common. Suspicion has taken the place of goodwill. Once we could debate with impunity along a wide range of inquiry. Once we could safely explore to the edges of a problem, challenge orthodoxy without qualms, and run the gamut of ideas in search of solutions to perplexing problems. Once we had confidence in each other. Now there is suspicion. Innocent acts become telltale marks of disloyalty. The coincidence that an idea parallels Soviet Russia's policy for a moment of time settles an aura of suspicion around a person.

Suspicion grows until only the orthodox idea is the safe one. Suspicion grows until only the person who loudly proclaims that orthodox view, or who, once having been a Communist, has been converted, is trustworthy. Competition for embracing the new orthodoxy increases. Those who are unorthodox are suspect. Everyone who does not follow the military policymakers is suspect. Everyone who voices opposition to the trend away from diplomacy and away from political tactics takes a chance. Some who are opposed are indeed "subversive." Therefore, the thundering edict commands that all who are opposed are "subversive." Fear is fanned to a fury. Good and honest men are pilloried. Character is assassinated. Fear runs rampant. . . .

Fear has driven more and more men and women in all walks of life either to silence or to the folds of the orthodox. Fear has mounted— fear of losing one's job, fear of being investigated, fear of being pilloried. This fear has stereotyped our thinking, narrowed the range of free public discussion, and driven many thoughtful people to despair. This fear has even entered universities, great citadels of our spiritual strength, and corrupted them. We have the spectacle of university officials lending themselves to one of the worst witch-hunts we have seen since early days.

This fear has affected the youngsters. . . .

Youth—like the opposition party in a parliamentary system—has served a powerful role. It has cast doubts on our policies, challenged our inarticulate major premises, put the light on our prejudices, and exposed our inconsistencies. Youth has made each generation indulge in self-examination.

But a great change has taken place. Youth is still rebellious; but it is largely holding its tongue. There is the fear of being labeled a "subversive" if one departs from the orthodox party line. That charge — if leveled against a young man or young woman — may have profound effects. It may ruin a youngster's business or professional career. No one wants a Communist in his organization nor anyone who is suspect. . . .

This pattern of orthodoxy that is shaping our thinking has dangerous implications. No one man, no one group can have the answer to the many perplexing problems that today confront the management of world affairs. The scene is a troubled and complicated one. The problems require the pooling of many ideas, the exposure of different points of view, the hammering out in public discussions of the pros and cons of this policy or of that. . . .

The great danger of this period is not inflation, nor the national debt, nor atomic warfare. The great, the critical danger is that we will so limit or narrow the range of permissible discussion and permissible thought that we will become victims of the orthodox school. If we do, we will lose flexibility. We will lose the capacity for expert management. We will then become wedded to a few techniques, to a few devices. They will define our policy and at the same time limit our ability to alter or modify it. Once we narrow the range of thought and discussion, we will surrender a great deal of our power. We will become like the man on the toboggan who can ride it but who can neither steer it nor stop it.

The mind of man must always be free. The strong society is one that sanctions and encourages freedom of thought and expression. . . .

Our real power is our spiritual strength, and that spiritual strength stems from our civil liberties. If we are true to our traditions, if we are tolerant of a whole market place of ideas, we will always be strong. Our weakness grows when we become intolerant of opposing ideas, depart from our standards of civil liberties, and borrow the policeman's philosophy from the enemy we detest.

Glossary

Atomic Energy Commission (AEC) The AEC was the successor to the Manhattan Project. It was established by the U.S. government in 1946 to control the development and production of atomic energy for both military and civilian uses.

Aesopian language The term refers to the Communist party's supposed reliance on language that actually meant the opposite of what is said. The concept came from a passage in one of Lenin's early works in which he notes the need to use misleading language to evade the censorship of the Russian tsar. The concept figured prominently in the federal government's criminal prosecution of the American Communist party because it enabled the prosecutors and their witnesses to discount anything that the Communist leaders said in their defense.

American Civil Liberties Union (ACLU) Established during World War I, the ACLU is the nation's leading organization devoted to the protection of individual civil and political rights.

American Federation of Labor (AFL) Founded in 1886, the AFL was the nation's foremost labor organization, a group of unions representing skilled workers. Because of the AFL's reluctance to organize unskilled workers in the 1930s, some of its members split off to form the CIO. In 1955 the two organizations merged.

Cadre A full-time worker within the Communist movement, usually either a party official or a staff member in a labor union or in one of the many organizations associated with the Communist party.

COINTELPRO A covert FBI program of subversion and harassment directed initially against the American Communist party. It was begun in 1956 after it had become clear that Supreme Court decisions might stand in the way of using criminal prosecutions to undermine American communism. In the 1960s, COINTELPRO operations were directed against the Ku Klux Klan, Black Power, and other New Left and radical groups.

Comintern This Moscow-based organization coordinated the worldwide Communist movement after the Bolshevik Revolution. The American Communist party was a member of the Comintern and usually tried to follow its directives. Although initially designed to encourage Communist revolutions throughout the world, the Comintern soon became a vehicle for Soviet foreign policy and was dissolved by Stalin in 1943 as a gesture of goodwill toward his Western allies.

Congress of Industrial Organizations (CIO)   Organized in 1937, the CIO was one of the nation's two leading federations of labor unions. Most of the unions that belonged to the CIO originally represented workers in mass-production industries. In 1955 it merged with the AFL.

Dies Committee   See *HUAC*.

Fellow travelers   People who did not actually belong to the American Communist party but who worked closely with it and supported its policies. During the McCarthy period, anti-Communist investigators made few distinctions between fellow travelers and party members.

Fifth column   An undercover arm of the enemy that seeks to sabotage the defense of a nation from within. The phrase first came into use during the Spanish Civil War when fascist general Francisco Franco encircled Madrid with four columns of troops and boasted that he would be victorious because of the activities of the "fifth column," his supporters within the city.

Friendly witnesses   The men and women who were willing to tell anti-Communist investigating committees about their activities within the Communist party and to give the names of other members. *Unfriendly witnesses* usually relied on the Fifth Amendment and refused to name names.

Front groups   Organizations associated with the American Communist party. Often, but not always, established to carry out a program that promoted causes the party supported, front groups often attracted liberals and other non-Communists.

GRU   The Soviet Union's military intelligence organization ran an espionage operation within the United States that may have included Alger Hiss.

House Un-American Activities Committee (HUAC)   This committee was established in 1938 to investigate Nazi and Communist propaganda. In its early years, when its chair was the Texas Democrat Martin Dies, HUAC was also known as the *Dies Committee*. After World War II, it became the most active and powerful anti-Communist investigating committee in the country.

KGB   The KGB, the Soviet secret police, operated in the realms of internal security and foreign espionage.

McCarran Committee   See *Senate Internal Security Subcommittee*.

Manhattan Project   This top-secret U.S. military program developed the atomic bomb during World War II. Most of its scientific research was conducted at the laboratory at Los Alamos, New Mexico.

Marshall Plan Named for Secretary of State George Marshall who proposed it in a Harvard commencement address in 1947, the Marshall Plan was the program of American economic assistance to the nations of Western Europe during the early years of the cold war.

National Labor Relations Board (NLRB) The NLRB was established by the Wagner Act in 1935 to regulate and protect unions by running union representation elections and deciding on such matters as unfair labor practices and the jurisdiction of bargaining units.

Office of Strategic Services (OSS) The OSS was the main U.S. intelligence-gathering and covert operations agency during World War II. It was disbanded at the end of the war, and its activities were later taken up by the CIA.

Popular Front When the Soviet Union recognized the need for allies against the threat of Nazi Germany, it called on the world's Communists to moderate their revolutionary rhetoric and join democrats and liberals in a Popular Front against fascism. Lasting from 1935 until the Nazi-Soviet Pact of 1939, it was resurrected after Hitler attacked Russia in June 1941.

Senate Internal Security Subcommittee (SISS) This subcommittee of the Senate Judiciary Committee was set up by the 1950 Internal Security Act to investigate subversive activities and monitor the administration of the act. Also known as the *McCarran Committee* for its first chair, the powerful Nevada Democratic Senator Pat McCarran, the SISS conducted many of the McCarthy era's most important anti-Communist investigations. In the mid-1950s its chairs were Indiana Senator William Jenner and Mississippi Senator James O. Eastland.

Subversive Activities Control Board (SACB) The SACB was set up by the Internal Security Act of 1950 to register Communist organizations and thus indirectly to drive them out of business.

Truman Doctrine Proclaimed by President Harry Truman in March 1947 as he petitioned Congress for economic and military aid for Greece and Turkey, the Truman Doctrine pledged the United States to the defense of all nations that were threatened by a Communist takeover.

VENONA This top-secret code-breaking project deciphered the texts of the intercepted KGB telegraphic correspondence between its operatives in the United States and their Moscow superiors. These documents revealed that hundreds of Americans had spied for the Soviet Union during World War II.

Unfriendly witnesses See *Friendly witnesses.*

Yalta Conference In February 1945 at Yalta, Franklin Delano Roosevelt, Joseph Stalin, and Winston Churchill discussed the postwar future of the world. During the McCarthy period, Yalta was attacked by anti-Communists within the Republican party and elsewhere as having sold out Eastern Europe and China to the Soviet Union.

A McCarthyism Chronology
(1917–1976)

1917

November: Bolshevik Revolution.

1919

July–August: Founding of American Communist party.
November 7–January 2, 1920: Palmer Raids during Red scare.

1933

March: Franklin Delano Roosevelt takes office; New Deal begins.

1935

August: Communist International inaugurates Popular Front as antifascist coalition.

1936

July 18: Spanish Civil War begins.

1936–38

Through the Moscow purge trials at which Bolshevik leaders were forced to make false public confessions, Stalin liquidated all opposition within the Soviet Communist party.

1938

August: House Un-American Activities Committee established.

1939

August 24: Nazi-Soviet Pact creates Soviet alignment with Germany until 1941.

September 1: World War II begins in Europe.

1940

June 28: Smith Act prohibits teaching or advocating the overthrow of the government.

1941

June 22: Hitler's invasion of the Soviet Union returns Communist party to Allied camp.

December 7: Japanese attack Pearl Harbor.

1944

May 20: American Communist party becomes Communist Political Association under Earl Browder.

1945

February: At Yalta Conference, Roosevelt, Churchill, and Stalin negotiate postwar settlement for Europe.

April: Duclos Letter criticizes American Communists; forces reorganization of American Communist party.

April 12: Franklin Roosevelt dies; Harry Truman becomes president.

May 8: Germany surrenders.

June 6: *Amerasia* case begins with arrest of six journalists and government employees for leaking classified documents.

July: American Communist party reorganized; General Secretary Earl Browder expelled. Potsdam Conference settles postwar boundaries of Poland and divides Germany into four Allied zones.

August 6: United States drops atomic bomb on Hiroshima.

August 13: Japan surrenders.

September: Igor Gouzenko defects in Canada; reveals Soviet espionage in North America.

October 11: Louis Budenz quits Communist party.

November: Elizabeth Bentley tells FBI about espionage ring.

1946

November: Republicans win majority in Congress.

November 25: Truman appoints Temporary Commission on Employee Loyalty, which formulates loyalty-security program.

1947

March 12:   Truman Doctrine proclaimed in presidential request for aid to Greece and Turkey.

March 21:   Executive Order 9835 creates loyalty-security program for federal employees.

June: Marshall Plan proposed for postwar economic rehabilitation in Western Europe.

June 18:   Taft-Hartley Act curtails unions' power and Communist leadership of unions.

October 27–30:   Hollywood Ten hearings call screenwriters and directors before HUAC.

November: Attorney General prepares list of subversive groups.

December 3:   Waldorf Statement: studios fire Hollywood Ten.

1948

January: University of Washington fires three professors.

February: Communists take over Czechoslovakia.

June: Berlin blockade begins.

July 20:   Eugene Dennis and eleven other Communist leaders arrested under Smith Act.

August: Hiss-Chambers hearings begin HUAC's pursuit of Communists in government.

November: Truman wins reelection.

November 17:   Chambers reveals stolen government documents.

December 2:   Chambers gives "Pumpkin Papers" to HUAC.

December 15:   Alger Hiss indicted for perjury.

1949

January 17–October 21:   *Dennis* trial; first Smith Act trial of party leaders results in guilty verdict.

January 22:   University of Washington regents dismiss three professors for alleged Communist connections.

March 4:   Judith Coplon arrested on espionage charges.

June 12:   University of California regents impose loyalty oath on faculty.

July: First Hiss trial ends in hung jury.

Summer: Chinese Communists take over China.

August: State Department issues white paper on China.

August: Soviet Union detonates atomic bomb.

November: CIO convention expels left-led unions.

1950

January 21: Hiss convicted of perjury in second trial.

February 2: Klaus Fuchs arrested for atomic espionage.

February 9: Joseph McCarthy's speech in Wheeling, West Virginia, alleges presence of Communist agents in State Department.

May 23: Harry Gold arrested for atomic espionage.

June 15: David Greenglass confesses to espionage and names Julius Rosenberg.

June 22: *Red Channels* blacklists alleged Communists in entertainment industry.

June 25: Korean War begins.

June–July: Tydings Committee investigates McCarthy's charges of Communists in government.

July 14: Tydings Committee majority report concludes that McCarthy is "a hoax and a fraud."

July 17: Julius Rosenberg arrested for espionage. (Ethel Rosenberg arrested in August.)

August 1: U.S. Court of Appeals upholds conviction of *Dennis* defendants.

September 22: McCarran Act (Internal Security Act) forces registration of Communist organizations; passes over Truman's veto.

1951

February 17: FBI inaugurates Responsibilities Program to weed out communism in state employment.

March 6: Julius and Ethel Rosenberg trial begins.

April 5: Judge Irving Kaufman sentences Rosenbergs to death.

June 4: Supreme Court upholds convictions in *Dennis* case.

June 20: Second round of Smith Act prosecutions follows sweeping arrests of party leaders across the country.

July 1951–June 1952: SISS hears testimony on Institute of Pacific Relations and Communist subversion of foreign policy in China.

December 13: John Stewart Service fired from State Department.

1952

November: Dwight D. Eisenhower elected president.

December: Johns Hopkins professor Owen Lattimore indicted for perjury.

1953

March: Joseph Stalin dies.

April 27:   Executive Order 10450 tightens loyalty-security program.

June 19:   Julius and Ethel Rosenberg executed.

July 27:   Korean War ends.

November: SISS resurrects charges of espionage against Harry Dexter White.

December 23:   Manhattan Project physicist J. Robert Oppenheimer's security clearance revoked pending investigation.

1954

April–June: In Army-McCarthy hearings, Senate investigates McCarthy for alleged improprieties.

May 17:   In *Brown v. Board of Education,* Supreme Court rules against segregated schools.

June 1:   AEC hearing panel revokes Oppenheimer's security clearance.

August 19:   Communist Control Act authorizes Subversive Activities Control Board to register Unions as Communist-infiltrated.

December 2:   Senate censures McCarthy.

1955

June 28:   Justice Department drops prosecution of Owen Lattimore.

1956

February: Twentieth Congress of the Soviet Communist Party; Khrushchev reveals Stalin's crimes.

April: Supreme Court voids state sedition laws being used against Communists.

June: Khrushchev speech to Twentieth Congress published in United States.

August: FBI launches COINTELPRO against Communist party.

November 4:   Soviet Union invades Hungary.

1957

May 2: Joseph McCarthy dies.

June 17: Supreme Court reinstates John Stewart Service; overrules California Smith Act convictions; limits HUAC power.

1961

June 5: Supreme Court upholds Scales's conviction; upholds SACB registration of Communist party.

1962

December: Scales receives clemency from President John F. Kennedy.

1976

Amendments to the Freedom of Information Act allow access to previously unavailable government documents.

Intepreting McCarthyism:
A Bibliographic Essay

McCarthyism does not inspire calm reflection. More than fifty years have passed, yet controversy still rages. Recently released documents have settled some issues—like the guilt of Julius Rosenberg—but others remain unresolved, mainly because they involve much larger issues of historical interpretation and national identity. To examine McCarthyism is to raise troubling questions about the nature of cold war America. Was the political repression of the period an unfortunate overreaction to a genuine threat or a deliberate attempt to stifle dissent? There is no neutral ground, for avoiding these questions is in itself a political gesture; and even the most dispassionate historian has to take sides.

The scholarship on McCarthyism has been undergoing revision since the 1950s, as much in response to changes in the political climate as to the discovery of new sources and the rereading of old ones. Each new wave of interpretation emphasized a different aspect of the phenomenon. Just as the figure of Joseph McCarthy dominated early attempts at explanation, that of Harry Truman suffused the second, and J. Edgar Hoover the third (and it seems likely that the new wave of post–cold war revisionism may boost Joseph Stalin into this cohort)—each of these men a symbolic representation of the forces that scholars believed were primarily responsible for what happened. Concurrent with the continuing search for an explanation of McCarthyism was the less ambitious scholarly project of filling in the record and showing how the anti-Communist campaign operated in different areas of society. This scholarship often reinforced or revised prevailing interpretations, but it also had the independent virtue of adding to our overall knowledge of what went on.

The first wave of interpretation was the most imaginative. Among the scholars and intellectuals who tried to understand the phenomenon during the 1950s were some of the best minds of the period and their work established the parameters within which most later scholarship took place. Both their interpretations and their choice of subject matter reflected their own engagement with the politics of anticommunism. Civil libertarians who were distressed by the injustices they witnessed offered victim-centered accounts of the phenomenon. Cold war liberals who endorsed what they considered a more responsible version of anticommunism put Joseph McCarthy at the heart of their story.

The most influential contemporary interpretation appeared in a 1955 collection of essays edited by Daniel Bell, *The New American Right* (New York: Criterion, 1955). The historians and sociologists who contributed to that volume argued that, in the words of the brilliant historian Richard Hofstadter, McCarthyism represented a "pseudo-Conservative revolt," an essentially irrational phenomenon motivated in large part by the status anxieties of downwardly mobile WASPs and upwardly mobile ethnics. These authors tended to take McCarthy's anti-elitist rhetoric at face value and to regard his supporters as the direct heirs of the populist movements of the late nineteenth century. This interpretation, despite its slender empirical base and narrow view of what was going on, was extraordinarily influential. By presenting McCarthyism as a psychosocial problem, Hofstadter, Bell, and their colleagues, offered a comforting vision of contemporary political life in which the anti-Communist crusade figured as a passing aberration.

By the late 1960s as the Vietnam War brought cold war liberalism into question, the Hofstadter version came under attack. Scholars began to do serious historical research, placing McCarthyism within a broader political context that removed McCarthy himself from the center of the story. The most important studies, Michael Paul Rogin's *The Intellectuals and McCarthy: The Radical Specter* (Cambridge: MIT Press, 1967) and Robert Griffith's *The Politics of Fear: Joseph R. McCarthy and the Senate,* 2d ed. (1970; Amherst: University of Massachusetts Press, 1987) discarded the notion that McCarthy was a populist and showed how his career evolved as part of ordinary partisan politics. Similar investigations of the political struggles that surrounded McCarthyism are Earl Latham's *The Communist Controversy in Washington: From the New Deal to McCarthy* (Cambridge: Harvard University Press, 1966); Alan D. Harper's *The Politics of Loyalty: The White House and the Communist Issue, 1946–1952* (Westport, Conn.: Greenwood, 1969); Richard Fried's *Men Against McCarthy* (New York:

Columbia University Press, 1976); and the more recent Jeff Broadwater's *Eisenhower and the Anti-Communist Crusade* (Chapel Hill: University of North Carolina Press, 1992).

While these scholars were downgrading the importance of Senator McCarthy, they and others were also offering a new interpretation that viewed the political repression of the 1940s and 1950s as integral to the Truman administration's conduct of the cold war. Athan Theoharis's *Seeds of Repression: Harry S. Truman and the Origin of McCarthyism* (Chicago: Quadrangle, 1971) and Richard Freeland's *The Truman Doctrine and the Origins of McCarthyism: Foreign Policy, Domestic Politics, and Internal Security, 1946–1948* (New York: Knopf, 1971) were the most important early expressions of that thesis. Many of the essays in *The Specter: Original Essays on the Cold War and the Origins of McCarthyism,* edited by Robert Griffith and Athan Theoharis (New York: Franklin Watts, 1974) touched on related themes.

The notion that the federal government bore much responsibility for McCarthyism was reinforced in the mid-1970s with the revelations of official wrongdoing that Watergate produced. The passage of the revised Freedom of Information Act and the opening of the FBI's records to scholars led to yet another revision, one that assigned a much more central role to J. Edgar Hoover and his agents. Athan Theoharis has been particularly diligent in tracing Hoover's footsteps. See, in particular, Athan Theoharis and John Stuart Cox, *The Boss: J. Edgar Hoover and the Great American Inquisition* (Philadelphia: Temple University Press, 1988). Other useful studies of the FBI include Richard Gid Powers, *Secrecy and Power: The Life of J. Edgar Hoover* (New York: Free Press, 1987); Kenneth O'Reilly, *Hoover and the Un-Americans: The FBI, HUAC, and the Red Menace* (Philadelphia: Temple University Press, 1983); Curt Gentry, *J. Edgar Hoover: The Man and the Secrets* (New York: Norton, 1991); and Athan Theoharis, ed., *Beyond the Hiss Case: The FBI, Congress, and the Cold War* (Philadelphia: Temple University Press, 1982).

Documents that have been released from the previously unavailable Soviet and American files have stimulated a new wave of revisionism that harks back to the cold war liberalism of the 1950s. Emphasizing the connection between American Communism and Soviet espionage, it treats much of the political repression of the McCarthy era as a justifiable response to a genuine danger. Harvey Klehr and John Earl Haynes are the most prolific of these scholars, with several books and documentary collections, most notably, Klehr, Haynes, and Fridrikh

Igorevich Firsov, *The Secret World of American Communism* (New Haven: Yale University Press, 1995); Klehr, Haynes, and Kyrill M. Anderson, *The Soviet World of American Communism* (New Haven: Yale University Press, 1998); and Haynes and Klehr, *VENONA: Decoding Soviet Espionage in America* (New Haven: Yale University Press, 1999).

New theoretical approaches as well as new types of sources are also beginning to change our interpretations of the anti-Communist crusade. As scholars reexamine American culture using some of the theoretical tools provided by post-structuralism, they are once again granting more explanatory power to nonrational forces. Michael Rogin has done the most important work here. His discussion of the countersubversive tradition within American politics in *Ronald Reagan: The Movie and Other Episodes in Political Demonology* (Berkeley: University of California Press, 1988) is enormously suggestive. I am not convinced, however, that acknowledging the power of the countersubversive tradition requires us to toss out the earlier vision of McCarthyism as a partisan political operation. There is much to be said for a messy multicausality, including the fact that it may most closely approximate the complexity of real life.

GENERAL

Although there are dozens of books on different aspects of the anti-communist crusade, only a few general surveys exist. For the most recent work that expands on the themes introduced in this volume, see Ellen Schrecker, *Many Are the Crimes: McCarthyism in America* (Boston: Little, Brown, 1998). Other general surveys include David Caute's encyclopedic *The Great Fear: The Anti-Communist Purge under Truman and Eisenhower* (New York: Simon & Schuster, 1978); John Earl Haynes's conservative *Red Scare or Red Menace? American Communism and Anticommunism in the Cold War* (Chicago: Ivan R. Dee, 1996); and Richard Fried, *Nightmare in Red: The McCarthy Era in Perspective* (New York: Oxford University Press, 1990). Michael J. Heale, *American Anticommunism: Combating the Enemy Within, 1830–1970* (Baltimore: Johns Hopkins University Press, 1990); David H. Bennett, *The Party of Fear: From Nativist Movements to the New Right in American History* (Chapel Hill: University of North Carolina Press, 1988); and, most importantly, Robert Goldstein, *Political Repression in Modern America: From 1879 to 1976* (Urbana: University of Illinois Press, 2001) all treat McCarthyism within a longer historical timeframe.

COMMUNISM

The quality of the more specialized literature varies widely. It is not always the case that the most recent studies are the best. Much of the work from the 1950s has yet to be superseded. The following studies are only a sampling; there are literally hundreds of books that treat one or another aspect of American communism and anticommunism. In fact, historians have been doing so much work on American communism they have even formed their own professional association, but they have yet to produce a first-rate overview of the party. Until one does appear, students can consult Irving Howe and Louis Coser's dated polemic, *The American Communist Party, A Critical History, 1919–1957* (Boston: Beacon, 1957) and Harvey Klehr and John Earl Haynes's more recent one, *The American Communist Movement: Storming Heaven Itself* (New York: Twayne, 1992). The most useful of the monographic studies include Theodore Draper, *The Roots of American Communism* (New York: Viking, 1957); Draper, *American Communism and Soviet Russia, The Formative Period* (New York: Viking, 1960); Klehr, *The Heyday of American Communism: The Depression Decade* (New York: Basic Books, 1984); Fraser M. Ottanelli, *The Communist Party of the United States: From the Depression to World War II* (New Brunswick, N.J.: Rutgers University Press, 1991); Maurice Isserman, *Which Side Were You On? The American Communist Party During the Second World War* (Middletown, Conn.: Wesleyan University Press, 1982); Joseph Starobin, *American Communism in Crisis, 1943–1957* (Cambridge: Harvard University Press, 1972); Isserman, *If I Had a Hammer . . . The Death of the Old Left and the Birth of the New Left* (New York: Basic Books, 1987); and Michael E. Brown, Randy Martin, Frank Rosengarten, and George Snedeker, *New Studies in the Politics and Culture of U.S. Communism* (New York: Monthly Review Press, 1993). Biographies include James R. Barrett, *William Z. Foster and the Tragedy of American Radicalism* (Urbana: University of Illinois Press, 1999); Edward P. Johanningsmeier, *Forging American Communism: The Life of William Z. Foster* (Princeton, N.J.: Princeton University Press, 1994); and James G. Ryan, *Earl Browder: The Public Life of an American Communist* (Tuscaloosa: University of Alabama Press, 1997).

A problem with much of the scholarly literature on the party is that, with a few exceptions, it focuses on leadership and policy issues and overlooks the significance of rank-and-file activism. Studies of the front groups and other elements of the broader Communist movement may rectify some of these omissions. There are two outstanding books on the Communist party's work with African Americans in the 1930s: Mark Naison, *Communists in Harlem during the Depression* (Urbana: University of Illinois Press, 1983) and Robin D. G. Kelley, *Hammer and Hoe: Alabama Communists During the Great Depression* (Chapel Hill: University of North Carolina Press, 1990). Gerald Horne, *Black and Red: W. E. B. Du Bois and the Afro-American Response to the Cold War, 1944–1963* (Albany: State University of New York Press, 1986) deals with a later period.

Among the more useful studies of party activities in specific areas are Peter N. Carroll, *The Odyssey of the Abraham Lincoln Brigade: Americans in the Spanish Civil War* (Stanford: Stanford University Press, 1994); Robert Cohen, *When the Old Left Was Young: Student Radicals and America's First Mass Student Movement, 1929–1941* (New York: Oxford University Press, 1993); Lowell K. Dyson, *Red Harvest: The Communist Party and American Farmers* (Lincoln: University of Nebraska Press, 1982); Gerald Horne, *Communist Front? The Civil Rights Congress, 1946–1956* (Rutherford, N.J.: Fairleigh Dickinson University Press, 1988); Robbie Lieberman, *"My Song Is My Weapon": People's Songs, American Communism and the Politics of Culture 1930–1950* (Urbana: University of Illinois Press, 1989); Lieberman, *The Strangest Dream: Communism, Anticommunism, and the U.S. Peace Movement, 1945–1963* (Syracuse, N.Y.: Syracuse University Press, 2000); Paul Mischler, *Raising Reds: The Young Pioneers, Radical Summer Camps, and Communist Political Culture in the United States* (New York: Columbia University Press, 1999); and Kate Weigand, *Red Feminism: American Communism and the Making of Women's Liberation* (Baltimore: Johns Hopkins University Press, 2001).

An even more valuable source of information about the day-to-day texture of party life are the oral histories and memoirs of former Communists. There are dozens of these. Among the better oral histories are Paul Lyons, *Philadelphia Communists, 1936–1956* (Philadelphia: Temple University Press, 1982) and Griffin Fariello, *Red Scare: Memories of the American Inquisition* (New York: Norton, 1995). Some useful memoirs are John J. Abt with Michael Myerson, *Advocate and Activist: Memoirs of an American Communist Lawyer* (Urbana: University of Illinois Press, 1993); Peggy Dennis, *The Autobiography of an American Communist* (Westport and Berkeley: Lawrence Hill & Co., Creative Arts Book Co., 1977); Dorothy Healey and Maurice Isserman, *Dorothy Healey Remembers: A Life in the American Communist*

Party (New York: Oxford University Press, 1990; the University of Illinois Press paperback version is called *California Red*); Nell Irvin Painter, *The Narrative of Hosea Hudson: His Life as a Negro Communist in the South* (Cambridge: Harvard University Press, 1979); Jessica Mitford, *A Fine Old Conflict* (New York: Knopf, 1977); Steve Nelson, James Barrett, and Rob Ruck, *Steve Nelson: American Radical* (Pittsburgh: University of Pittsburgh Press, 1981); Al Richmond, *A Long View from the Left: Memoirs of an American Revolutionary* (Boston: Houghton Mifflin, 1973); and Junius Irving Scales and Richard Nickson, *Cause at Heart: A Former Communist Remembers* (Athens: University of Georgia Press, 1987). There are also memoirs by the children of Communists. See, for example, Judy Kaplan and Linn Shapiro, eds., *Red Diapers: Growing Up in the Communist Left* (Urbana: University of Illinois Press, 1998); Kim Chernin, *In My Mother's House: A Daughter's Story* (Boston: Ticknor and Fields, 1983); and Sally Belfrage, *Un-American Activities: A Memoir of the Fifties* (New York: HarperCollins, 1994). Although in need of updating, an immensely useful tool is John Earl Haynes's bibliography, *Communism and Anti-Communism in the United States: An Annotated Guide to Historical Writings* (New York: Garland, 1987).

The relationship among communism, anticommunism, and American cultural and intellectual life has spawned a large literature, much of it looking at the so-called New York Intellectuals. Among the most interesting studies are Michael Denning, *The Cultural Front: The Laboring of American History in the Twentieth Century* (London and New York: Verso, 1996); Daniel Aaron, *Writers on the Left: Episodes in American Literary Communism* (New York: Harcourt, Brace and World, 1961); Richard H. Pells, *Radical Visions and American Dreams: Culture and Social Thought in the Depression Years* (New York: Harper and Row, 1973); Terry A. Cooney, *The Rise of the New York Intellectuals: Partisan Review and Its Circle* (Madison: University of Wisconsin Press, 1986); and Alan M. Wald, *The New York Intellectuals: The Rise and Decline of the Anti-Stalinist Left from the 1930s to the 1980s* (Chapel Hill: University of North Carolina Press, 1987).

ANTICOMMUNISM

Scholars are also beginning to pay some attention to anticommunism and to the conservatives who contributed so much to it. See, for example, Richard Gid Powers, *Not Without Honor: The History of American Anticommunism* (New York: Free Press, 1995) and for an earlier period George Sirgiovanni, *An Undercurrent of Suspicion: Anti-Communism in America during World War II* (New Brunswick: Transaction, 1990). The few studies of the far right like Leo Ribuffo's splendid *The Old Christian Right: The Protestant Far Right from the Great Depression to the Cold War* (Philadelphia: Temple University Press, 1983) and William Pencak's, *For God and Country: The American Legion, 1919–1941* (Boston: Northeastern University Press, 1989) do not cover the McCarthy years.

On the Catholic Church, see Joshua B. Freeman and Steve Rosswurm, "The Education of an Anti-Communist: Father John Cronin and the Baltimore Labor Movement," *Labor History* 33, 2 (Spring 1992): 217–47; Donald F. Crosby, S. J., *God, Church, and Flag: Senator Joseph R. McCarthy and the Catholic Church, 1950–1957* (Chapel Hill: University of North Carolina Press, 1978); and Douglas P. Seaton, *Catholics and Radicals: The Association of Catholic Trade Unionists and the American Labor Movement, from Depression to Cold War* (Lewisburg, Penn.: Bucknell University Press, 1981).

On cold war liberals, see Mary Sperling McAuliffe, *Crisis on the Left: Cold War Politics and American Liberals* (Amherst: University of Massachusetts Press, 1978); Steven M. Gillon, *Politics and Vision: The ADA and American Liberalism* (New York: Oxford University Press, 1987); William W. Keller, *The Liberals and J. Edgar Hoover: Rise and Fall of a Domestic Intelligence State* (Princeton, N.J.: Princeton University Press, 1989); and Samuel Walker, *In Defense of American Liberties: A History of the ACLU* (New York: Oxford University Press, 1990).

SPYING AND POLITICAL TRIALS

Probably no other topic has engendered as much interest as espionage. Problematic because its research cannot be replicated but somewhat more balanced than the Klehr-Haynes oeuvre is Allen Weinstein and Alexander Vassiliev, *The Haunted Wood: Soviet Espionage in America—The Stalin Era* (New York: Random House, 1999). See also Robert J. Lamphere and Tom Schachtman, *The FBI-KGB War: A Special Agent's Story* (New York: Random House, 1983); Christopher Andrew and Oleg Gordievsky, *KGB: The Inside Story of Its Foreign Operations from Lenin to Gorbachev* (New York: HarperCollins, 1990); Nigel West and Oleg Tsarev, *The Crown Jewels: The British Secrets at the Heart of the KGB Archives* (London: HarperCollins, 1998); and the unreliable Pavel Sudoplatov and Anatolii Sudoplatov with Jerrold L. Schechter and Leona P. Schechter, *Special Tasks: The Memoirs of an*

Unwanted Witness—A Soviet Spymaster (Boston: Little, Brown, 1994). The most important VENONA documents are reproduced in Robert Louis Benson and Michael Warner, eds., *VENONA: Soviet Espionage and the American Response* (Washington, D.C.: National Security Agency, Central Intelligence Agency, 1996). The texts of the decrypts are also available on the World Wide Web at the National Security Agency's Web site <www.nsa.gov>.

On specific espionage cases, see Allen Weinstein, *Perjury: The Hiss-Chambers Case* (New York: Knopf, 1978); Ronald Radosh and Joyce Milton, *The Rosenberg File: A Search for the Truth* (New York: Holt, Rinehart, and Winston, 1983); Robert Chadwell Williams, *Klaus Fuchs, Atom Spy* (Cambridge: Harvard University Press, 1987); Joseph Albright and Marcia Kunstel, *Bombshell: The Secret Story of America's Unknown Atomic Spy Conspiracy* (New York: Times Books, 1997) (on Theodore Hall); Gary May, *Un-American Activities: The Trials of William Remington* (New York: Oxford University Press, 1994); Merrily Weisbord, *The Strangest Dream: Canadian Communists, the Spy Trials, and the Cold War* (Toronto: Lester and Orpen Dennys, 1983); Reg Whitaker and Gary Marcuse, *Cold War Canada: The Making of a National Insecurity State, 1945–1957* (Toronto: University of Toronto Press, 1994).

Other high-profile cases did not involve espionage. On Oppenheimer, see Philip M. Stern, *The Oppenheimer Case* (New York: Harper and Row, 1969) and Barton J. Bernstein, "The Oppenheimer Loyalty-Security Case Reconsidered," *Stanford Law Review* 42 (July 1990): 1383–484. On the cases involving China, see Harvey Klehr and Ronald Radosh's mistitled *The* Amerasia *Spy Case: Prelude to McCarthyism* (Chapel Hill: University of North Carolina Press, 1996); Robert Newman, *Owen Lattimore and the "Loss" of China* (Berkeley: University of California Press, 1992); E. J. Kahn Jr., *The China Hands: America's Foreign Service Officers and What Befell Them* (New York: Viking, 1975); and Gary May, *China Scapegoat: The Diplomatic Ordeal of John Carter Vincent* (Washington, D.C.: New Republic Books, 1979). Both Michal Belknap, *Cold War Political Justice: The Smith Act, the Communist Party, and American Civil Liberties* (Westport, Conn.: Greenwood, 1977) and Peter Steinberg, *The Great "Red Menace": United States Prosecution of American Communists, 1947–1952* (Westport, Conn.: Greenwood, 1984) do a fine job on the Smith Act trials of the Communist party. Stanley Kutler's *The American Inquisition: Justice and Injustice in the Cold War* (New York: Hill and Wang, 1982) deals with several other key cold war prosecutions.

There is no complete study of the Supreme Court and the communist issue, although it is possible to piece together a fairly coherent account from such general works as C. Herman Pritchett, *Civil Liberties and the Vinson Court* (Chicago: University of Chicago Press, 1954); Robert McCloskey, *The Modern Supreme Court* (Cambridge: Harvard University Press, 1972); and Lucas A. Powe Jr., *The Warren Court and American Politics* (Cambridge: Harvard University Press, 2000). My own favorite reference for constitutional matters is actually a casebook, Thomas I. Emerson, David Haber, and Norman Dorsen, *Political and Civil Rights in the United States*, 3rd ed. (Boston: Little, Brown, 1967; later editions carry less material on the 1950s).

The professional witnesses deserve attention. The standard survey, Herbert L. Packer's *Ex-Communist Witnesses, Four Studies in Fact Finding* (Stanford: Stanford University Press, 1962) predates the Freedom of Information Act (FOIA). Sam Tanenhaus's overpraised but highly readable *Whittaker Chambers: A Biography* (New York: Random House, 1997) does use FBI files. Many of the witnesses wrote their memoirs, which are interesting artifacts. The classic is Whittaker Chambers, *Witness* (New York: Random House, 1952). See also Harvey Matusow, *False Witness* (New York: Cameron and Kahn, 1955); Louis Budenz, *This Is My Story* (New York: McGraw-Hill, 1947); Herbert Philbrick, *I Led Three Lives: Citizen, "Communist," Counterspy* (New York: McGraw-Hill, 1952); and Elizabeth Bentley, *Out of Bondage, The Story of Elizabeth Bentley* (New York: Devin-Adair, 1951).

LOYALTY PROGRAMS AND INVESTIGATIONS

The loyalty-security program attracted more scholarly attention in the 1950s than it did later. The best studies are Eleanor Bontecou, *The Federal Loyalty-Security Program* (Ithaca, N.Y.: Cornell University Press, 1953) and Ralph S. Brown Jr., *Loyalty and Security: Employment Tests in the United States* (New Haven: Yale University Press, 1958). For more victim-oriented accounts see the material in Caute's *Great Fear* mentioned above, as well as Selma R. Williams, *Red-Listed: Haunted by the Washington Witch Hunt* (Reading, Mass.: Addison-Wesley, 1993) and Carl Bernstein's surprisingly revealing *Loyalties: A Son's Memoir* (New York: Simon & Schuster, 1989).

Much of the good work on the congressional investigating committees was also done in the 1950s and 1960s. See, for example, Robert K. Carr, *The House Committee on Un-American Activities* (Ithaca, N.Y.: Cornell University Press, 1952); Telford Taylor, *Grand Inquisition: The*

Story of Congressional Investigations (New York: Simon & Schuster, 1955); Frank Donner, *The Un-Americans* (New York: Ballantine, 1961); and Walter Goodman, *The Committee: The Extraordinary Career of the House Committee on Un-American Activities* (New York: Farrar, Straus, and Giroux, 1968). In addition to Richard H. Rovere's lively polemic, *Senator Joe McCarthy* (New York: Harcourt, Brace, Jovanovich, 1959), there are two large biographies of McCarthy—David Oshinsky, *A Conspiracy So Immense: The World of Joe McCarthy* (New York: Free Press, 1983) and Thomas Reeves, *The Life and Times of Joe McCarthy* (New York: Stein and Day, 1982)—and two of McCarthy's chief counsel, Roy Cohn—Nicholas von Hoffman, *Citizen Cohn: The Life and Times of Roy Cohn* (New York: Doubleday, 1988) and Sidney Zion, *The Autobiography of Roy Cohn* (Secaucus, N.J.: Lyle Stuart, 1988). Roger Morris *Richard Milhous Nixon: The Rise of an American Politician* (New York: Henry Holt, 1990) contains useful material on HUAC's most successful alumnus.

Much work still needs to be done on McCarthyism's local manifestations. Among the recent studies are M. J. Heale, *McCarthy's Americans: Red Scare Politics in State and Nation, 1935–1965* (Athens: University of Georgia Press, 1998) (on Georgia, Massachusetts, and Michigan) and Philip Jenkins, *The Cold War at Home: The Red Scare in Pennsylvania* (Chapel Hill: University of North Carolina Press, 1999). Also useful are Walter Gellhorn, ed., *The States and Subversion* (Ithaca, N.Y.: Cornell University Press, 1952); James T. Selcraig, *The Red Scare in the Midwest, 1945–1955: A State and Local Study* (Ann Arbor: UMI Research, 1982); Don E. Carleton, *Red Scare! Right-Wing Hysteria, Fifties Fanaticism, and Their Legacy in Texas* (Austin: Texas Monthly Press, 1985); Edward Barrett, *The Tenney Committee: Legislative Investigation of Subversive Activities in California* (Ithaca, N.Y.: Cornell University Press, 1951); Lawrence H. Chamberlain, *Loyalty and Legislative Action: A Survey of Activity by the New York State Legislature, 1919–1949* (Ithaca, N.Y.: Cornell University Press, 1951); and Vern Countryman, *Un-American Activities in the State of Washington: Canwell Committee* (Ithaca, N.Y.: Cornell University Press, 1951).

IMPACT OF McCARTHYISM

For exploring the impact of McCarthyism on its most important target, the labor movement, see Harvey A. Levenstein, *Communism, Anticommunism, and the CIO* (Westport, Conn.: Greenwood, 1981); Steve Rosswurm, ed., *The CIO's Left-Led Unions* (New Brunswick,

N.J.: Rutgers University Press, 1992); Bert Cochran, *Labor and Communism: The Conflict that Shaped American Unions* (Princeton, N.J.: Princeton University Press, 1977); Roger Keeran, *The Communist Party and the Auto Workers Unions* (Bloomington: Indiana University Press, 1980); Joshua B. Freeman, *In Transit: The Transport Workers Union in New York City, 1933–1960* (New York: Oxford University Press, 1989); Howard Kimeldorf, *Reds or Rackets? The Making of Radical and Conservative Unions on the Waterfront* (Berkeley: University of California Press, 1988); and Ronald L. Filippelli and Mark McColloch, *Cold War in the Working Class: The Rise and Decline of the United Electrical Workers* (Albany: State University of New York Press, 1995). George Lipsitz, *Rainbow at Midnight: Labor and Culture in the 1940s* (Urbana: University of Illinois Press, 1994) is an important study of working class culture, just as Howell J. Harris, *The Right to Manage: Industrial Relations Policies of American Business in the 1940s* (Madison: University of Wisconsin Press, 1982) and Elizabeth A. Fones-Wolf, *Selling Free Enterprise: The Business Assault on Labor and Liberalism, 1945–1960* (Urbana: University of Illinois Press, 1994) are equally valuable studies of management.

There is a vast literature on McCarthyism and the entertainment industry. Start with Larry Ceplair and Steven Englund, *The Inquisition in Hollywood: Politics in the Film Community, 1930–1960* (Garden City, N.Y.: Anchor Press/Doubleday, 1979). See also Victor Navasky, *Naming Names* (New York: Viking, 1980); Patrick McGilligan and Paul Buhle, *Tender Comrades: A Backstory of the Hollywood Blacklist* (New York: St. Martin's, 1997); Merle Miller, *The Judges and the Judged* (Garden City, N.Y.: Doubleday, 1952); and John Cogley's two-volume *Report on Blacklisting* (New York: Fund for the Republic, 1954). For McCarthyism and the academic community, see Ellen W. Schrecker, *No Ivory Tower: McCarthyism and the Universities* (New York: Oxford University Press, 1986); Jane Sanders, *Cold War on the Campus: Academic Freedom at the University of Washington* (Seattle: University of Washington Press, 1979); Sigmund Diamond, *Compromised Campus: The Collaboration of Universities with the Intelligence Community, 1945–1955* (New York: Oxford University Press, 1992); and David P. Gardner, *The California Oath Controversy* (Berkeley: University of California Press, 1967). For the world of science, see Jessica Wang, *American Science in an Age of Anxiety: Scientists, Anticommunism, and the Cold War* (Chapel Hill: University of North Carolina Press, 1999) and Walter Gellhorn, *Security, Loyalty and Science* (Ithaca, N.Y.: Cornell University Press, 1950). On the legal profession, see Jerold S. Auerbach,

Unequal Justice: Lawyers and Social Change in Modern America (New York: Oxford University Press, 1976). On the press, see Edwin R. Bayley, *Joe McCarthy and the Press* (Madison: University of Wisconsin Press, 1981) and James Aronson, *The Press and the Cold War* (Boston: Beacon, 1970). On social work, see Daniel J. Walkowitz, *Working with Class: Social Workers and the Politics of Middle-Class Identity* (Chapel Hill: University of North Carolina Press, 1999).

Many scholars have been looking at the impact of communism and anticommunism on American cultural and intellectual life. A good start for the cold war is Stephen J. Whitfield, *The Culture of the Cold War* (Baltimore: Johns Hopkins University Press, 1996). See also Lary May, ed., *Recasting America: Culture and Politics in the Age of the Cold War* (Chicago: University of Chicago Press, 1989) and Richard H. Pells, *The Liberal Mind in a Conservative Age: American Intellectuals in the 1940s and 1950s* (New York: Harper & Row, 1985).

DOCUMENTS

Finally, for anybody interested in a deeper immersion into the McCarthy era, there are the FBI files and congressional hearings of the period. Eric Bentley's *Thirty Years of Treason: Excerpts from Hearings Before the House Committee on Un-American Activities, 1938–1968* (New York: Viking, 1971) contains some of HUAC's finest moments. Athan Theoharis, ed., *From the Secret Files of J. Edgar Hoover* (Chicago: Ivan R. Dee, 1991) shows us Hoover's, while Edith Tiger, ed., In Re *Alger Hiss* (New York: Hill and Wang, 1979) reproduces the FBI files that Hiss felt would exonerate him. The FBI has also posted some of its cold war cases on its Web site at <www.fbi.gov>.

Acknowledgments (continued from p. ii)

William O. Douglas. Quote from "The Black Silence of Fear." Originally published in *The New York Times Magazine,* January 13, 1952, pp. 7, 37–38. Reprinted by permission of The Lantz Office on behalf of the Estate of William O. Douglas and Cathleen Douglas Stone.

William Z. Foster. Excerpt from "From the Communist Party's Perspective: William Z. Foster Looks at the World in 1947" in *The New Europe.* Copyright © 1947 by William Z. Foster. Reprinted by permission of International Publishers.

Sidney Hook. "Heresy, Yes—But Conspiracy, No." From *The New York Times Magazine,* July 9, 1950, pp. 12, 38–39. Copyright © 1950 by The New York Times Company. Reprinted by permission.

James Lein and Julia Reichert. Excerpts from interviews in *Seeing Red: Oral History of the American Left* by Howard Johnson, David Friedman, Marge Frantz, and Rose Krysak. Archived at the Tamiment Institute Library and Elmer Holmes Bobst Library, New York University. Reprinted by permission.

James F. O'Neil. Excerpt from "How You Can Fight Communism." Originally published in *The American Legion Magazine,* August 1948. Copyright © 1993. Reprinted with permission of *The American Legion Magazine.*

Ethel and Julius Rosenberg. Correspondence from *We Are Your Sons: The Legacy of Julius and Ethel Rosenberg,* Second Edition by Robert and Michael Meeropol. Copyright © 1975, 1986 by Robert and Michael Meeropol. Used with permission of Robert and Michael Meeropol and the University of Illinois Press.

Index

Abt, John, 138, 140
academic purgings, 18, 93–95
  AAUP response to, 101
  and "Fifth Amendment witnesses," 89, 94
  at University of Washington, 93–94
  See also education system
Acheson, Dean, 73, 237, 239, 240
ACLU. *See* American Civil Liberties Union
AEC. *See* Atomic Energy Commission
Aesopian language, 130, 198, 205, 206
African Americans
  in Communist party, 110–12
  and southern racism, 84–85
  See also civil rights movement; racial issues
Alien and Sedition Laws (1798), 219
Amerasia incident, 32, 77, 237, 279
American Association of University Professors (AAUP), 101
American Bar Association (ABA), 97, 101
American Business Consultants, 90, 91
American Civil Liberties Union (ACLU), 15, 268
  anticommunism of, 18
  detachment from anti-Communist crusade, 100–101
American Committee for Protection of Foreign Born, 58
American Communist party. *See* Communist party
American Federation of Labor (AFL), 15
American Federation of Television and Radio Artists (AFTRA), 101, 103, 250, 255–56
American Government (Magruder), 81
American Legion
  on fighting communism, 122–25
  and Hollywood blacklisting, 90, 91
  role in anti-Communist crusade, 14, 15, 16, 17, 18, 80
  support of HUAC, 64
Americans for Democratic Action (ADA), 99
anti-Communist crusade
  communists-in-government issue, 31–37
  congressional hearings, 63–70

  economic sanctions, 86–97
  ex-Communists in, 16–17
  federal government's role in promoting, 25–30
  against front groups, 58
  against left-wing labor unions, 58–62
  legacy of, 104–6
  liberal opposition to, 99–103
  loyalty-security programs, 43–47
  and political careerism, 71–74
  scope and longevity of, 1–3
  at state and local levels, 80–85
  See also McCarthyism
anti-Communist network, growth of, 12–19
Anti-Defamation League, 91
anti-Semitism, 102
Army-McCarthy hearings, 74, 282
Association of Motion Picture Producers, 243
Atlantic Treaty, 222, 223
atomic bomb, Soviet detonation of, 21, 38
Atomic Energy Commission (AEC)
  investigation of Oppenheimer, 41, 42, 282
  security clearances required by, 46
atomic espionage, 23, 38–42
  reasons for investigating, 71
  Rosenberg case, 39–41, 155–70
  See also espionage, Communist
attorney general's list, 102, 171, 190–96, 280
  impact on organizations, 46–47, 58
attorneys. *See* lawyers
AWARE, Incorporated, Faulk's case against, 250–57

Baldwin, Roger, 268
Belmont, A. H., 164
Bentley, Elizabeth, 49, 152
  Chambers's testimony on, 138, 139
  and Russian spy ring, 33–35, 68, 279
Berlin blockade, 21, 280
Bessie, Alvah, 215
Biberman, Herbert, 215
Birmingham, Alabama, anticommunism in, 83
Black, Justice Hugo, on *Dennis* case, 53, 207, 211–12

DATE DUE